THE WORLD IN PHOTOGRAPHS: 2001

AGENCE FRANCE-PRESSE

Harry N. Abrams, Inc., Publishers

INTRODUCTION

The idea of compiling a book of the best photos of the year 2001 was born a few days after the September 11th attacks on the World Trade Center in New York. It was at this point that the photojournalists at Agence France-Presse realized that, not only was the 20th century definitely over, but a next page in human history had been written, starting with a monumental disaster with unimaginable and unprecedented repercussions.

As professional photographers, they are accustomed to being daily witnesses to events that unfold around the globe. After the September 11th attacks it became essential to try to understand and make sense of this "Year 1" of the third millennium.

The World in Photographs : 2001 is a collection of photojournalism with no chronological constraints. The striking events are grouped together by a common theme or common location in an attempt to put the news of the past months into a coherent perspective. This retrospective can visually add to the news that has been collected from recent world events. The month of September 2000 proved a convenient point of departure, particularly the 28th, the day Israel's Prime Minister Ariel Sharon chose for his controversial visit to the Al-Aqsa mosque compound, Islam's third holiest shrine, thus triggering violent demonstrations by Palestinians and a relaunching of the Intifada against Israel. An entire chapter is devoted here to the Israeli-Palestinian conflict.

Of course, the other date which everyone will always remember is September 11, 2001. After the initial shock and horror of the video footage of jet airliners embedding themselves into the twin towers of Manhattan had past, photojournalism more than played its part in documenting the tragedy on a daily basis thereafter. From New York to Kabul, AFP's team of photojournalists went to action to relate, validate and portray every aspect of the aftermath of the murderous attack.

Those who believed that television, with its moving pictures and instant imagery, had left photoreportage as an outdated discipline, have had to face up to the fact that the two forms of media are rarely in direct competition. On the contrary, they are complementary. Nothing can replace the film footage of the aircraft slamming into the towers, nor the clouds of dust and debris raining down on the people of Manhattan. But, at the same time, nothing can improve on the pictures in this book, which allow a mature reflection of the events while

THE WORLD IN PHOTOGRAPHS: 2001

AGENCE FRANCE-PRESSE

Harry N. Abrams, Inc., Publishers

INTRODUCTION

The idea of compiling a book of the best photos of the year 2001 was born a few days after the September 11th attacks on the World Trade Center in New York. It was at this point that the photojournalists at Agence France-Presse realized that, not only was the 20th century definitely over, but a next page in human history had been written, starting with a monumental disaster with unimaginable and unprecedented repercussions.

As professional photographers, they are accustomed to being daily witnesses to events that unfold around the globe. After the September 11th attacks it became essential to try to understand and make sense of this "Year 1" of the third millennium.

The World in Photographs: 2001 is a collection of photojournalism with no chronological constraints. The striking events are grouped together by a common theme or common location in an attempt to put the news of the past months into a coherent perspective. This retrospective can visually add to the news that has been collected from recent world events. The month of September 2000 proved a convenient point of departure, particularly the 28th, the day Israel's Prime Minister Ariel Sharon chose for his controversial visit to the Al-Aqsa mosque compound, Islam's third holiest shrine, thus triggering violent demonstrations by Palestinians and a relaunching of the Intifada against Israel. An entire chapter is devoted here to the Israeli-Palestinian conflict.

Of course, the other date which everyone will always remember is September 11, 2001. After the initial shock and horror of the video footage of jet airliners embedding themselves into the twin towers of Manhattan had past, photojournalism more than played its part in documenting the tragedy on a daily basis thereafter. From New York to Kabul, AFP's team of photojournalists went to action to relate, validate and portray every aspect of the aftermath of the murderous attack.

Those who believed that television, with its moving pictures and instant imagery, had left photoreportage as an outdated discipline, have had to face up to the fact that the two forms of media are rarely in direct competition. On the contrary, they are complementary. Nothing can replace the film footage of the aircraft slamming into the towers, nor the clouds of dust and debris raining down on the people of Manhattan. But, at the same time, nothing can improve on the pictures in this book, which allow a mature reflection of the events while maintaining a certain distance so that one may understand the enormity of the occasion. For that reason, the "Newseum" in Arlington, near Washington, decided to exhibit as many photos as possible that were taken on that fatal day from all the photographic agencies to allow the American people the chance to fully measure the effect of what had taken place only a few weeks earlier.

As this book goes to press, the agency's photojournalists are active in the field on every front where the "Operation Enduring Freedom" is being fought, in Afghanistan, Pakistan, and Tajikistan. Technological advances, including the use of computers in the development and transmission of photos have liberated photojournalists and made it possible for them to roam freely wherever there is a story to be shot. Equipped with a satellite phone, the reporter can send his photos to the agency at any moment. However, this freedom means that the photographer must be more discerning with the subject matter he photographs and he must understand the events he is confronted with. In the daily execution of a dangerous calling, the photographers abilities are now less dependent on the quality of his equipment than on a certain passion he carries with him to capture and complete the task at hand.

The other themes in this book look back over the past year, perhaps unique in the number of important events that have erupted around the globe. The events are grouped around the big cultural, political and religious questions of the day—from the emergence of the anti-globilization lobby to the fall of Yugoslav president Slobodan Milosevic or the spectacular assembly of millions of Hindu pilgrims on the banks of the holy river Ganges. One can also not forget Algeria, the march of Subcommandante Marcos, the Zapatista National Liberation Army leader in Mexico, or the interminable wrangle over the American presidential election, hinging on a handful of ballot papers, recounted over and over again.

Through these pages, it is possible to evaluate just how much the global events of 2001 have marked and shaped our lives and how all the events that occur around the world will surely continue to do so.

Jean-Francois Le Mounier

Director of the AFP photographic service

DIVIDED TERRITORIES

ISRAEL-JERUSALEM
URGENT¥¥ SHOOTING AT AL-AQSA AFTER SHARON VISIT
JERUSALEM, SEPT 28 (AFP) – SHOOTING ERUPTED AT THE AL-AQSA MOSQUE COMPOUND IN JERUSALEM'S OLD CITY THURSDAY MORNING AFTER A VISIT TO THE SITE BY THE ISRAELI RIGHT-WING OPPOSITION LEADER ARIEL SHARON, AN AFP CORRESPONDENT AT THE SCENE REPORTED.
TXW/SS/DM

MIDEAST-UNREST-SOLDIER,LEAD
URGENT¥¥¥ TWO ISRAELI SOLDIERS LYNCHED BY MOB IN WEST BANK
RAMALLAH, WEST BANK, OCT 12 (AFP) – TWO MEMBERS OF A SPECIAL ISRAELI ARMY UNIT WERE LYNCHED THURSDAY BY AN ANGRY PALESTINIAN MOB IN THE WEST BANK TOWN OF RAMALLAH, AN AFP CORRESPONDENT SAID.
BUR/DB/MB

MIDEAST-UNREST-PFLP
URGENT ¥¥ LEADER OF PFLP KILLED BY ISRAELI ROCKETS IN WEST BANK
RAMALLAH, WEST BANK, AUG 27 (AFP) – THE LEADER OF POPULAR FRONT FOR THE LIBERATION OF PALESTINE (PFLP), ABU ALI MUSTAPHA, WAS KILLED IN AN ISRAELI ROCKET ATTACK ON HIS OFFICE IN THE WEST BANK TOWN OF RAMALLAH MONDAY, PALESTINIAN SECURITY OFFICIALS SAID.
JH/AL

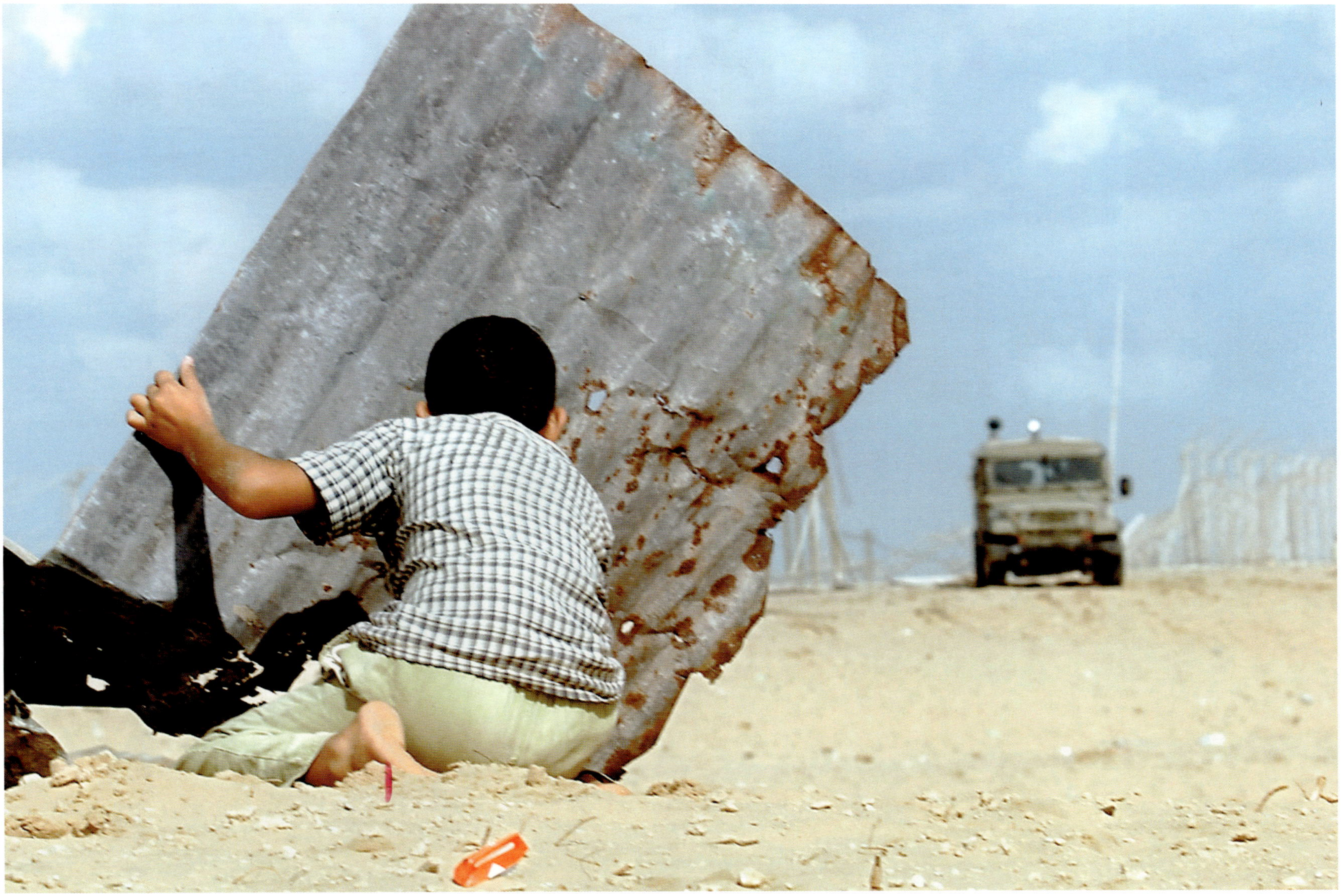

24TH OCTOBER 2000
– KHAN YUNES, GAZA STRIP –
A PALESTINIAN CHILD TAKES COVER BEHIND A SHEET OF CORRUGATED IRON DURING A VIOLENT CLASH IN THE GAZA STRIP. (THOMAS COËX)

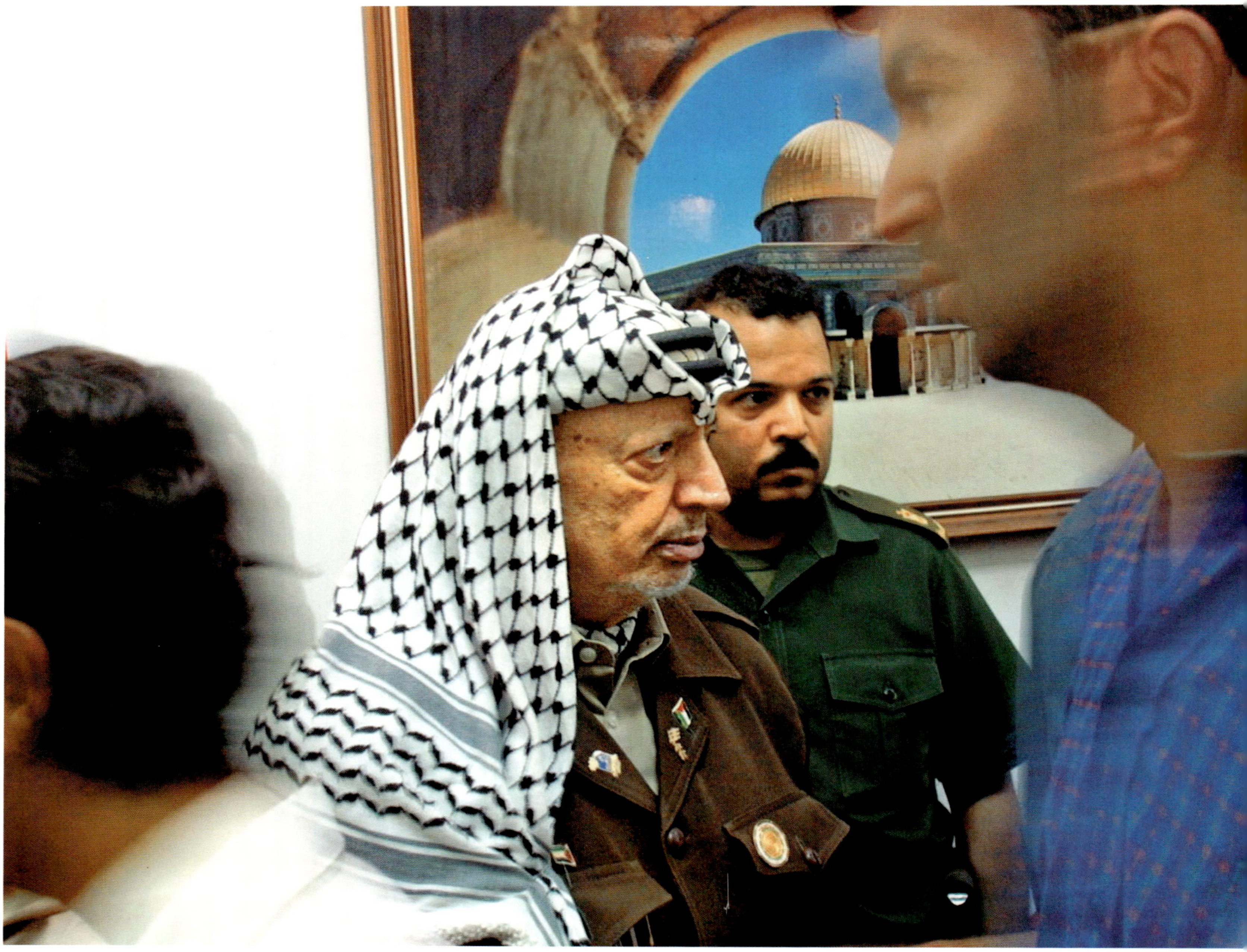

27TH AUGUST 2001 – GAZA CITY, GAZA STRIP – PALESTINIAN LEADER YASSER ARAFAT RECEIVES MOURNERS FOLLOWING THE ASSASSINATION OF ABU ALI MUSTAFA, THE POPULAR FRONT FOR THE LIBERATION OF PALESTINE LEADER, IN THE WEST BANK TOWN OF RAMALLAH. (EMMANUEL PAIN)

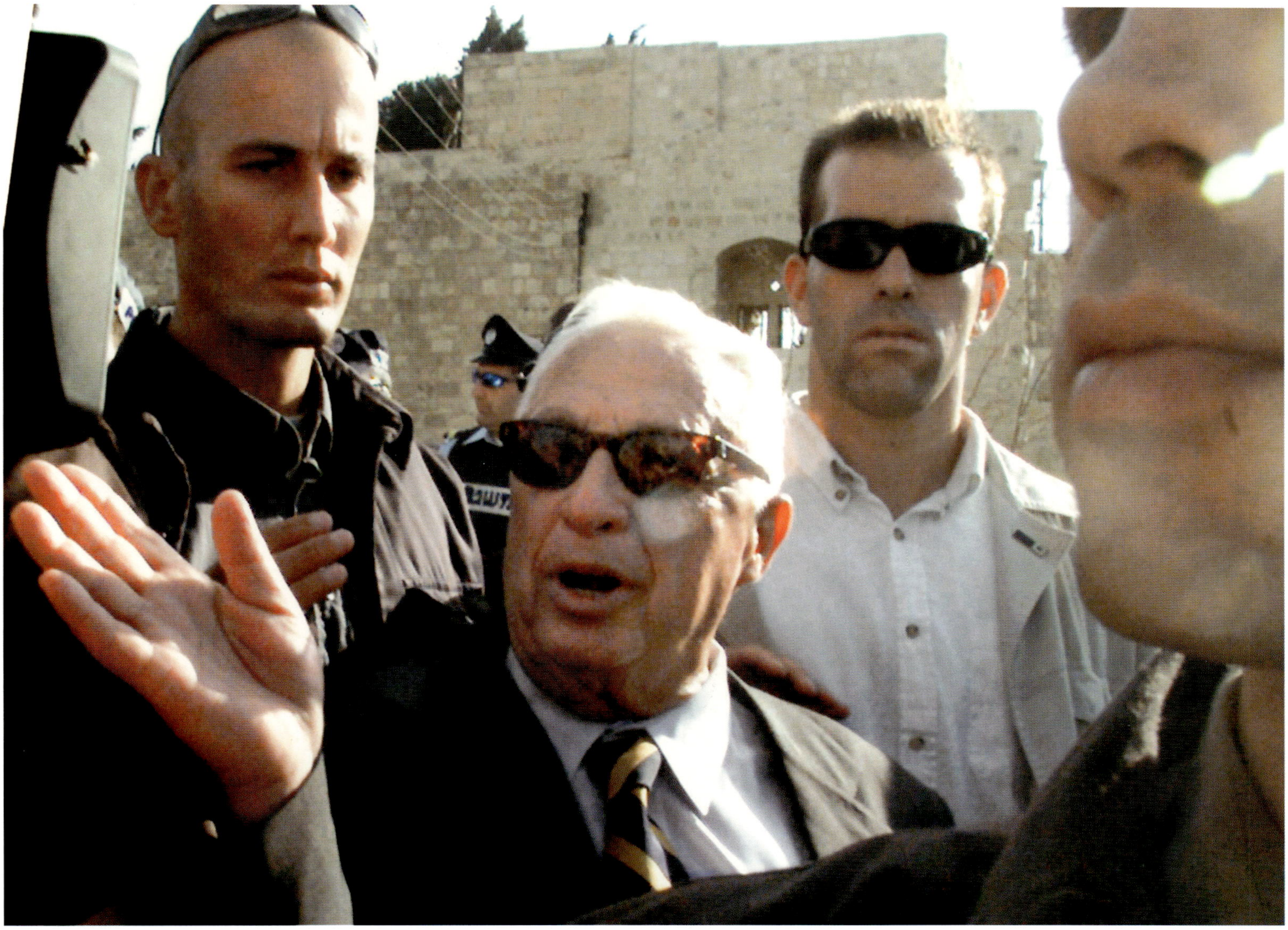

28TH SEPTEMBER 2000 – JERUSALEM – RIGHT-WING OPPOSITION LEADER ARIEL SHARON LEAVES THE AL-AQSA MOSQUE COMPOUND AFTER HIS CONTROVERSIAL VISIT TO ISLAM'S THIRD HOLIEST SHRINE, WHICH SPARKED VIOLENT DEMONSTRATIONS BY PALESTINIANS. (ANDRÉ DURAND)

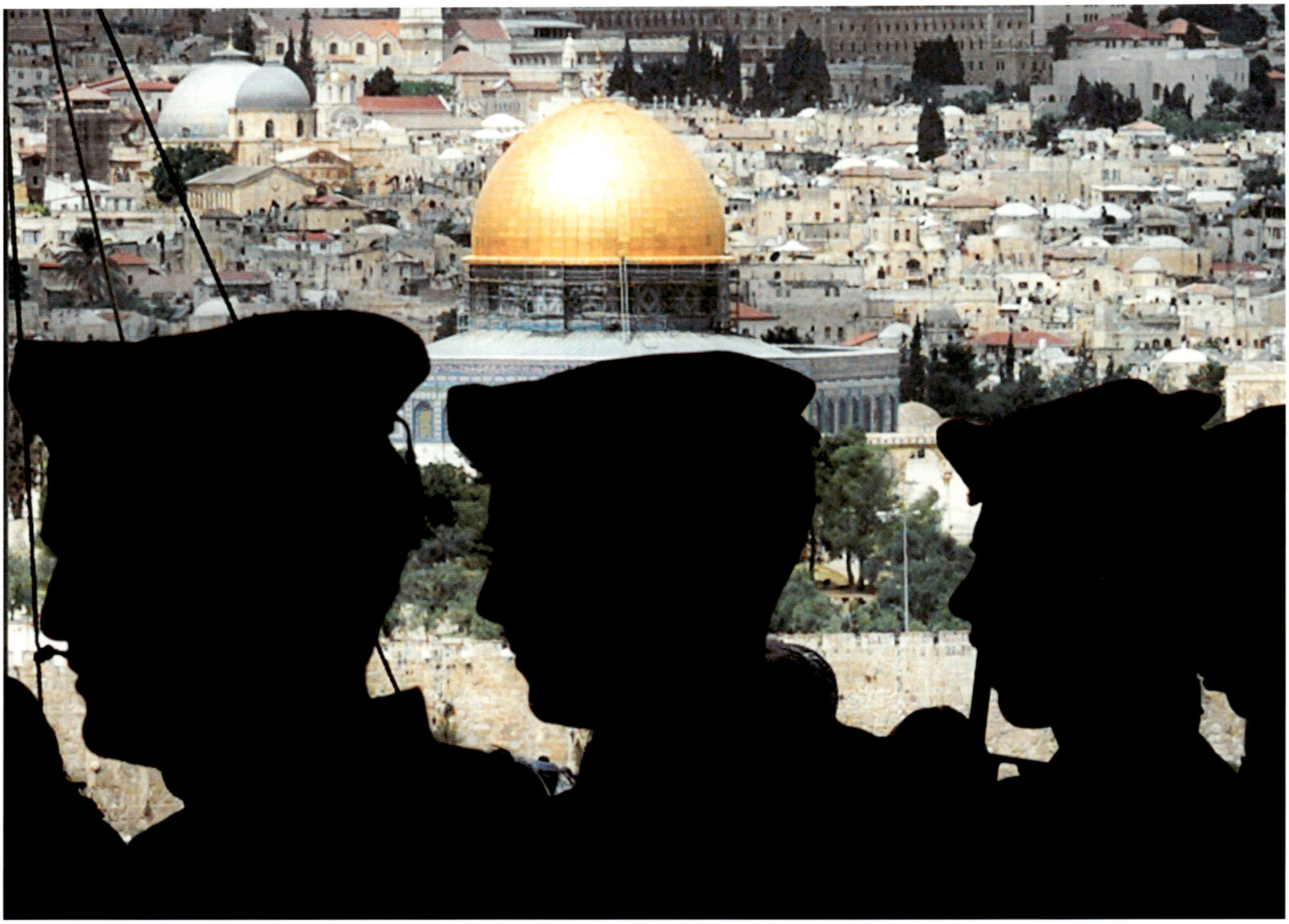

25TH APRIL 2001 – JERUSALEM –
ISRAELI SOLDIERS PICTURED AGAINST
THE DOME OF THE ROCK MOSQUE DURING
A REMEMBRANCE DAY CEREMONY ON THE
MOUNT OF OLIVES. (ANDRÉ DURAND)

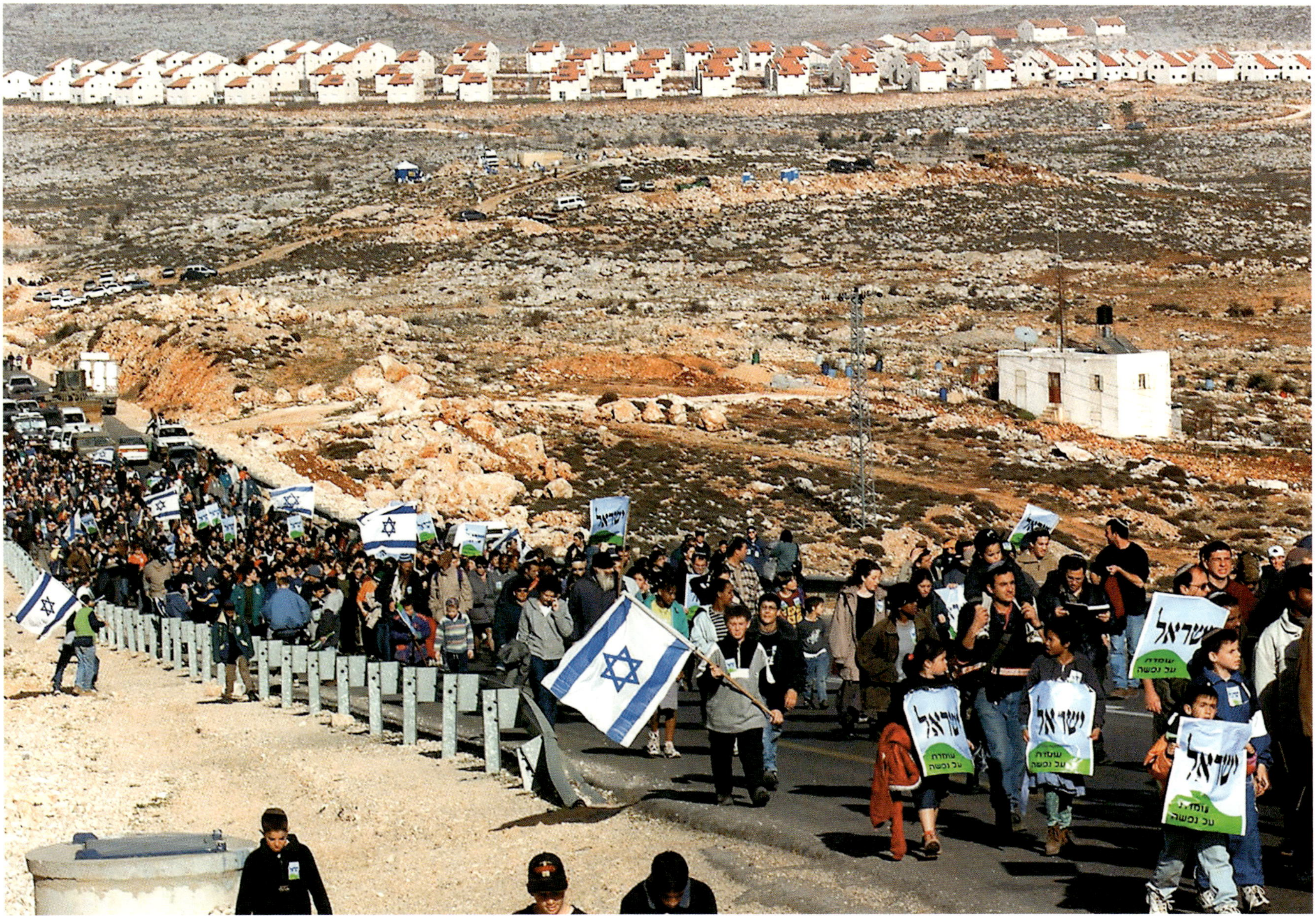

1ST JANUARY 2001 – OFRA, WEST BANK – ISRAELI SETTLERS MARCHING ON JERUSALEM TO PROTEST AGAINST A LACK OF SECURITY ON THE ROADS IN THE WEST BANK FOLLOWING THE MURDER OF A RIGHT-WING EXTREMIST AND HIS WIFE IN A PALESTINIAN AMBUSH. (MENAHEM KAHANA)

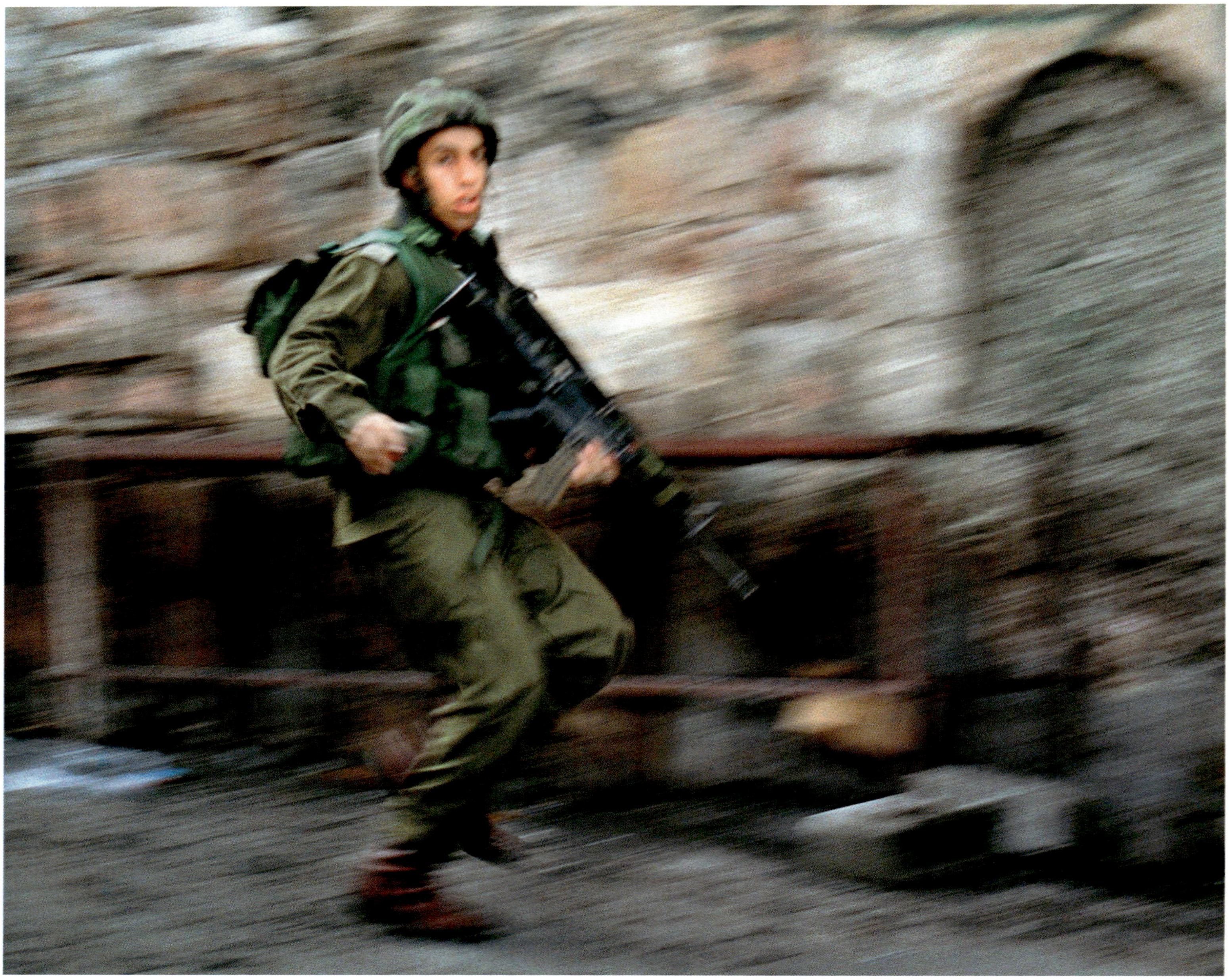

5TH JANUARY 2001 – HEBRON, WEST BANK – AN ISRAELI SOLDIER RUNS TO TAKE POSITION DURING CLASHES WITH STONE-THROWING PALESTINIANS. (HOSSAM ABOU ALLAN)

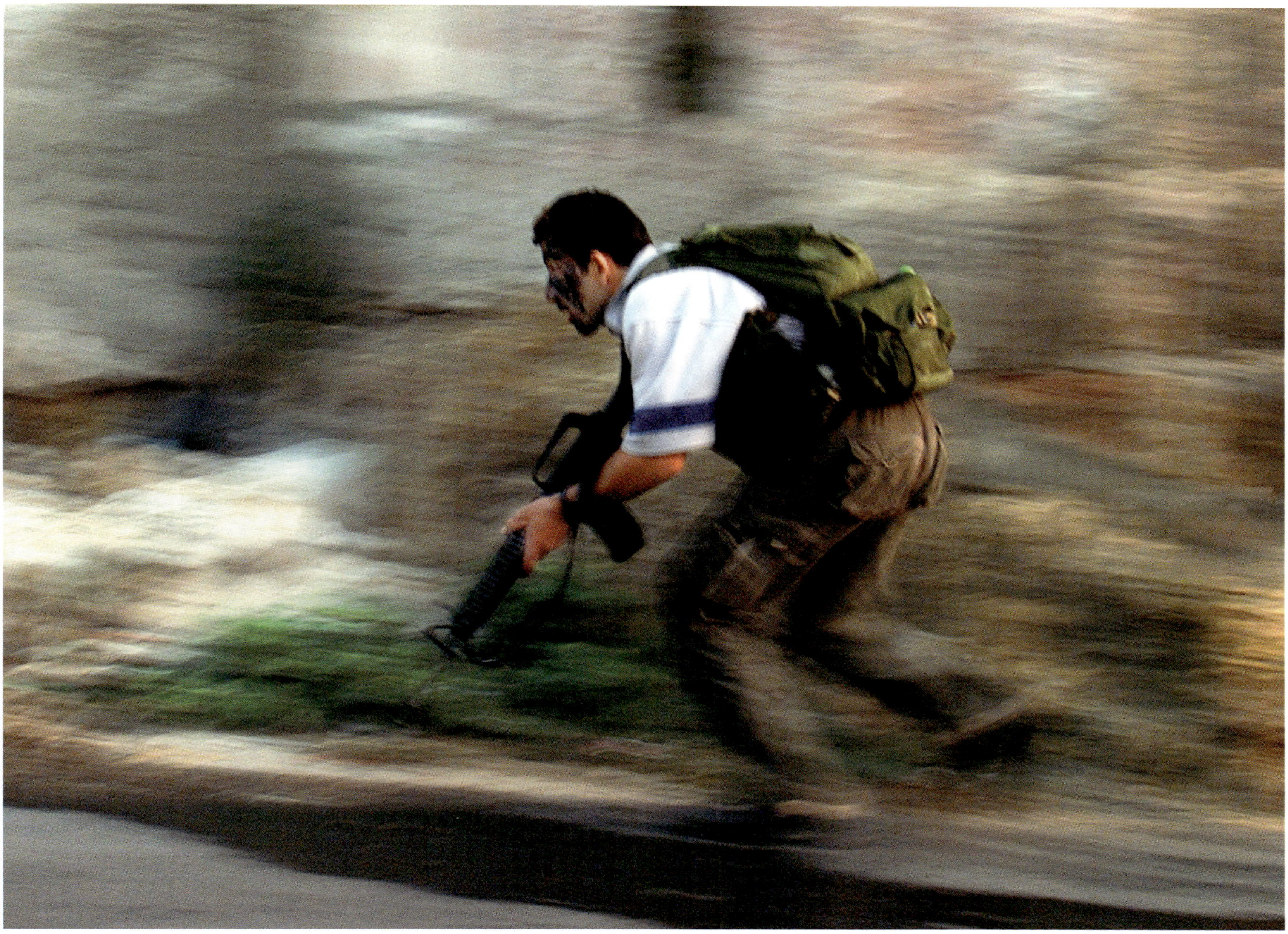

28TH AUGUST 2001 – BEIT JALA, WEST BANK – A PALESTINIAN GUNMAN TAKING PART IN FIGHTING AGAINST ISRAELI TROOPS ON THE OUTSKIRTS OF BETHLEHEM. (ANDRÉ DURAND)

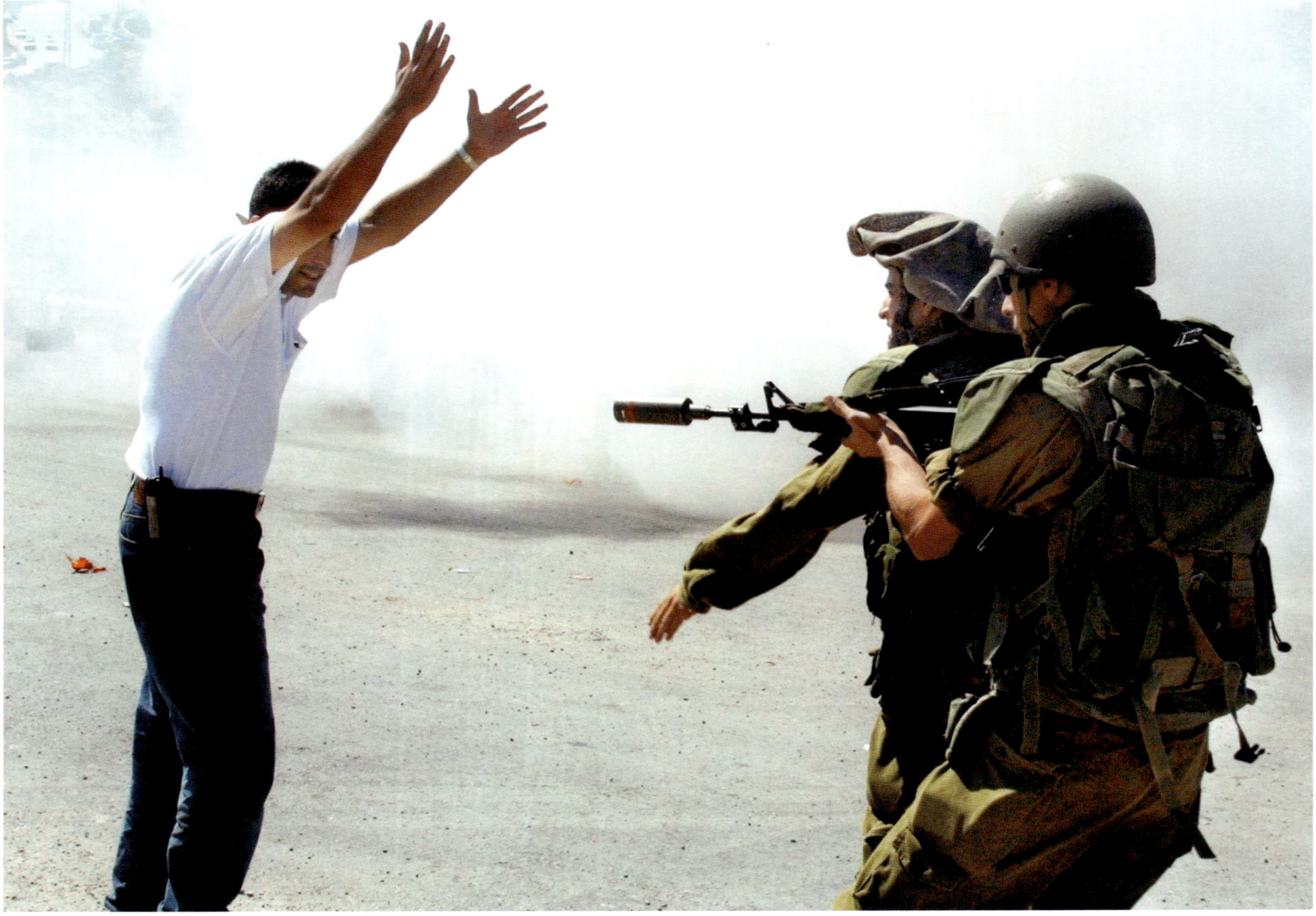

17TH SEPTEMBER 2001
– SURDA, WEST BANK –
NABIL HAMAD, A COORDINATOR FOR YASSER ARAFAT'S FATAH AL-SHABIBA YOUTH MOVEMENT, IS THREATENED BY ISRAELI SOLDIERS DURING A DEMONSTRATION BY BIR ZEIT UNIVERSITY STUDENTS.
(JAMAL ARURI)

5TH AUGUST 2001 – TEL AVIV, ISRAEL – ISRAELI POLICE SURROUND THE BODY OF PALESTINIAN GUNMAN ALI JOLANI, WHO SHOT AND INJURED EIGHT ISRAELI SOLDIERS AND TWO CIVILIANS IN FRONT OF THE DEFENSE MINISTRY. (SHAUL GOLAN/ YEDIOT AHARONOT)

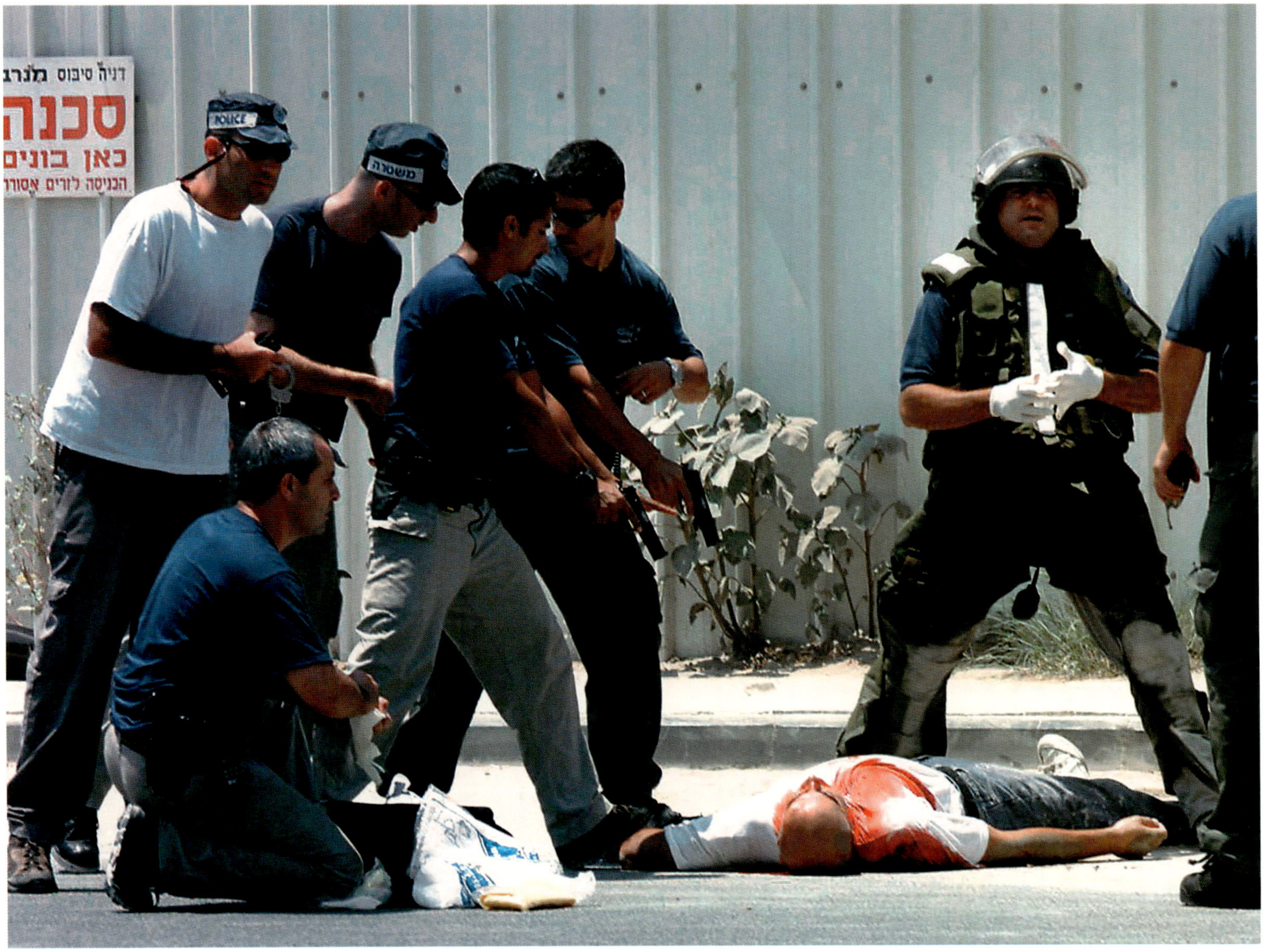

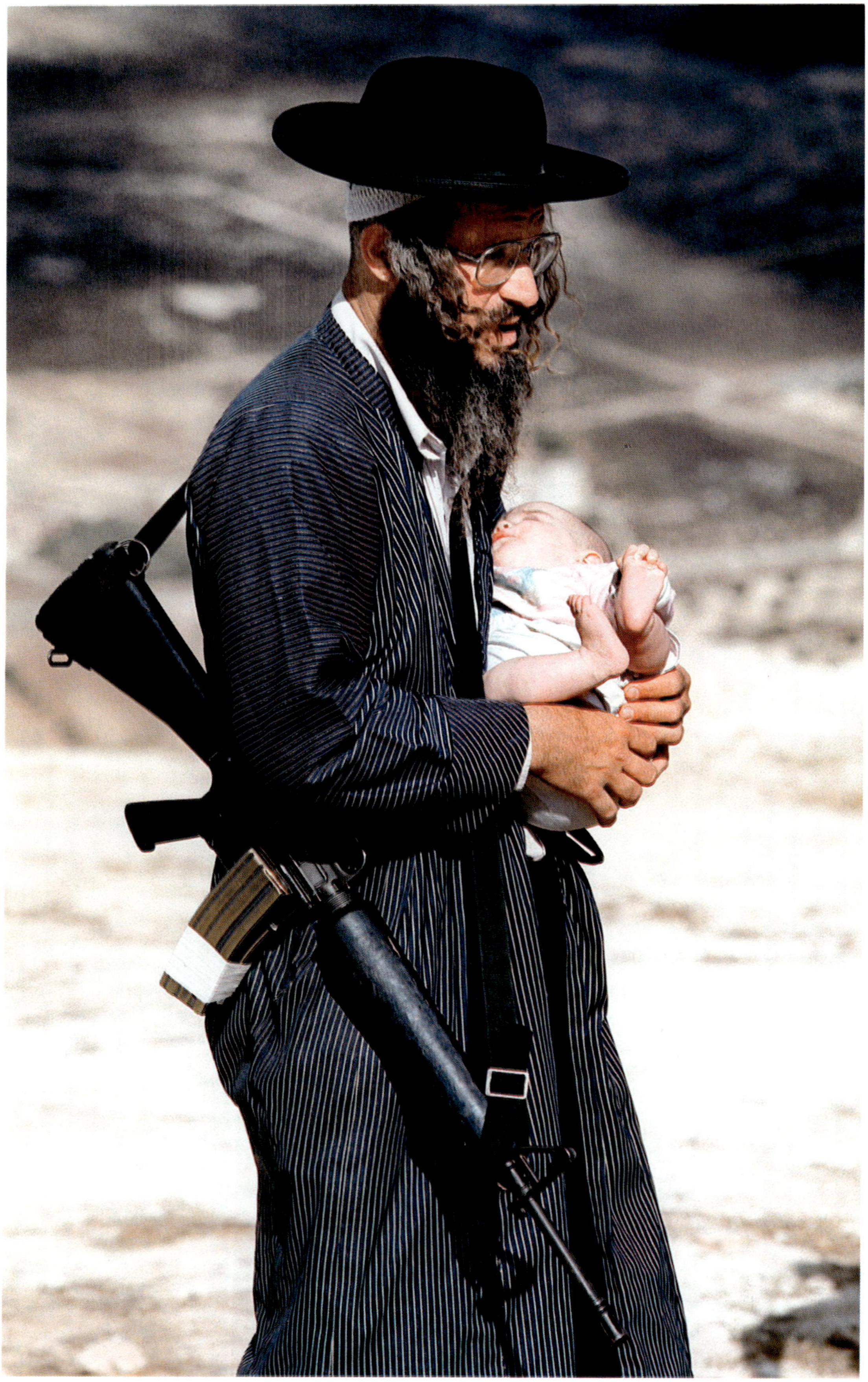

11TH OCTOBER 2000 – YITZHAR, WEST BANK – AN ARMED ULTRA-ORTHODOX JEWISH SETTLER CRADLES HIS BABY AT THE FUNERAL OF HILLEL LIEBERMAN, A US CITIZEN SHOT DEAD AT HIS HOME ON THE WEST BANK. (MENAHEM KAHANA)

8TH FEBRUARY 2001 – JERUSALEM – SECURITY MEN SHEPHERD ULTRA-ORTHODOX JEWS FROM THE SCENE OF A CAR BOMB WHICH EXPLODED IN WEST JERUSALEM TWO DAYS AFTER ARIEL SHARON WAS ELECTED ISRAELI PRIME MINISTER.

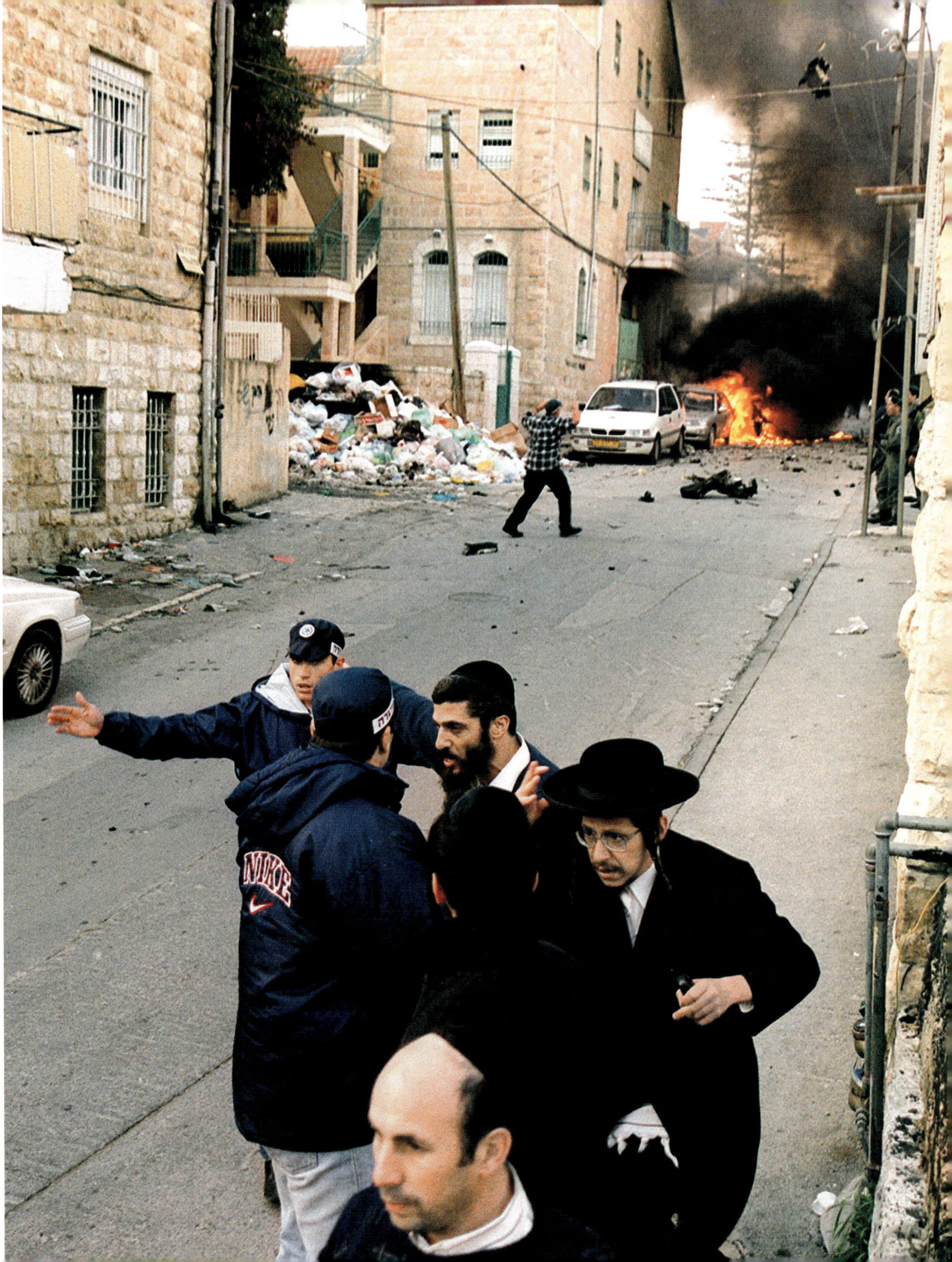
NIKE

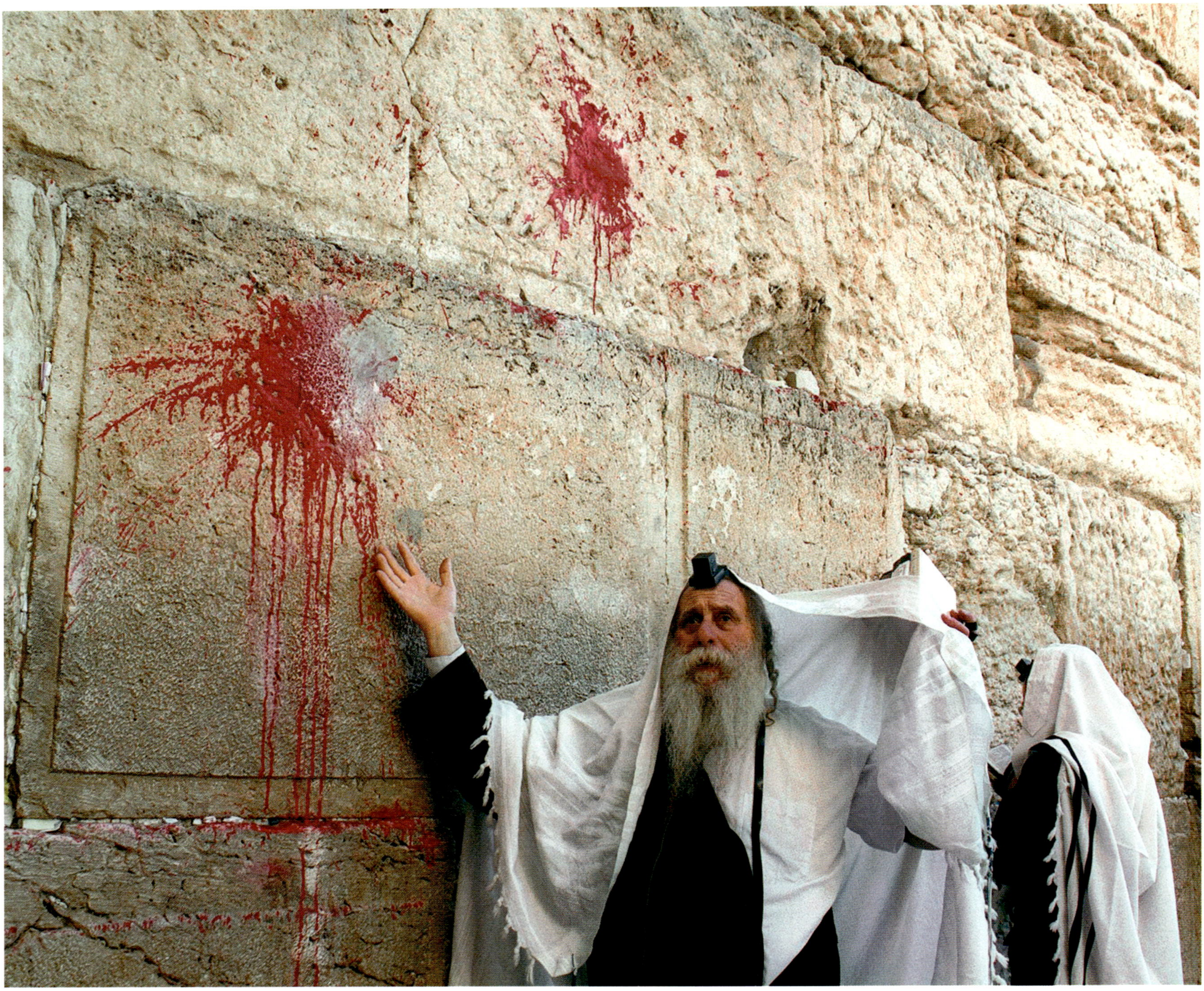

28TH DECEMBER 2000 – JERUSALEM – AN ULTRA-ORTHODOX JEW STANDS BESIDE THE WESTERN WALL, THE HOLIEST SITE IN JUDAISM, AFTER IT WAS DESECRATED BY AN AMERICAN TOURIST WHO HURLED BOTTLES OF RED PAINT AT THE WALL. (ISAAC HARARI)

3RD OCTOBER 2000 – NETZARIM CROSSING, GAZA STRIP – PALESTINIAN YOUTHS CARRY THE BODY OF A FELLOW-PROTESTOR SHOT DEAD BY ISRAELI SOLDIERS. (ANDRÉ DURAND)

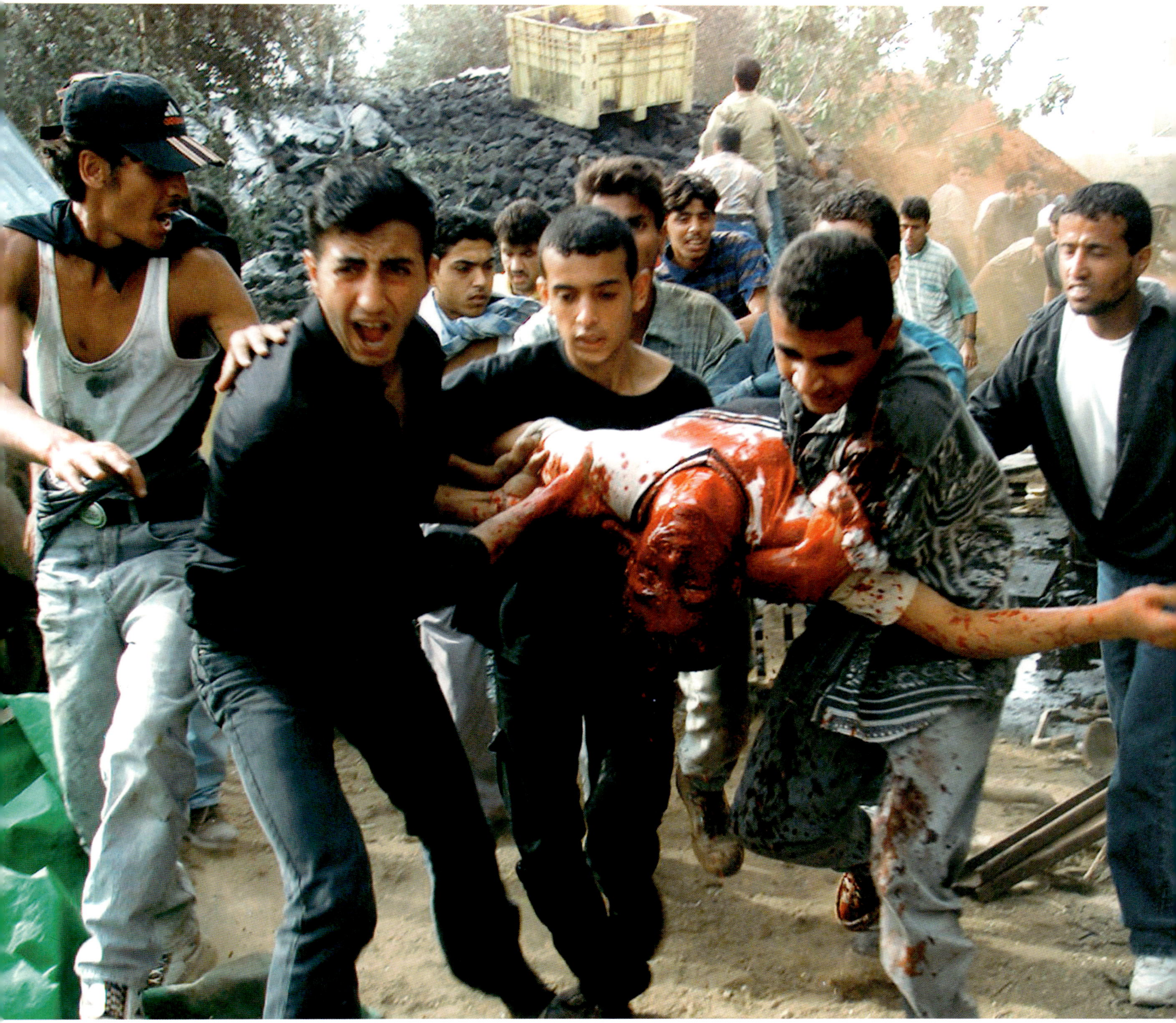

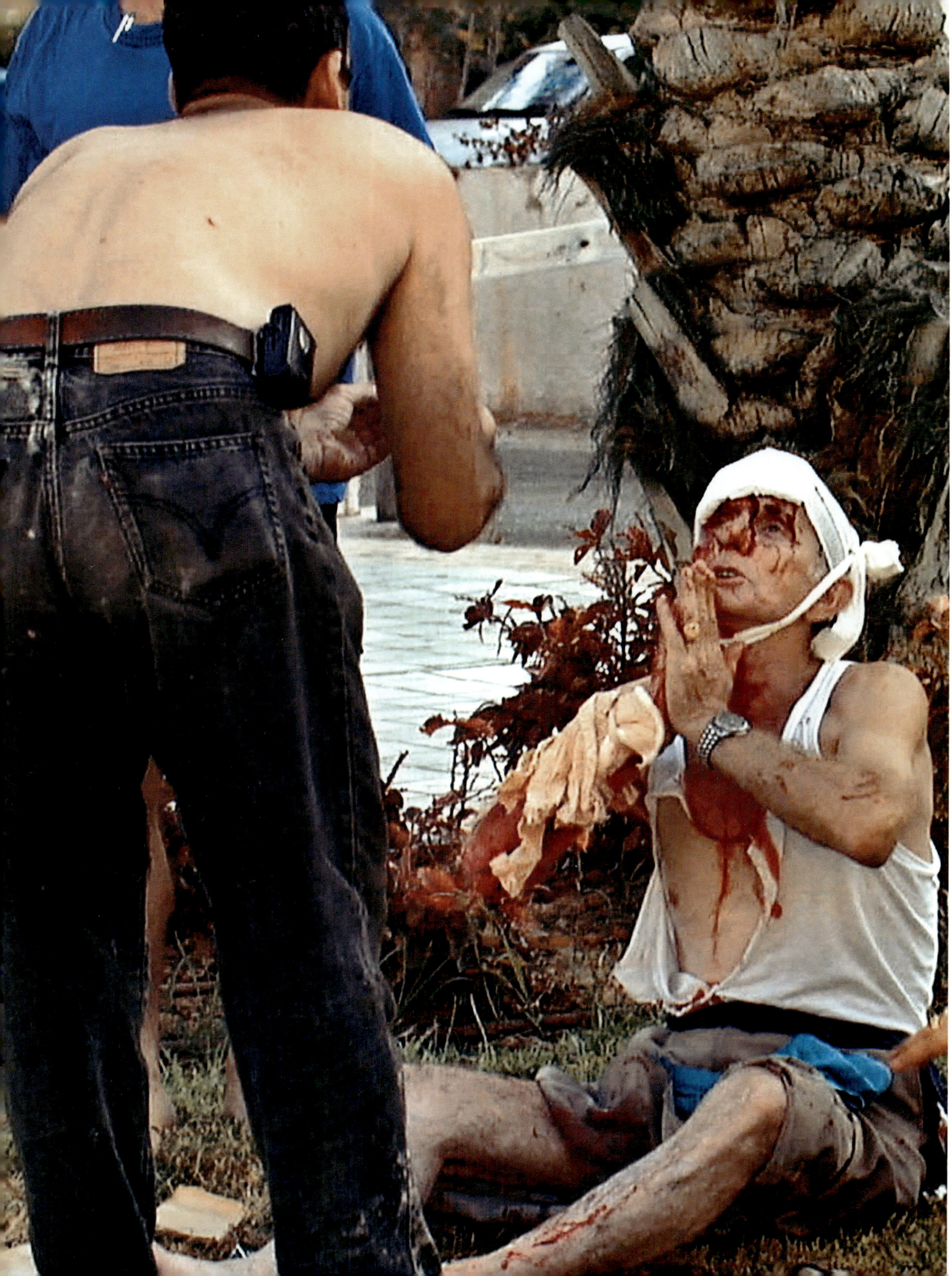

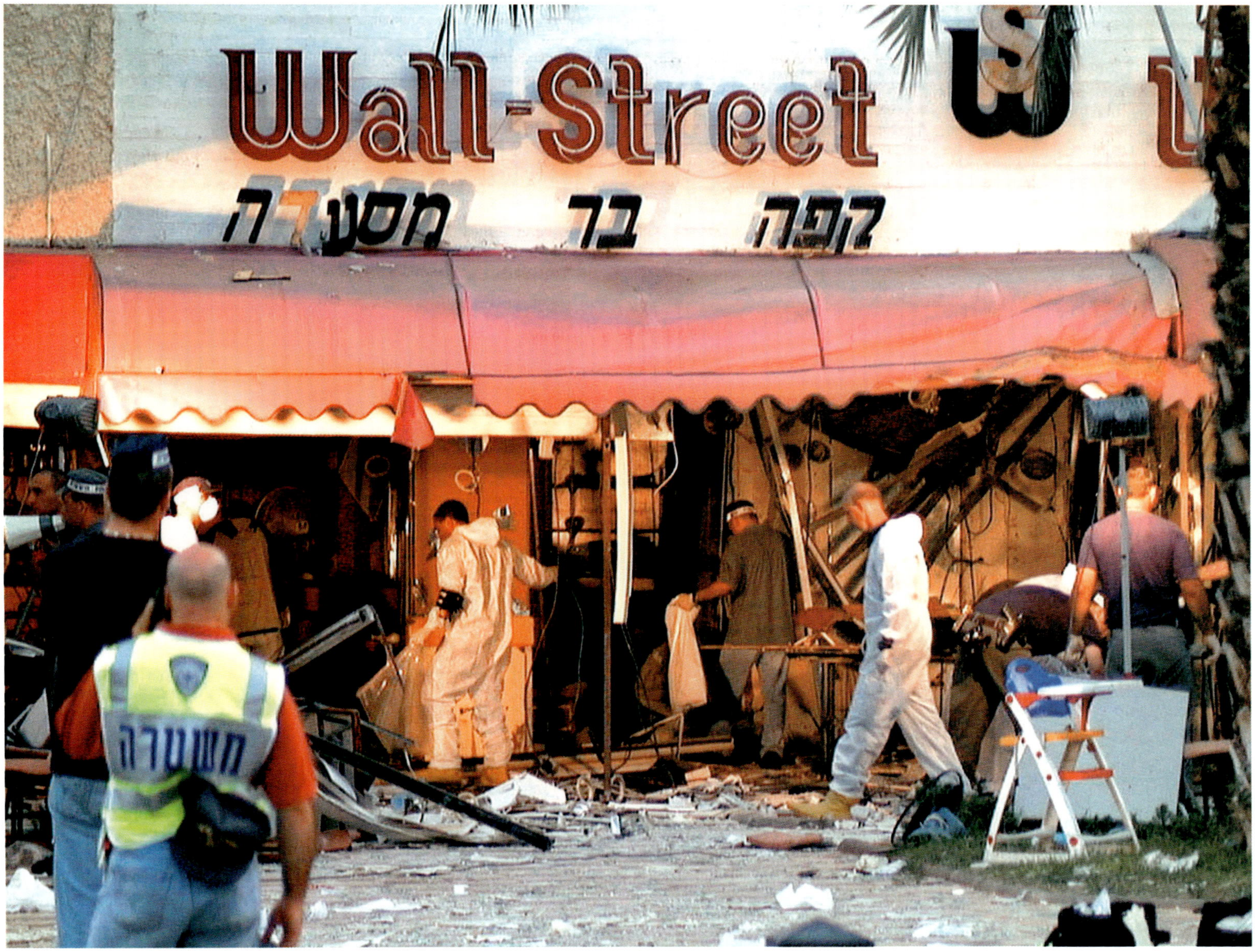

12TH AUGUST 2001 – KIRYAT MOTZKIN, ISRAEL – A WOUNDED ISRAELI ASKING FOR HELP AFTER THE SUICIDE-BOMBING OF THE BUSY WALL STREET CAFE. (ALEX KOLOMOISKY/ YEDIOT AHARONOT)

12TH AUGUST 2001 – KIRYAT MOTZKIN, ISRAEL – POLICE AND FORENSIC EXPERTS EXAMINE THE WRECKAGE OF THE WALL STREET CAFE AFTER A SUICIDE BOMB ATTACK. (ALEX KOLOMOISKY/ YEDIOT AHARONOT)

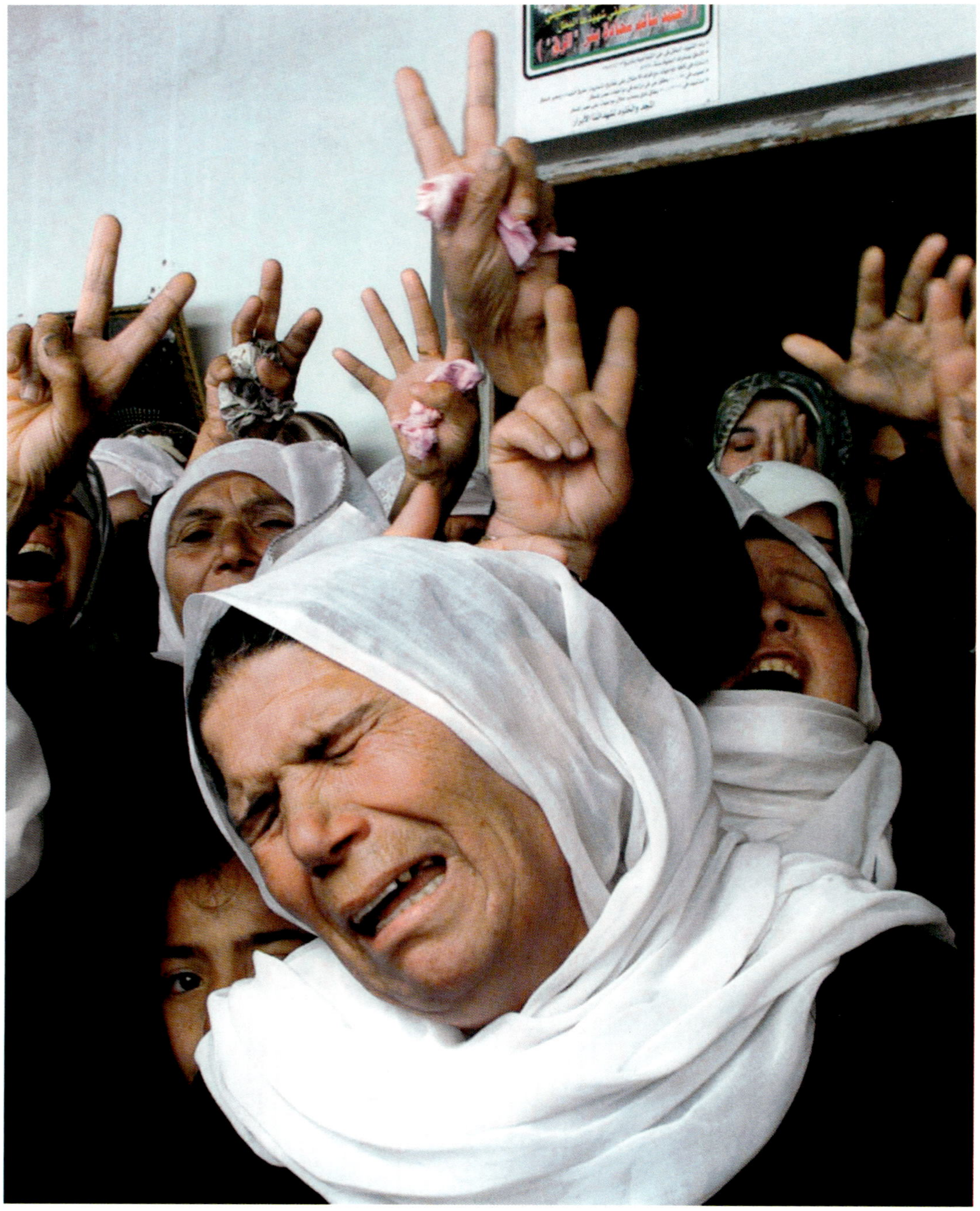

15TH MARCH 2001 – GAZA CITY, GAZA STRIP – A WOMAN MOURNS THE DEATH OF HER 19-YEAR-OLD GRANDSON, SHOT DEAD BY ISRAELI TROOPS WHO OPENED FIRE ON PALESTINIAN YOUTHS NEAR AN ARMY POST. (FAYEZ NURELDINE)

12TH OCTOBER 2000 – RAMALLAH, WEST BANK – A PALESTINIAN YOUTH SHOWS THE CROWD THE BLOOD ON HIS HANDS OF AN ISRAELI SOLDIER FROM INSIDE A PALESTINIAN POLICE STATION. (CHRIS GERALD)

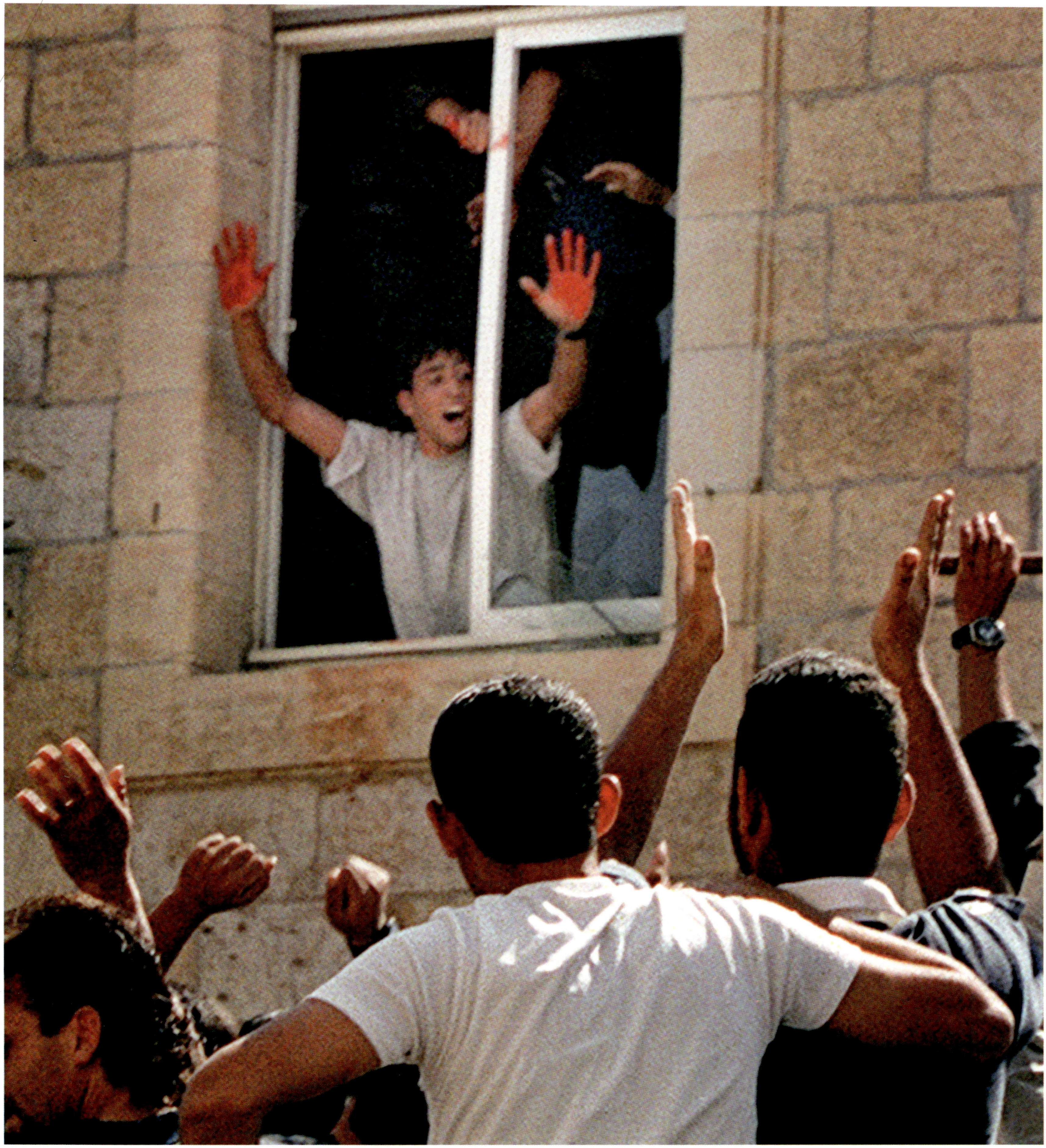

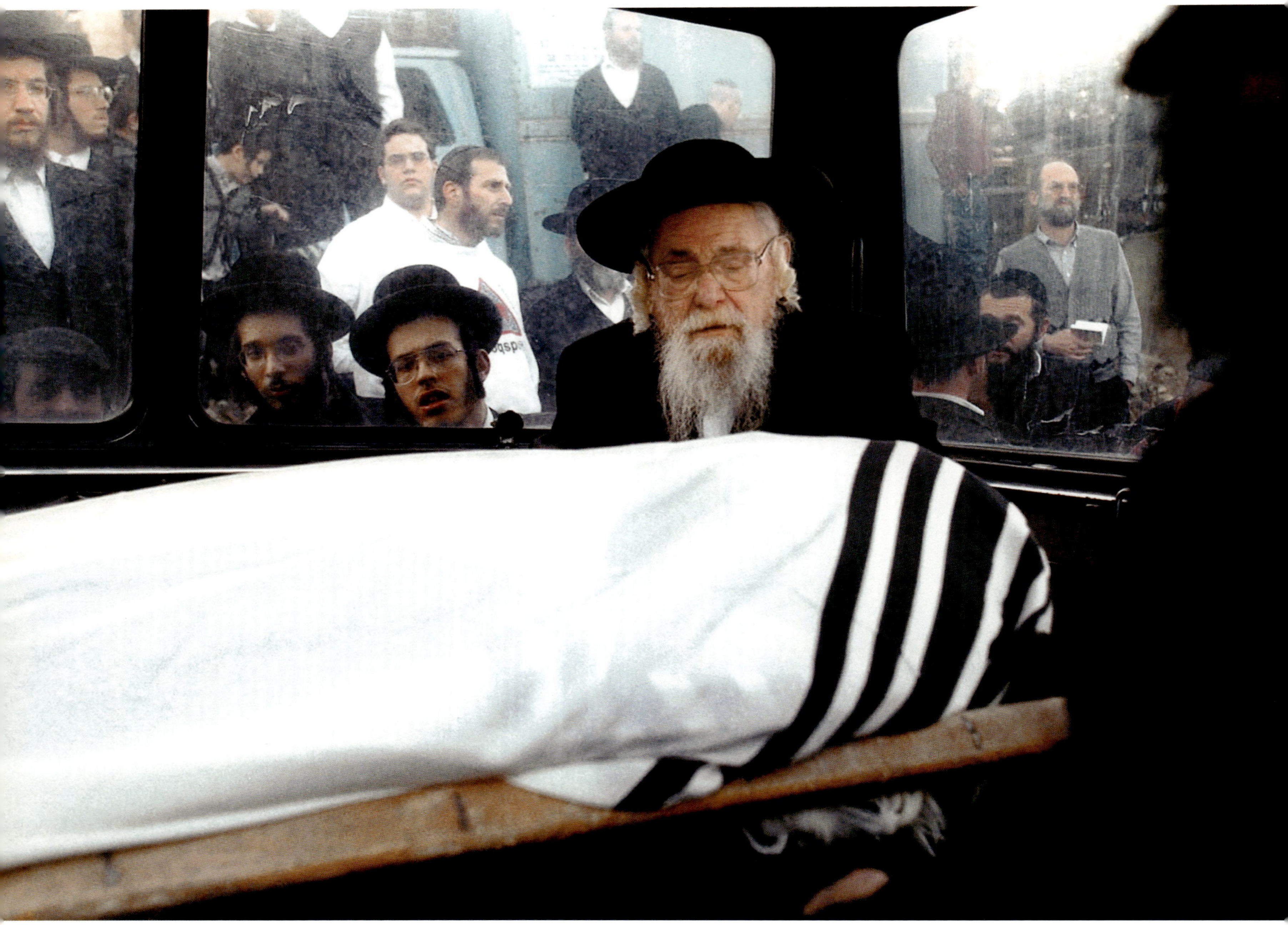

31ST DECEMBER 2000 – JERUSALEM – RABBIS WITH THE BODY OF AN ISRAELI EXTREMIST SHOT DEAD ALONG WITH HIS WIFE BY PALESTINIAN GUNMEN IN THE WEST BANK SETTLEMENT OF OFRA. (MENAHEM KAHANA)

6TH AUGUST 2001 – GINOT SHOMRON, WEST BANK – NOAM, THE ELDEST SON OF TEHIYA BLOMBERG, READS A PRAYER AS HIS YOUNGER BROTHER HAGAI LOOKS ON AT THEIR MOTHER'S FUNERAL FOLLOWING HER MURDER BY PALESTINIAN GUNMEN. (SHAUL GOLAN/YEDIOT AHARONOT)

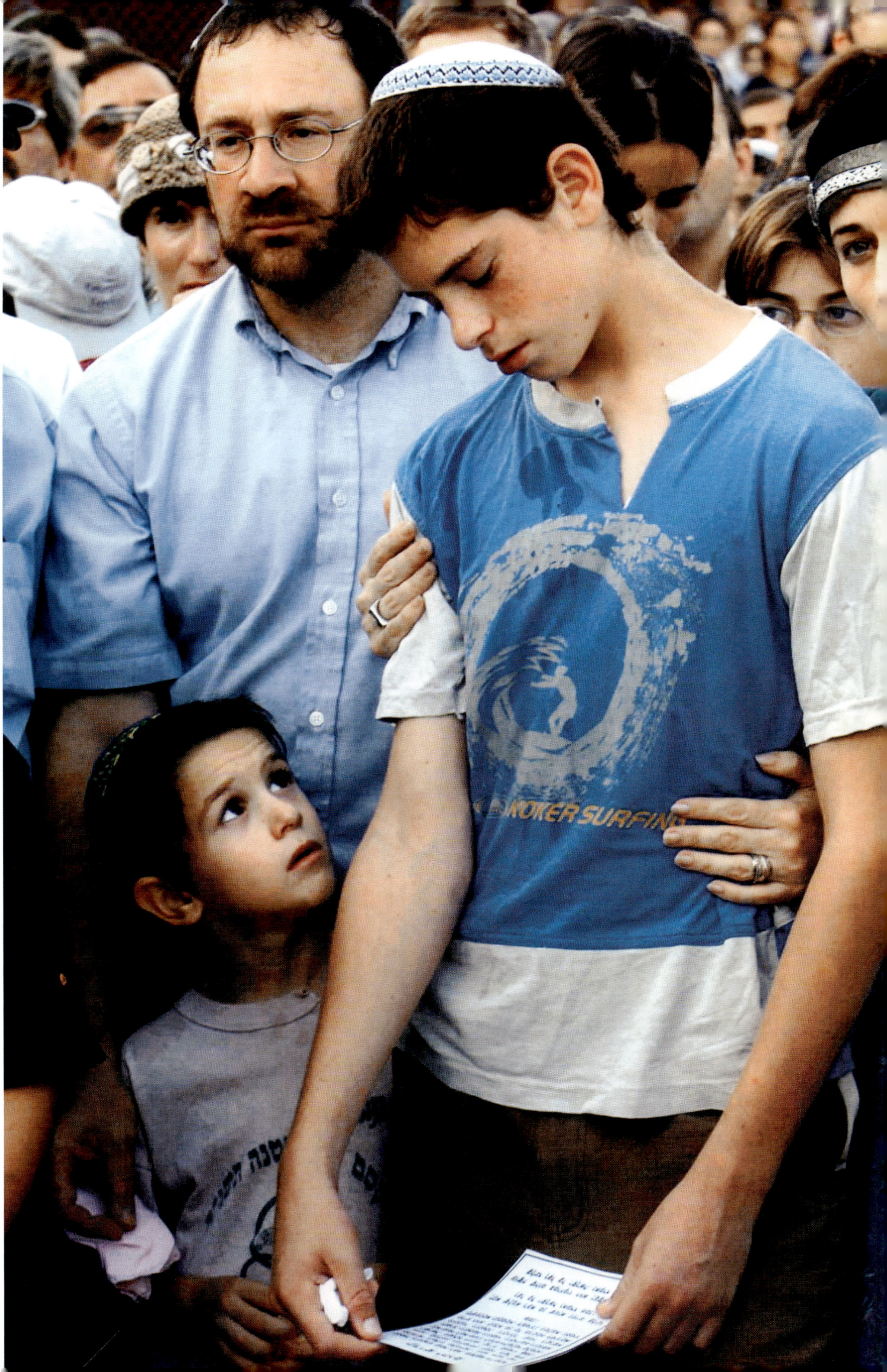

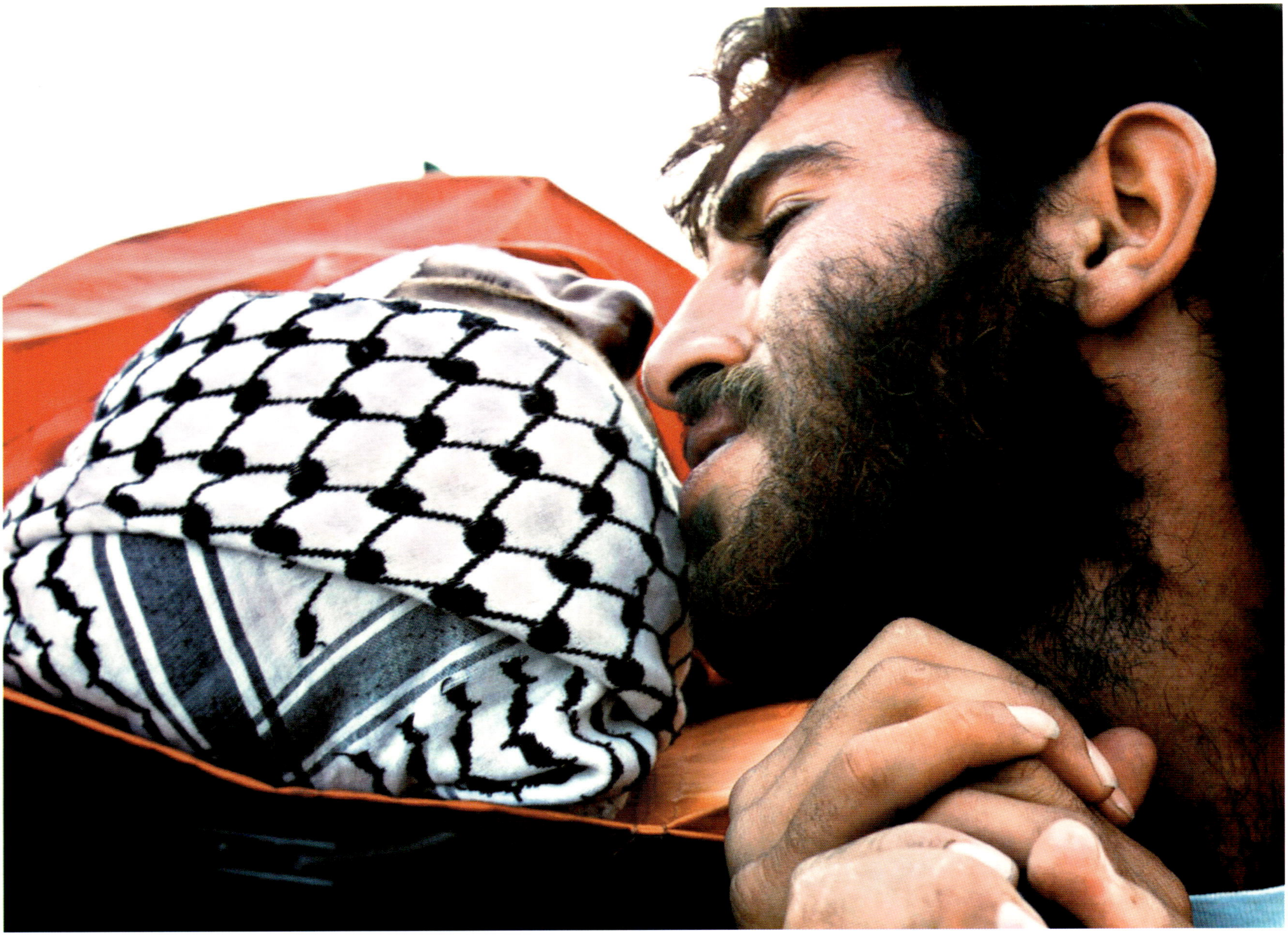

4TH NOVEMBER 2000 – HIZMA, WEST BANK – A PALESTINIAN CARRIES THE BODY OF A 19-YEAR-OLD YOUTH AT HIS FUNERAL AFTER BEING SHOT AND KILLED DURING CLASHES WITH ISRAELI TROOPS. (CHRISTOPHE SIMON)

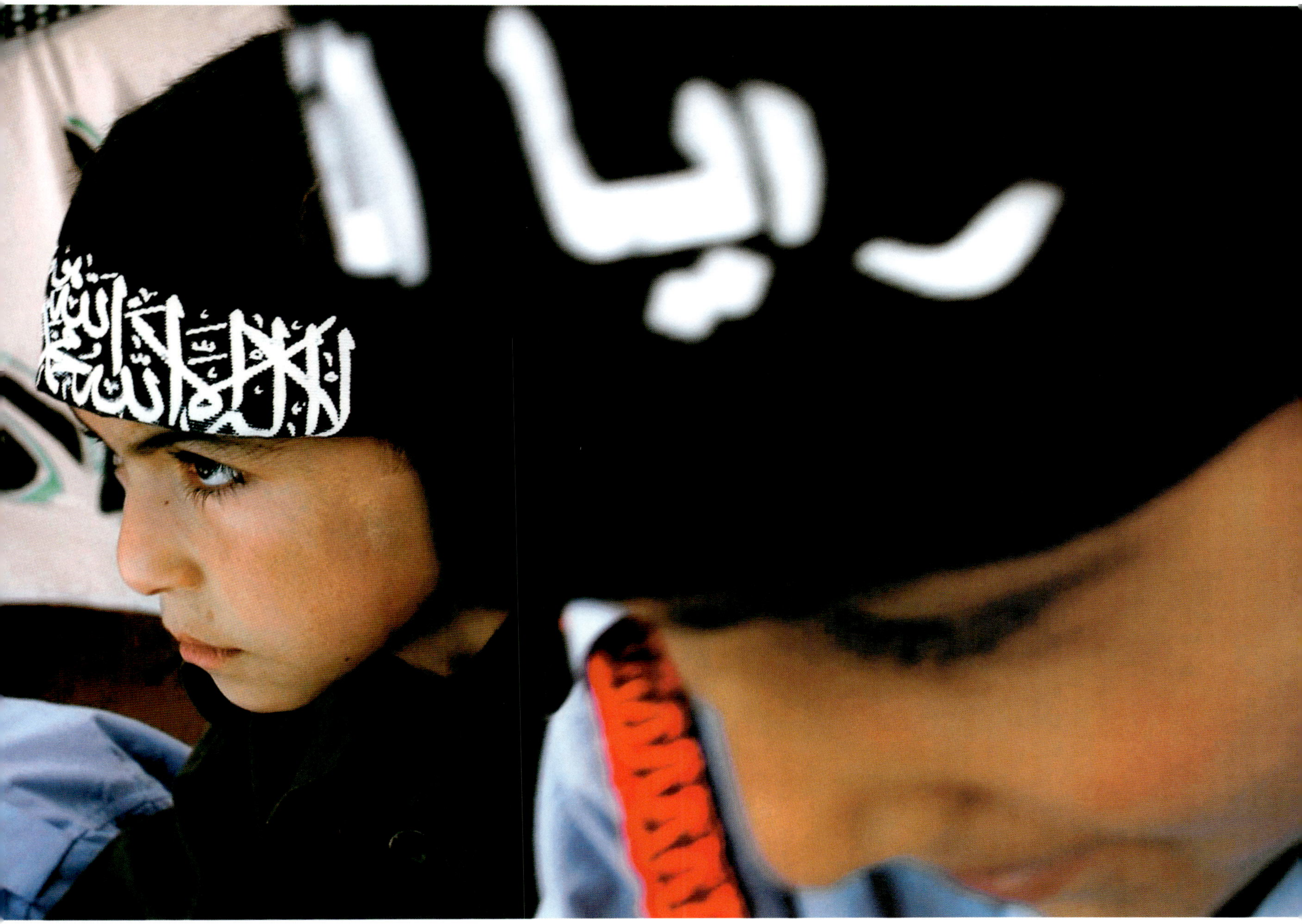

13TH APRIL 2001
– RAFAH, GAZA STRIP –
PALESTINIAN CHILDREN
AT A RALLY OF MILITANT
ISLAMIC JIHAD MEMBERS.
(CHRISTOPHE SIMON)

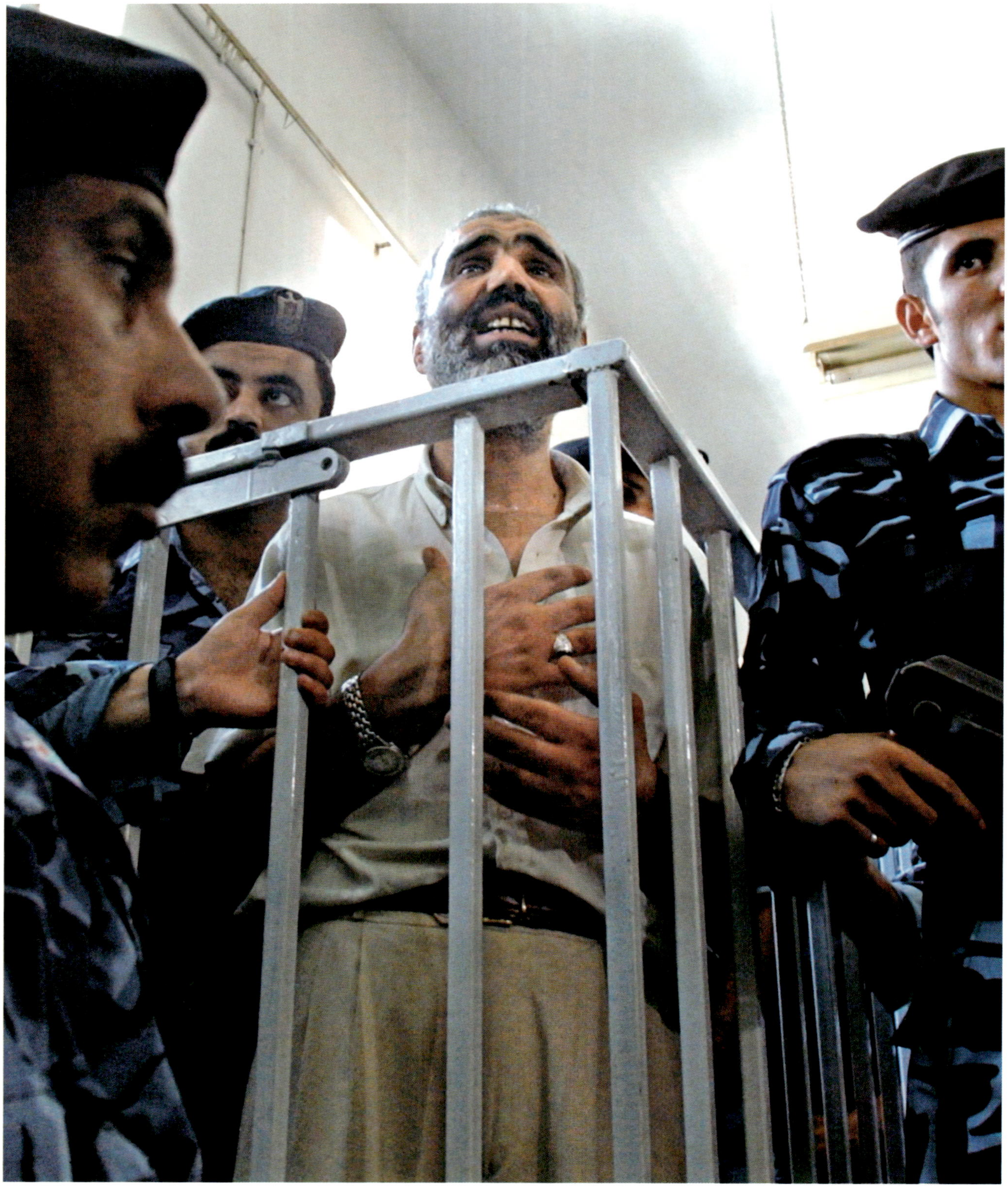

6TH AUGUST 2001 – NABLUS, WEST BANK – MONZER HAFNAWI SURROUNDED BY POLICE DURING HIS TRIAL FOR COLLABORATING WITH ISRAEL AND HIS INVOLVEMENT IN THE MURDER OF HAMAS ACTIVIST MAHMOUD EL-MADANI. (EMMANUEL PAIN)

CONFLICTS

YUGO-MILOSEVIC-END
URGENT¥¥¥ SLOBODAN MILOSEVIC SURRENDERS: OFFICIAL
BELGRADE, APRIL 1 (AFP) – SLOBODAN MILOSEVIC HAS SURRENDERED HIMSELF TO THE POLICE, A SPOKESMAN FOR THE SERBIAN GOVERNMENT TOLD AFP EARLY SUNDAY.
MAT/JH/DB

MEXICO-CHIAPAS-RALLY,LEAD
SUBCOMANDANTE MARCOS MAKES TRIUMPHANT ENTRANCE INTO MEXICAN CAPITAL
MEXICO CITY, MARCH 11 (AFP) – "SUBCOMANDANTE MARCOS" WAS GIVEN A TUMULTUOUS WELCOME SUNDAY AS HE ARRIVED IN THE HEART OF THE MEXICAN CAPITAL AT THE CONCLUSION OF A TWO-WEEK ZAPATISTA MARCH TO PROMOTE INDIGENOUS RIGHTS LEGISLATION.
A ROAR EMERGED FROM THE CROWD OF MORE THAN 150,000 PEOPLE WHO PACKED THE CENTRAL ZOCALO SQUARE AS MARCOS AND ANOTHER 24 REBEL COMMANDERS CLIMBED UP ON A PLATFORM FRONTING THE PRESIDENTIAL PALACE.
PM

COLOMBIA-VIOLENCE
COLOMBIAN ARMY CLAIMS 200 GUERRILLAS KILLED IN NORTHWEST
BOGOTA, OCT 22 (AFP) – A TOTAL OF 200 GUERRILLAS HAVE BEEN KILLED IN CLASHES WITH THE ARMY IN NORTHWEST COLOMBIA SINCE LAST WEDNESDAY, COLOMBIA'S AIR FORCE CHIEF GENERAL HECTOR VELASCO SAID SUNDAY.
MILITARY ACTION AGAINST THE COUNTRY'S MAIN LEFTIST GUERRILLA GROUP, THE REVOLUTIONARY ARMED FORCES OF COLOMBIA (FARC), AROUND THE NORTHWESTERN TOWN OF DABEIBA RESULTED IN "A LARGE NUMBER OF LOSSES" AMONG THE REBEL FORCES, HE SAID.
CRV/EB/MK

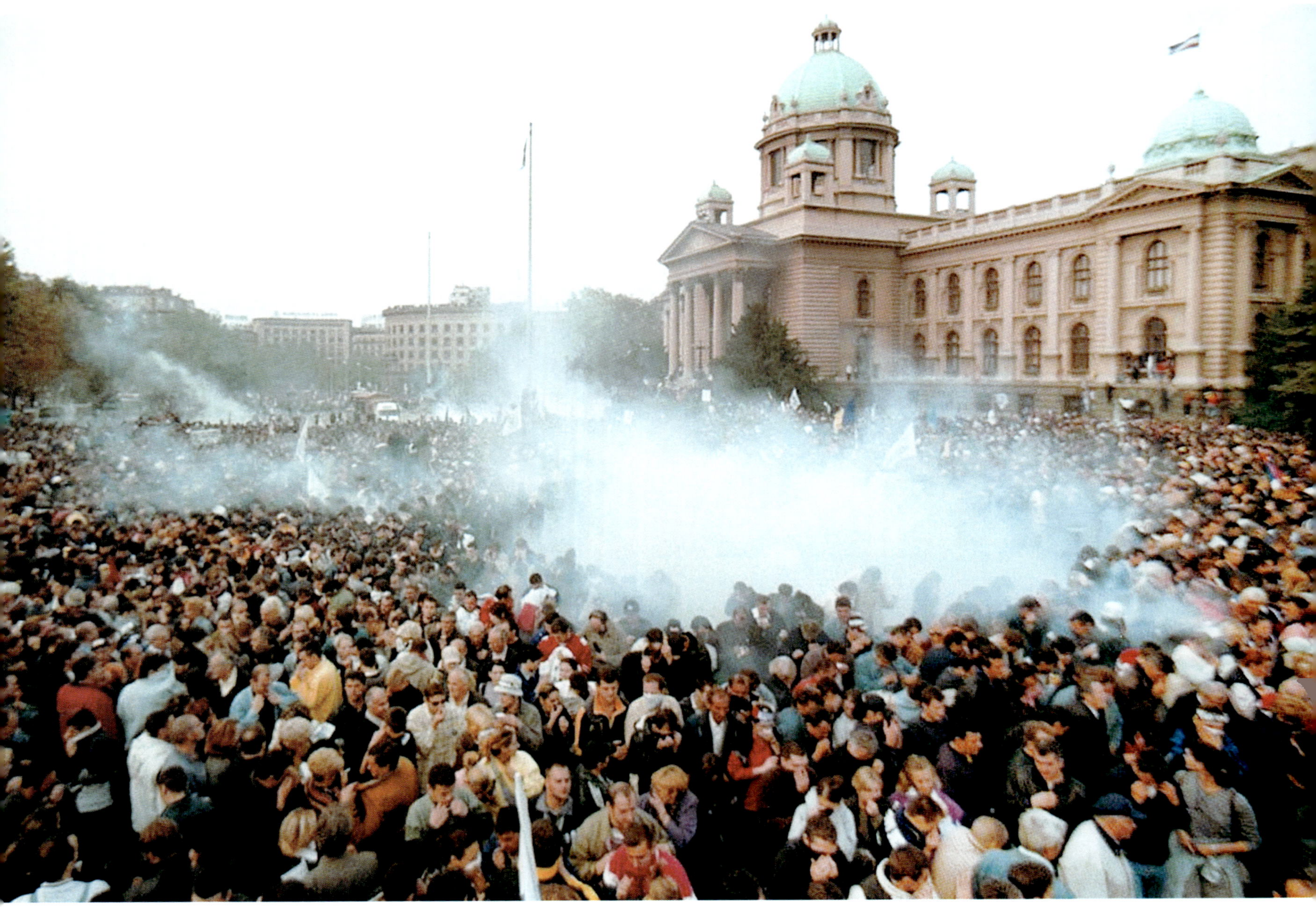

5TH OCTOBER 2000 – BELGRADE, YUGOSLAVIA – OPPOSITION SUPPORTERS GATHERED OUTSIDE PARLIAMENT TO DEMAND THE OUSTING OF PRESIDENT SLOBODAN MILOSEVIC RUN FROM TEAR GAS FIRED BY SERBIAN POLICE JUST BEFORE THE PROTESTORS STORM THE BUILDING. (AYPP)

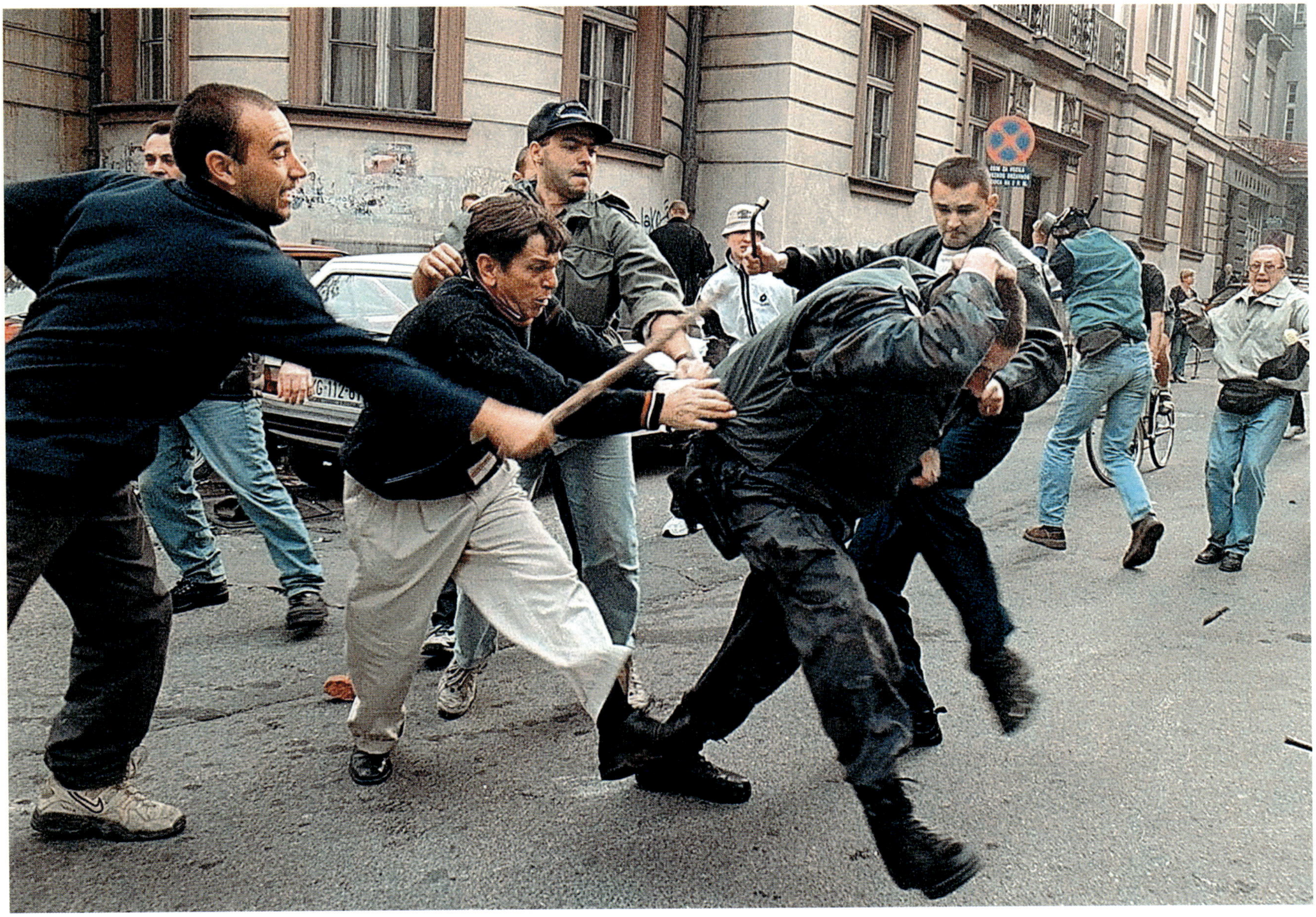

5TH OCTOBER 2000 – BELGRADE, YUGOSLAVIA – PROTESTERS ASSAULT A RIOT POLICEMAN DURING A DEMONSTRATION OF MORE THAN 300,000 PEOPLE CALLING FOR PRESIDENT SLOBODAN MILOSEVIC TO STEP DOWN.(DJORDJE TOMIC/EPA)

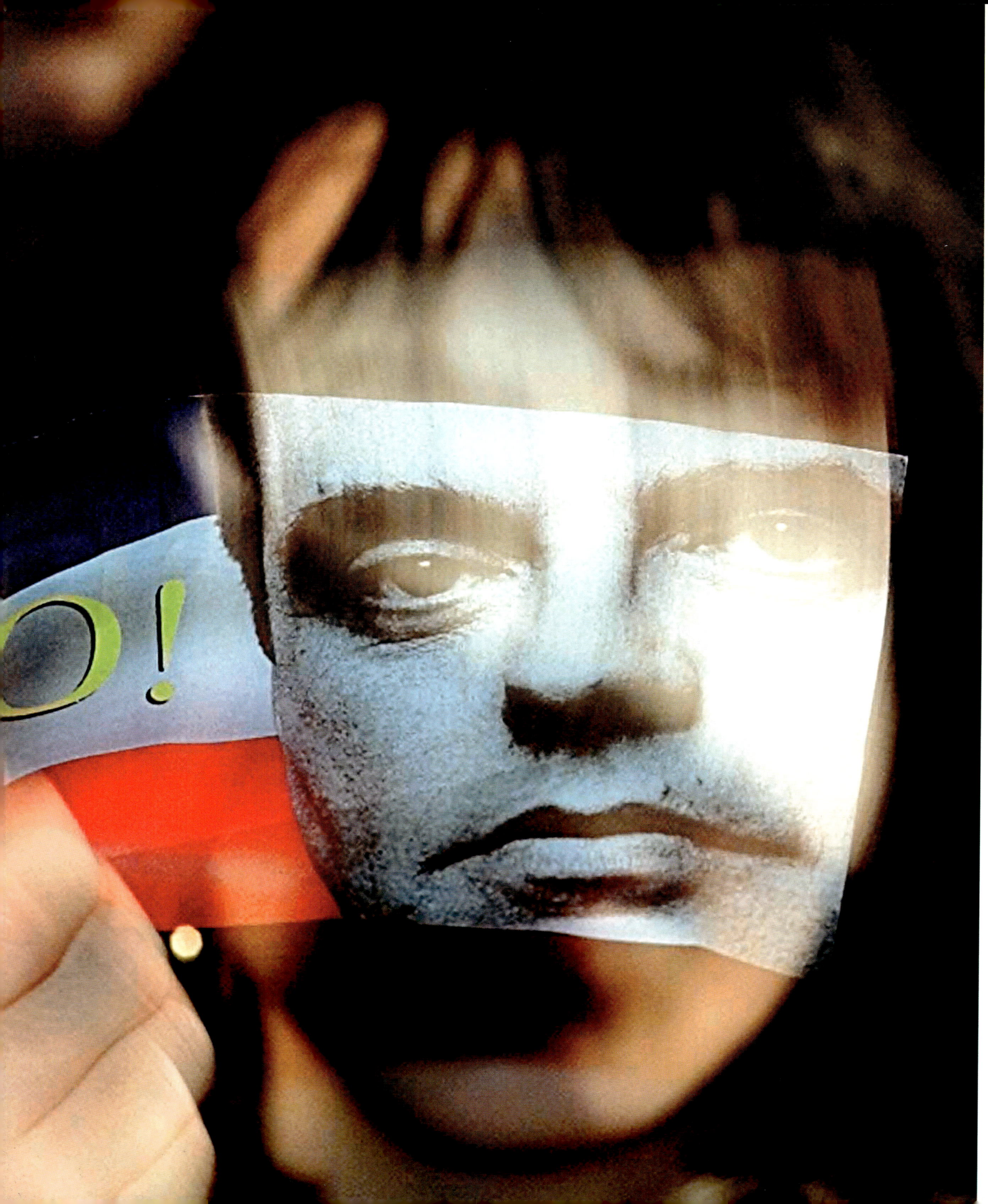
O!

21ST SEPTEMBER 2000
– NOVI SAD, YUGOSLAVIA –
AN OPPOSITION SUPPORTER DISPLAYS AN ELECTION LEAFLET WITH THE PICTURE OF PRESIDENTIAL CANDIDATE VOJISLAV KOSTUNICA. (SRDJAN SUKI/EPA)

6TH OCTOBER 2000
– BELGRADE, YUGOSLAVIA –
A DEMONSTRATOR BEARS A MOCK TOMBSTONE FOR FORMER YUGOSLAV PRESIDENT SLOBODAN MILOSEVIC AS CROWDS GATHER IN FRONT OF THE PARLIAMENT BUILDING FOR THE SWEARING IN OF HIS SUCCESSOR VOJISLAV KOSTUNICA. (SRDJAN SUKI/EPA)

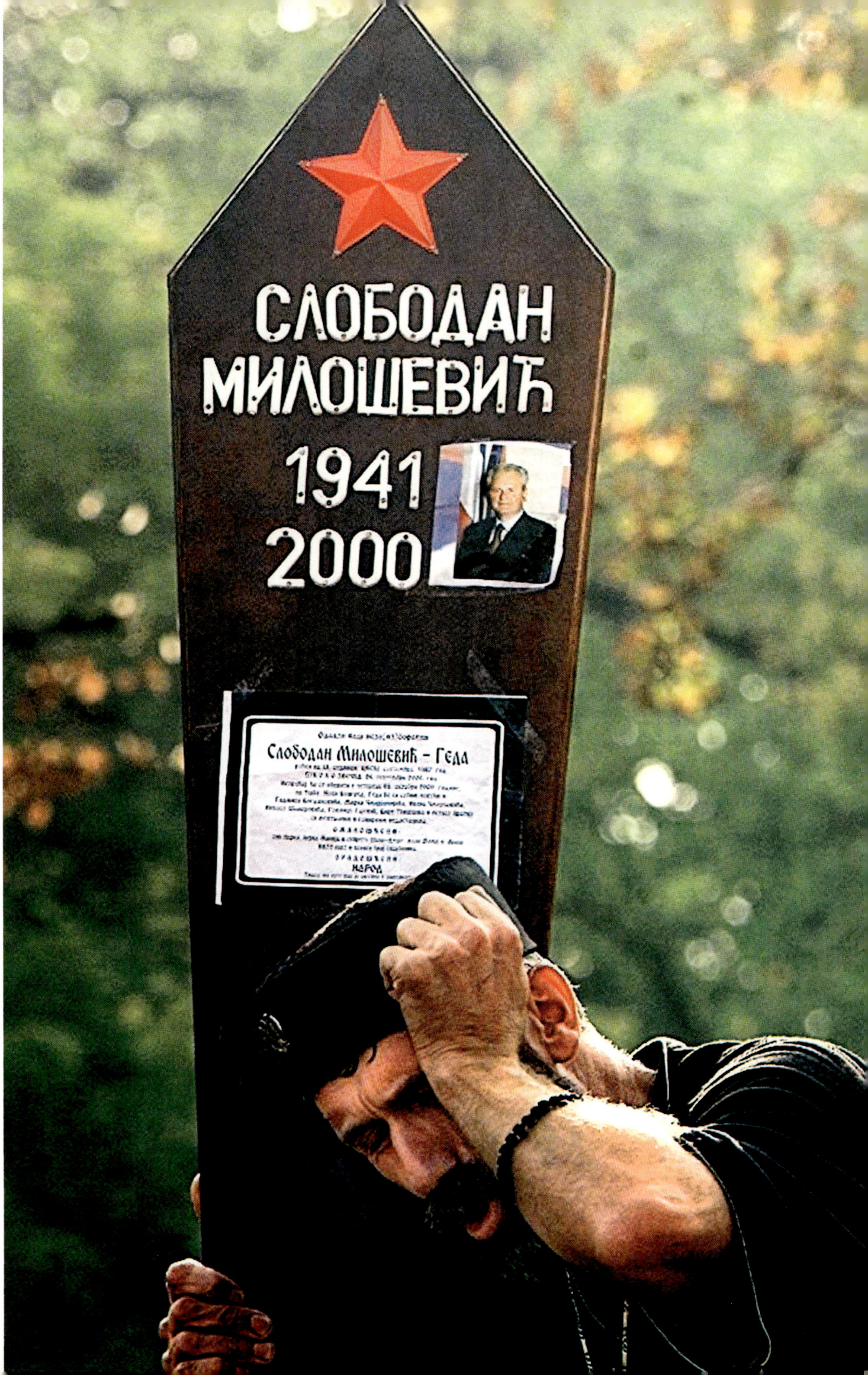

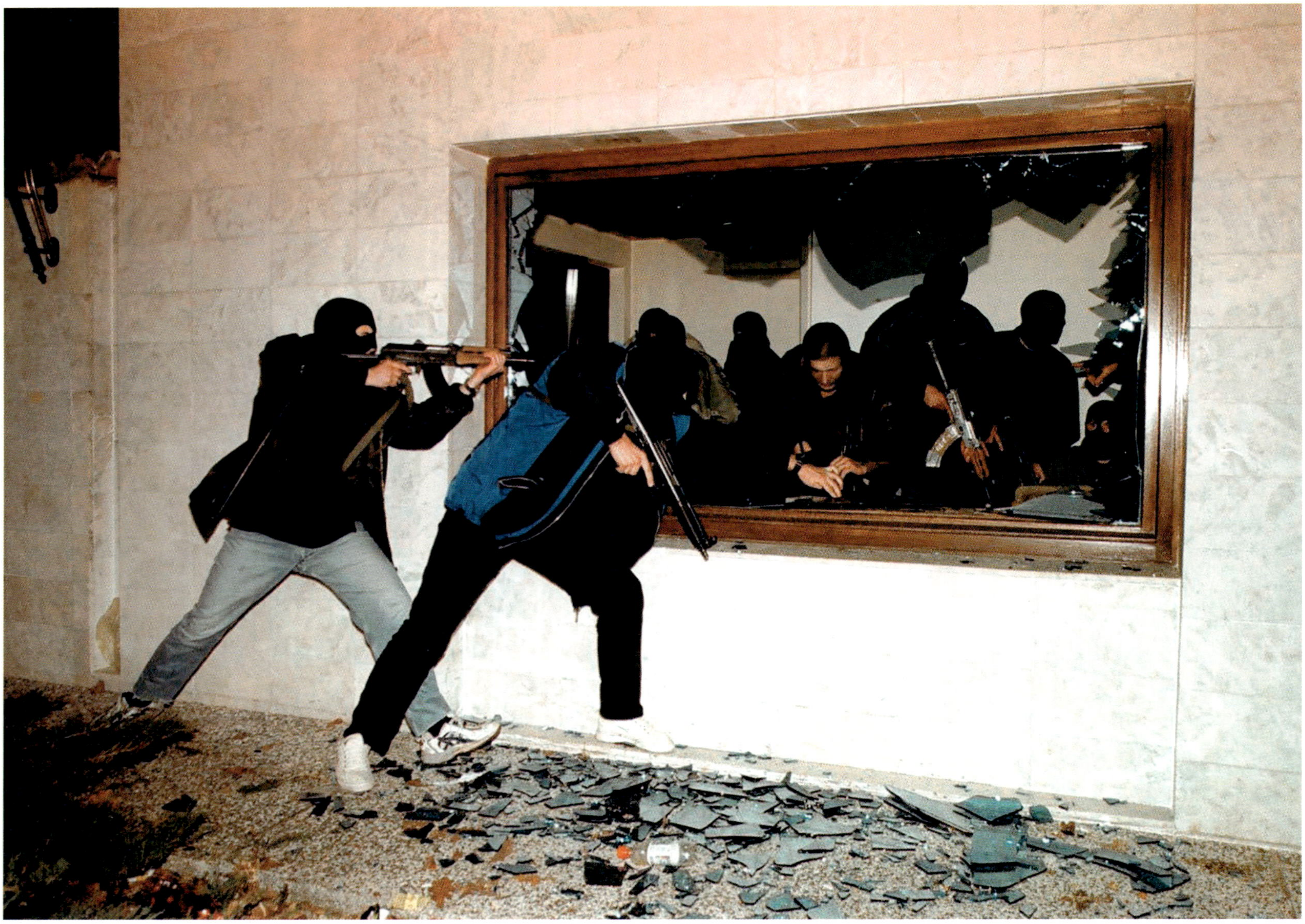

31ST MARCH 2001 – BELGRADE, YUGOSLAVIA – SERBIAN SPECIAL POLICE STORM THE HOME OF FORMER YUGOSLAV PRESIDENT SLOBODAN MILOSEVIC IN A MORNING RAID TO ARREST HIM ON CHARGES OF CRIMES AGAINST HUMANITY. (KOCA SULEJMANOVIC/EPA)

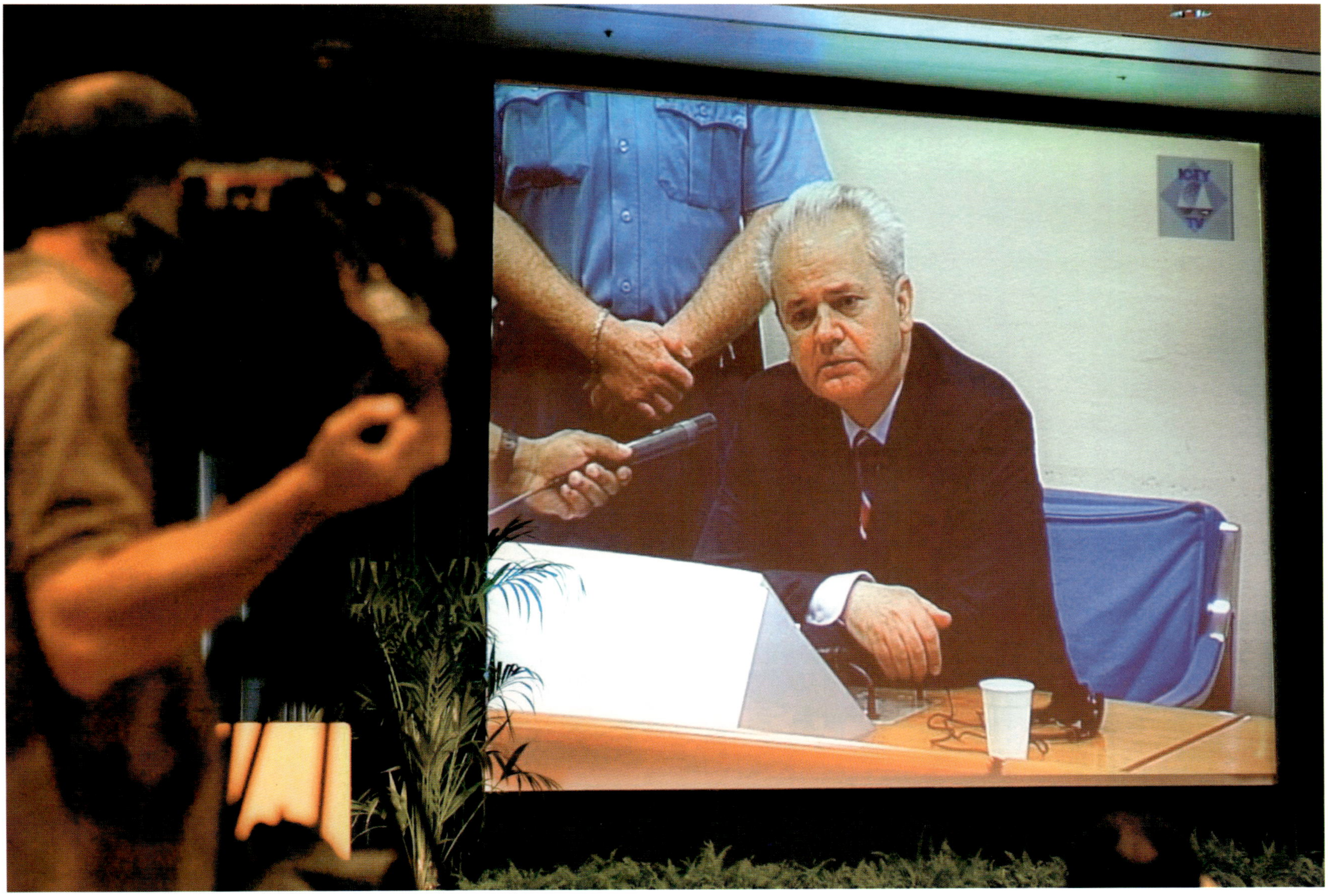

3RD JULY 2001 – THE HAGUE, NETHERLANDS – A CAMERAMAN WATCHES THE OPENING OF THE TRIAL OF FORMER YUGOSLAV PRESIDENT SLOBODAN MILOSEVIC ON A TV SCREEN MONITOR. (ÉRIC FEFERBERG)

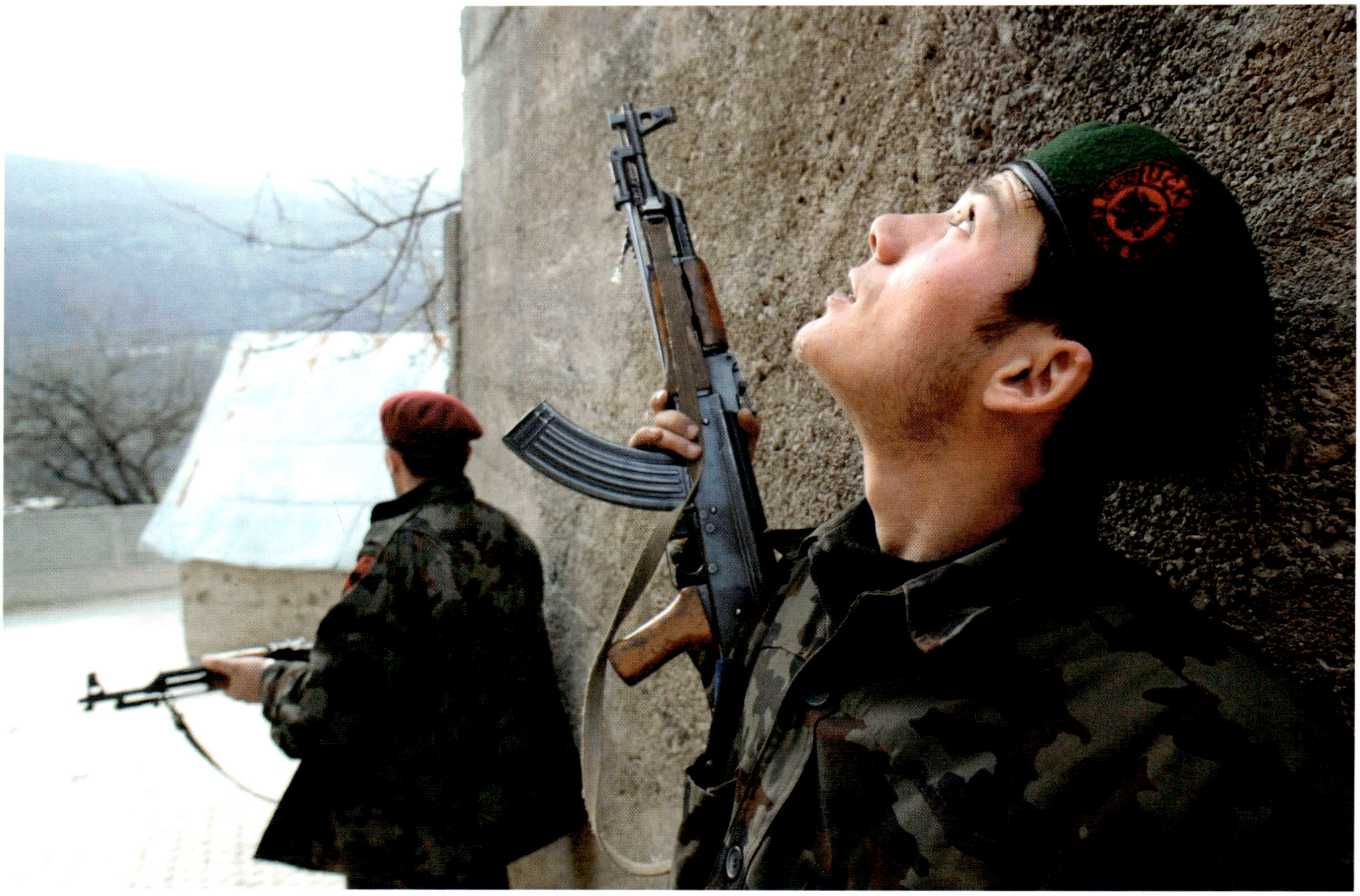

18TH MARCH 2001 – SELCE, MACEDONIA – ALBANIAN FIGHTERS TAKE COVER IN THE VILLAGE OF SELCE, ABOVE TETOVO, DURING EXCHANGES WITH MACEDONIAN FORCES. (ÉRIC FEFERBERG)

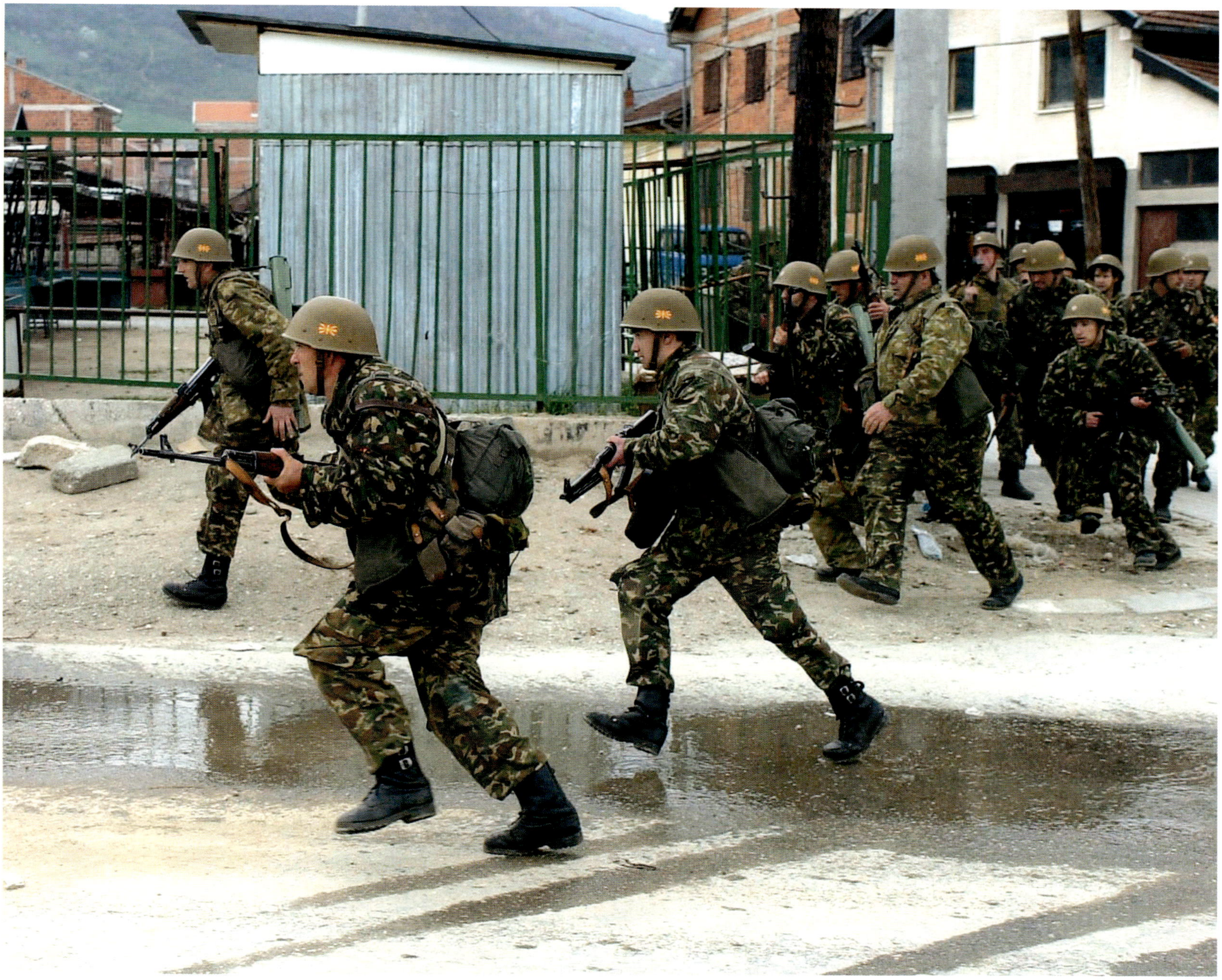

25TH MARCH 2001
– TETOVO, MACEDONIA –
MACEDONIAN INFANTRY TROOPS
LEAVE THE CENTER OF TETOVO AS
THEY LAUNCH AN OFFENSIVE AGAINST
ETHNIC ALBANIAN GUERRILLAS.
(ÉRIC FEFERBERG)

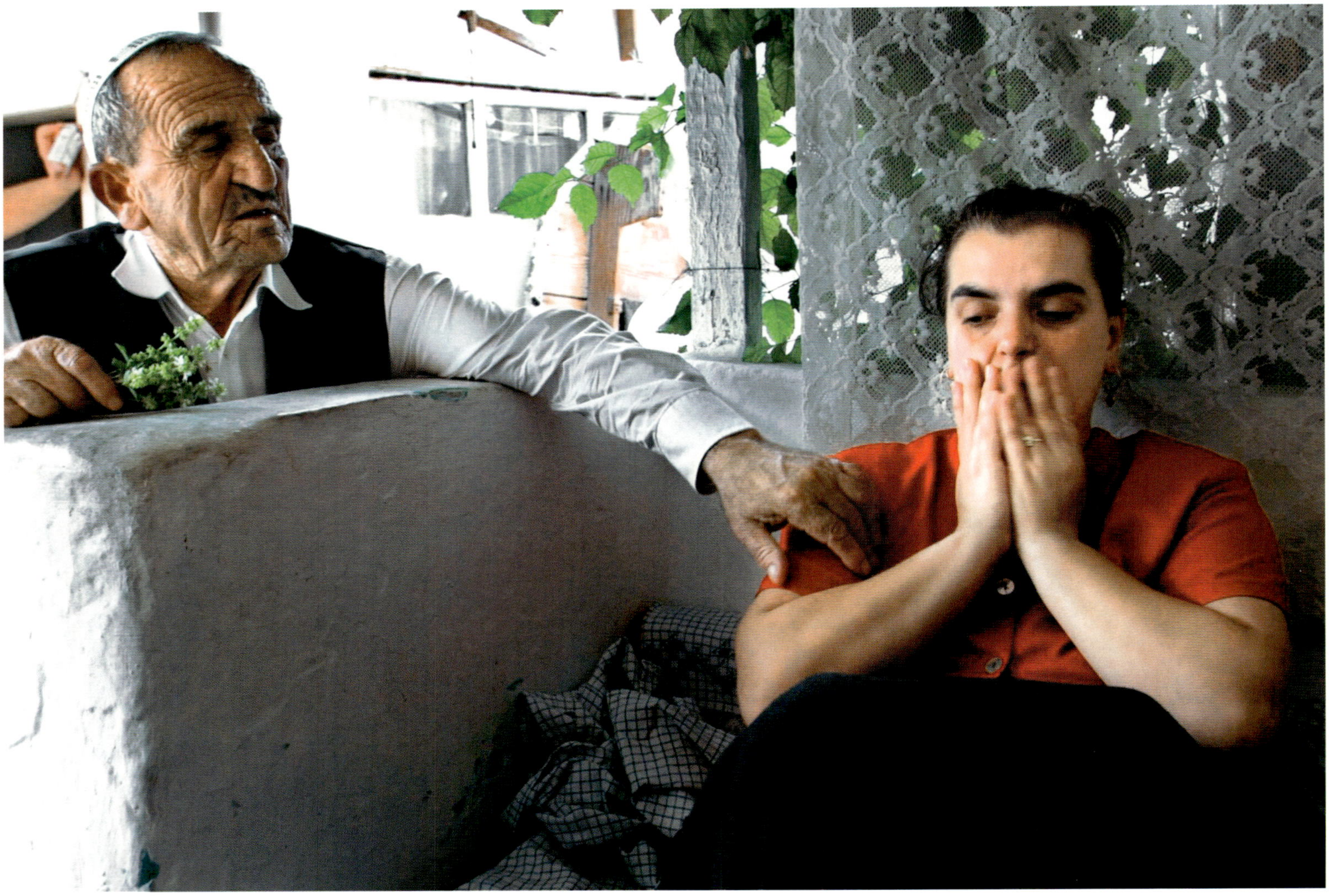

7TH AUGUST 2001 – SKOPJE, MACEDONIA – AN ALBANIAN MAN COMFORTS THE NEIGHBOUR OF ONE OF FIVE REBELS SHOT DEAD BY MACEDONIAN POLICE IN A DAWN RAID. (ALEXANDER NEMENOV)

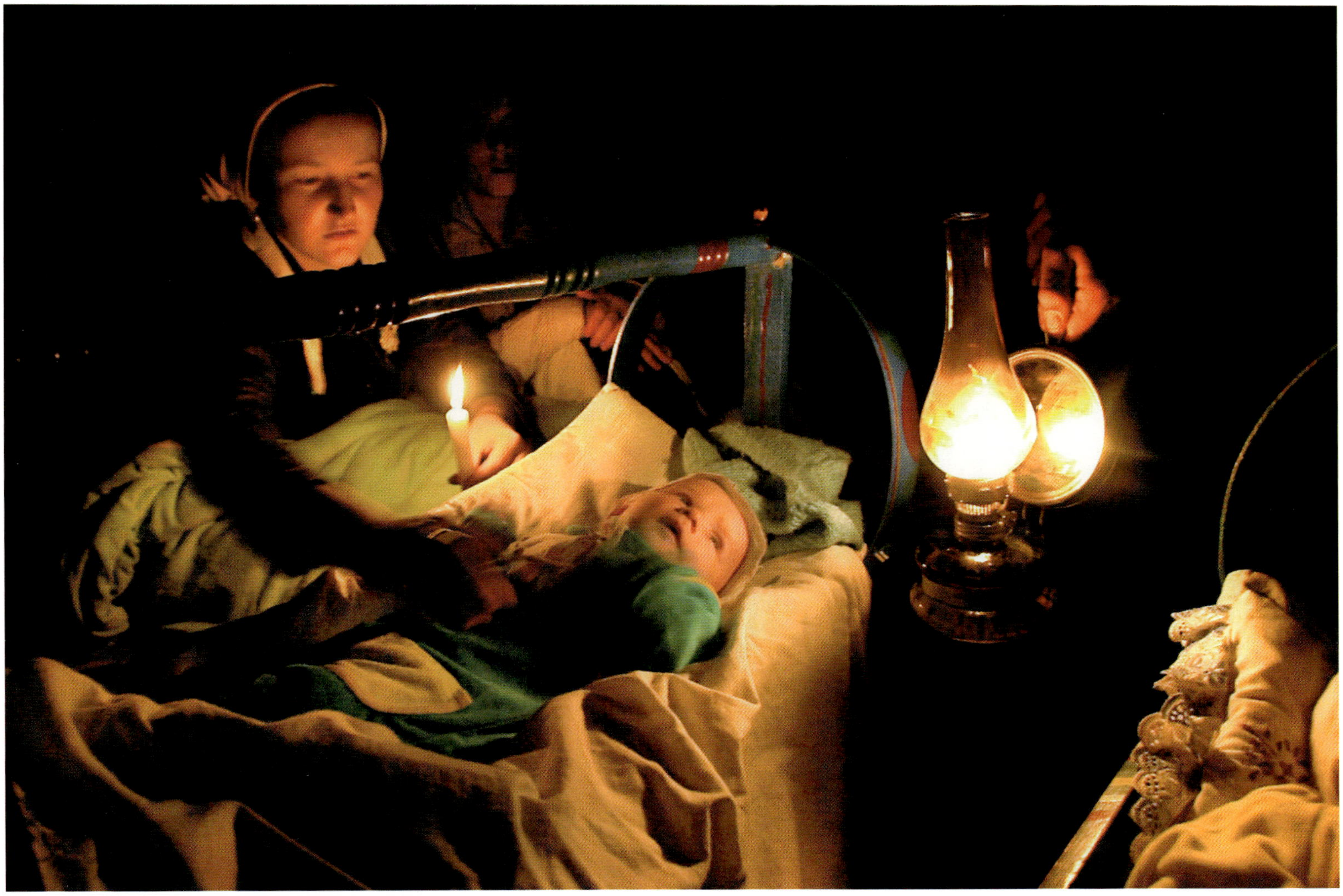

17TH MAY 2001 – SLUPCANE, MACEDONIA – AN ALBANIAN WOMAN ROCKS HER BABY IN A CELLAR, DURING CLASHES BETWEEN MACEDONIAN TROOPS AND ALBANIAN GUERRILLAS IN THIS FRONTLINE VILLAGE. (ÉRIC FEFERBERG)

8TH AUGUST 2001 – BOUDOUAOU, ALGERIA – ALGERIAN RIOT POLICE KEEP A CLOSE WATCH ON BERBER YOUTHS ON AN ANTI-GOVERNMENT PROTEST MARCH. (HOCINE)

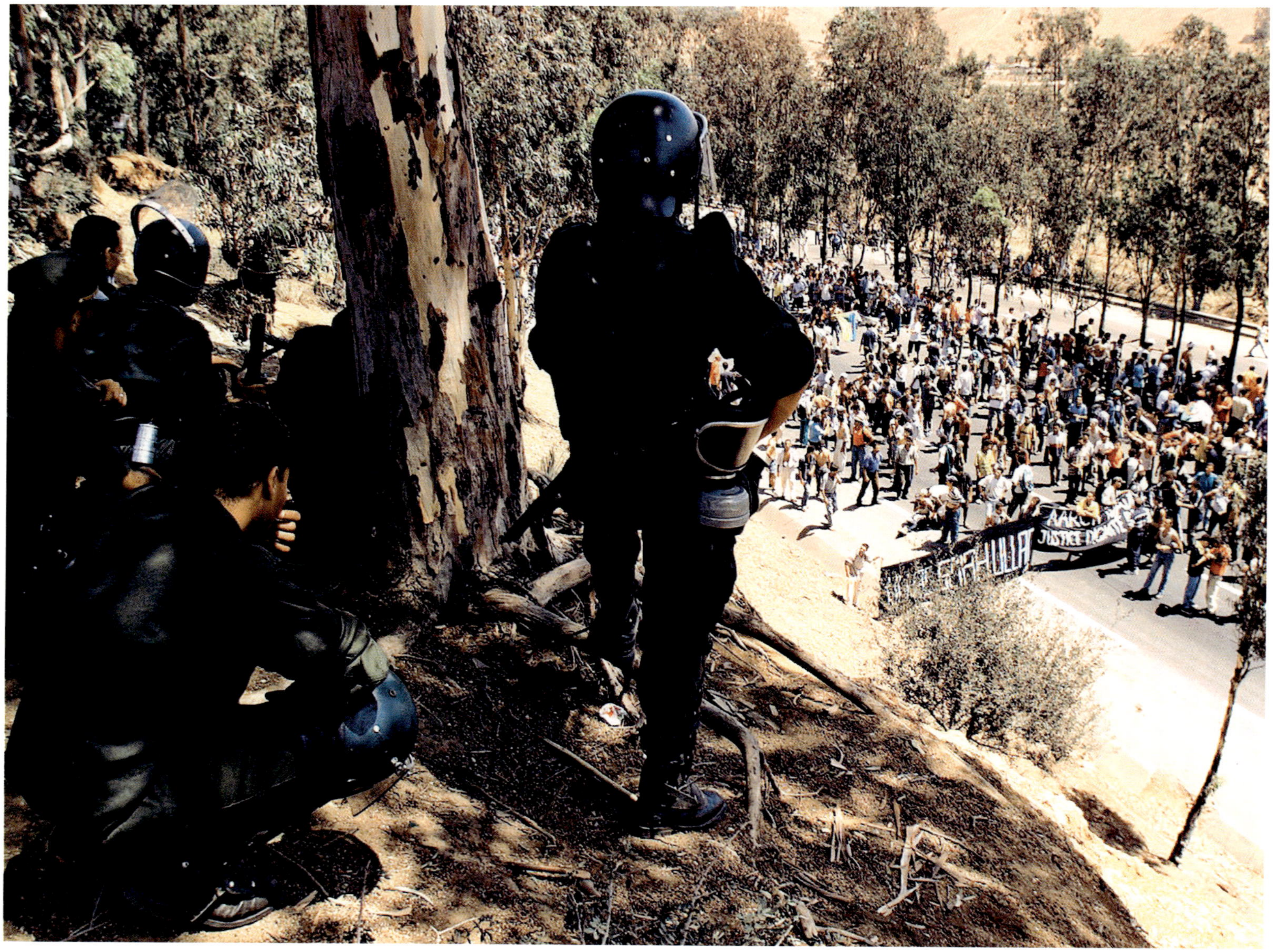

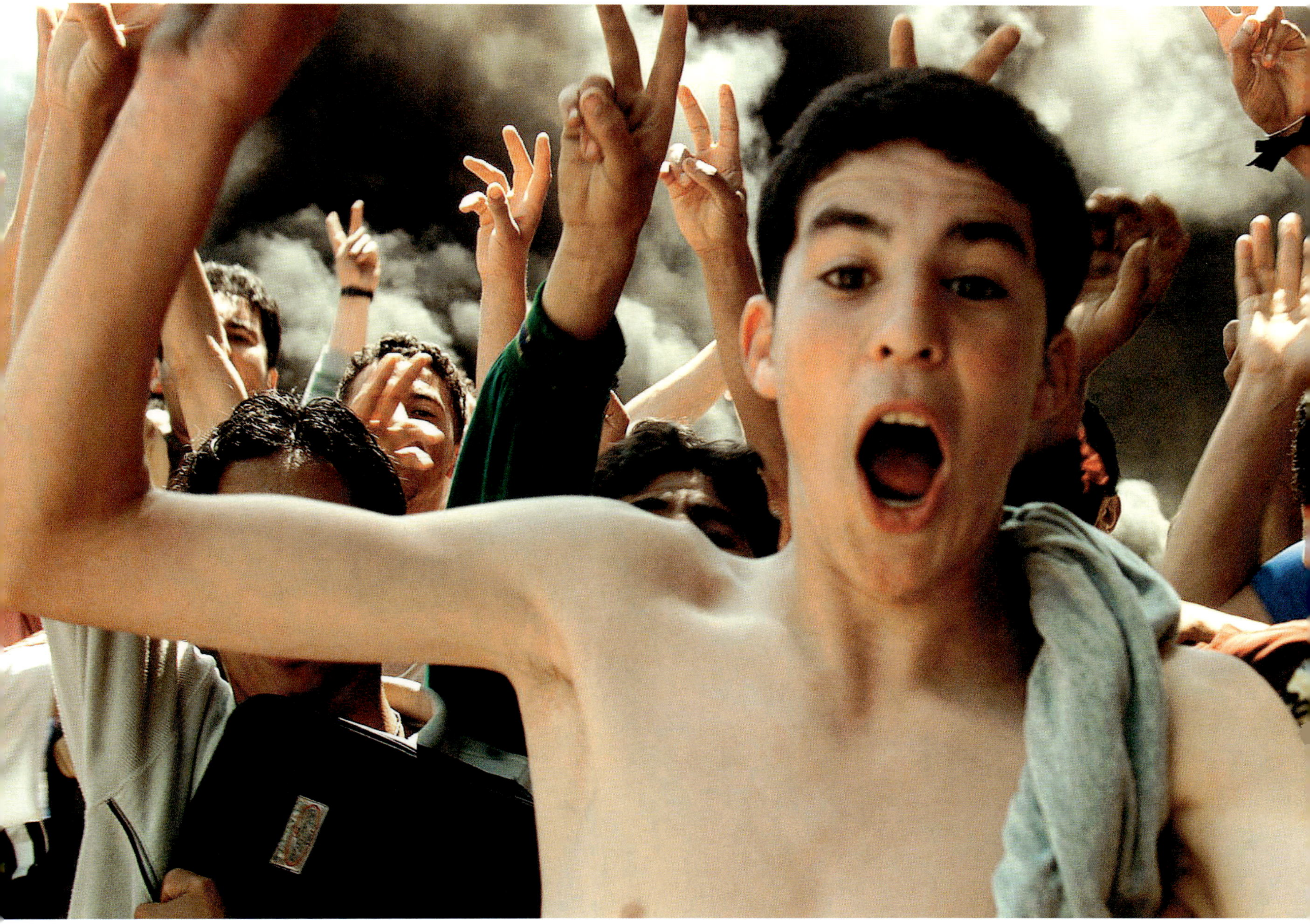

29TH MAY 2001
– SIDI-AICH, ALGERIA –
BERBER YOUTHS CONFRONT
SECURITY FORCES AND BURN
BARRICADES AS RIOT POLICE
FIRE TEAR GAS GRENADES,
INJURING A DOZEN PROTESTORS.

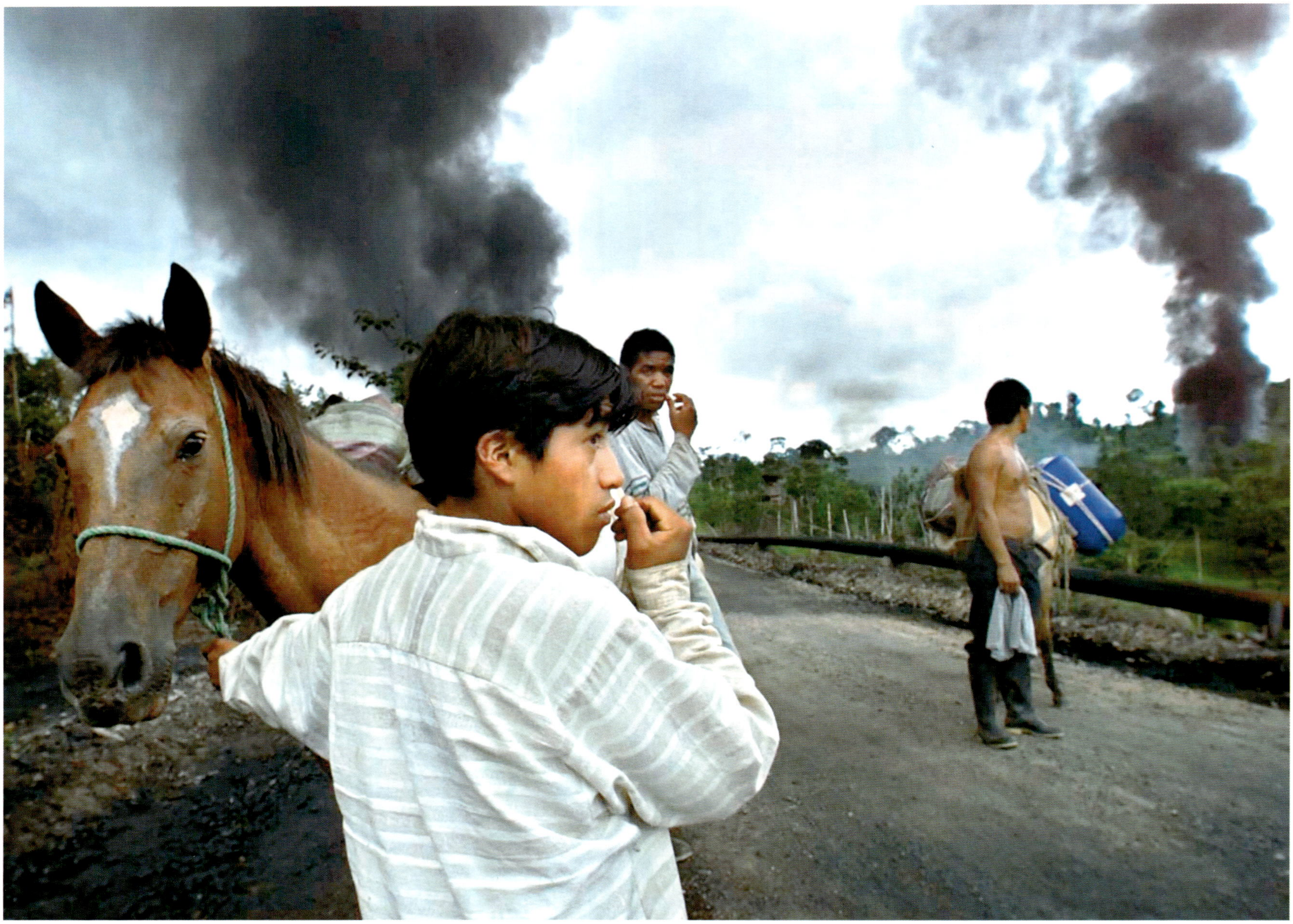

21ST OCTOBER 2000 – NUEVA ESPERANZA, COLOMBIA – FARMERS WATCH THE SMOKE RISING FROM AN OIL PIPELINE AFTER IT WAS DYNAMITED BY REVOLUTIONARY ARMED FORCES OF COLOMBIA GUERRILLAS. (PEDRO UGARTE)

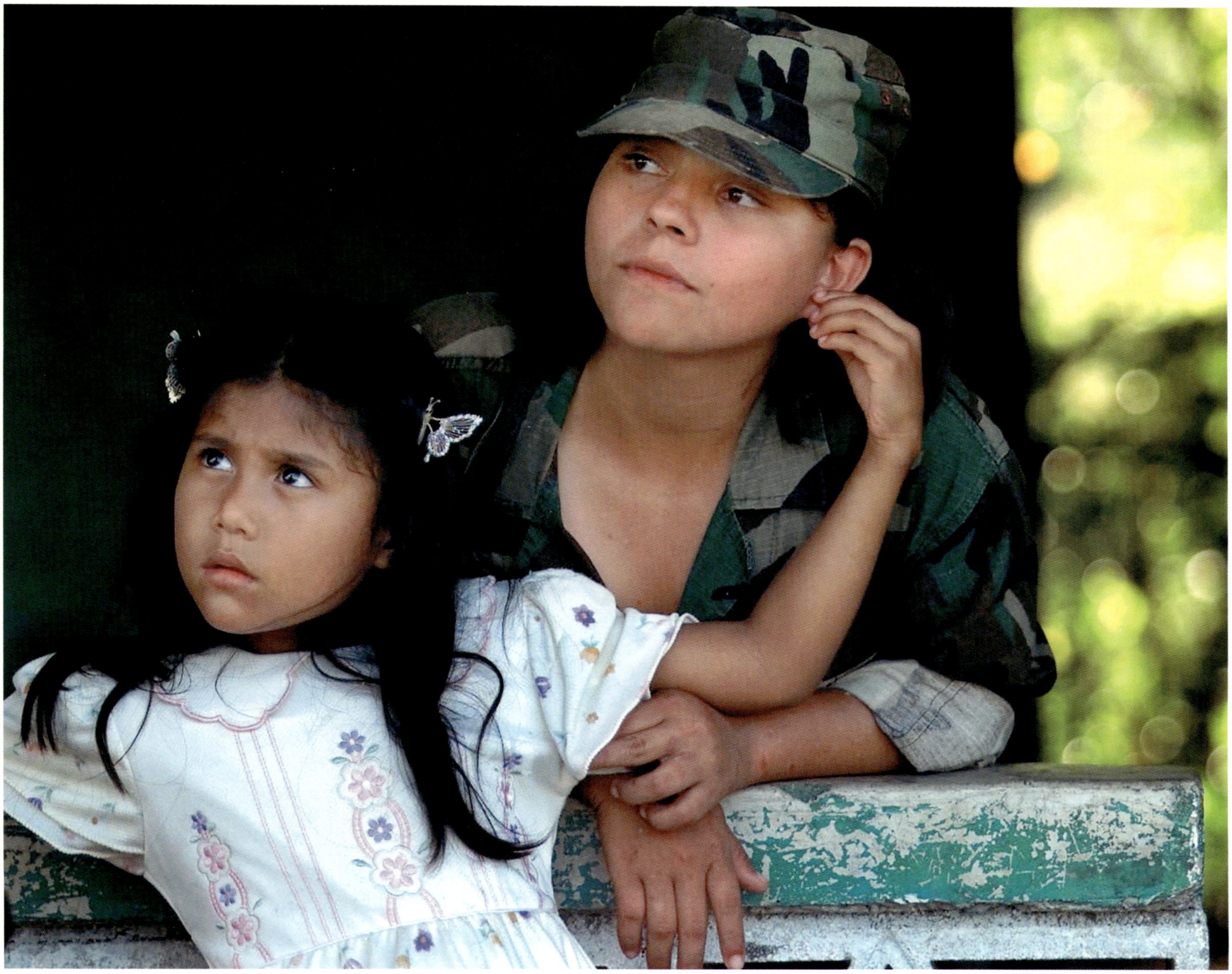

22ND OCTOBER 2000
– BLOQUE DE CASA, COLOMBIA –
A YOUNG GIRL PLAYS WITH A
MEMBER OF THE REVOLUTIONARY
ARMED FORCES OF COLOMBIA
GUERRILLA MOVEMENT.
(PEDRO UGARTE)

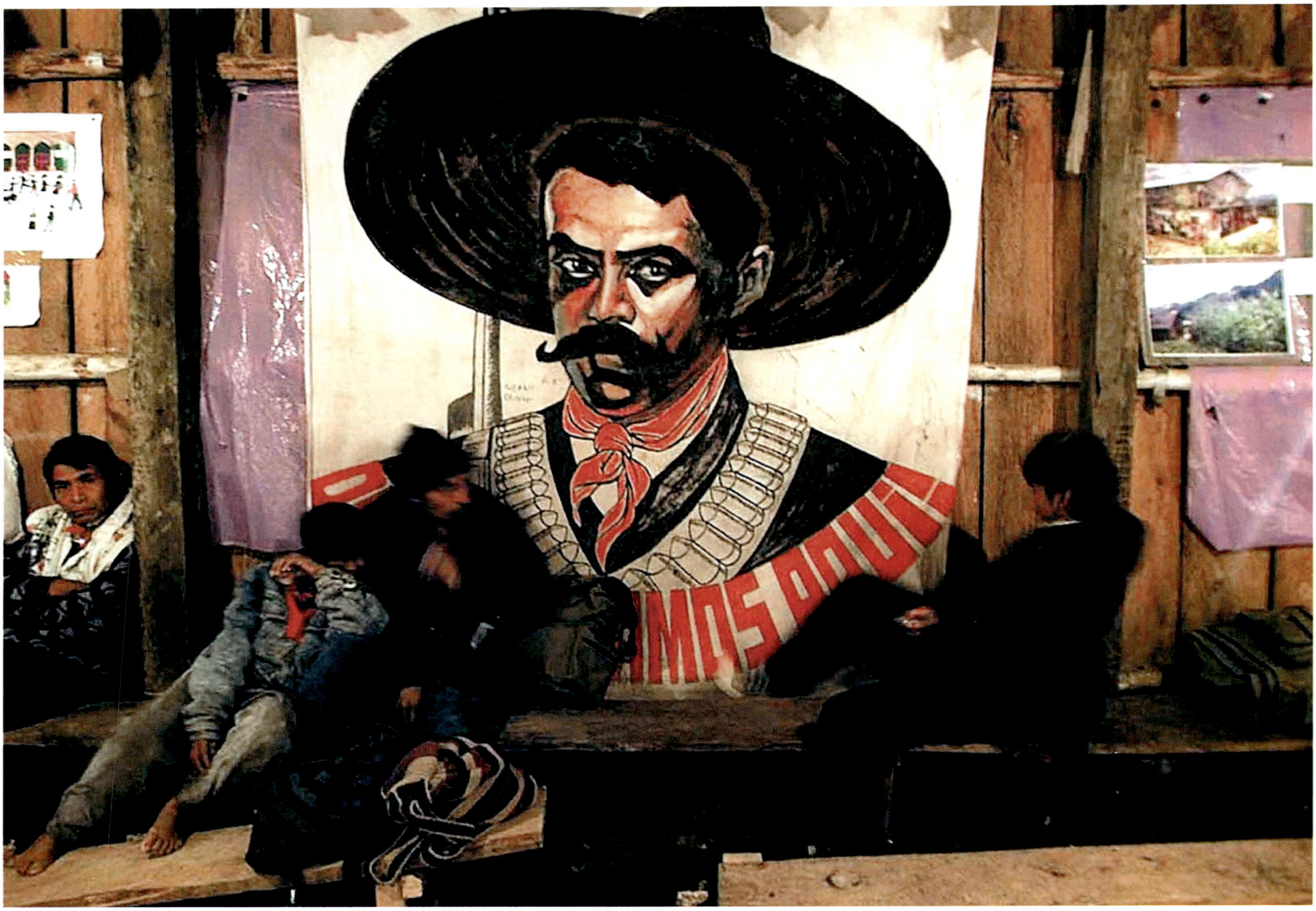

24TH FEBRUARY 2001 – OVENTIC, MEXICO – THE FACE OF POPULAR HERO EMILIANO ZAPATA LOOKS DOWN ON A GROUP OF INDIGENOUS PEOPLE PREPARING TO JOIN A PROTEST MARCH FROM SAN CRISTOBAL DE LAS CASAS TO MEXICO CITY. (JORGE UZON)

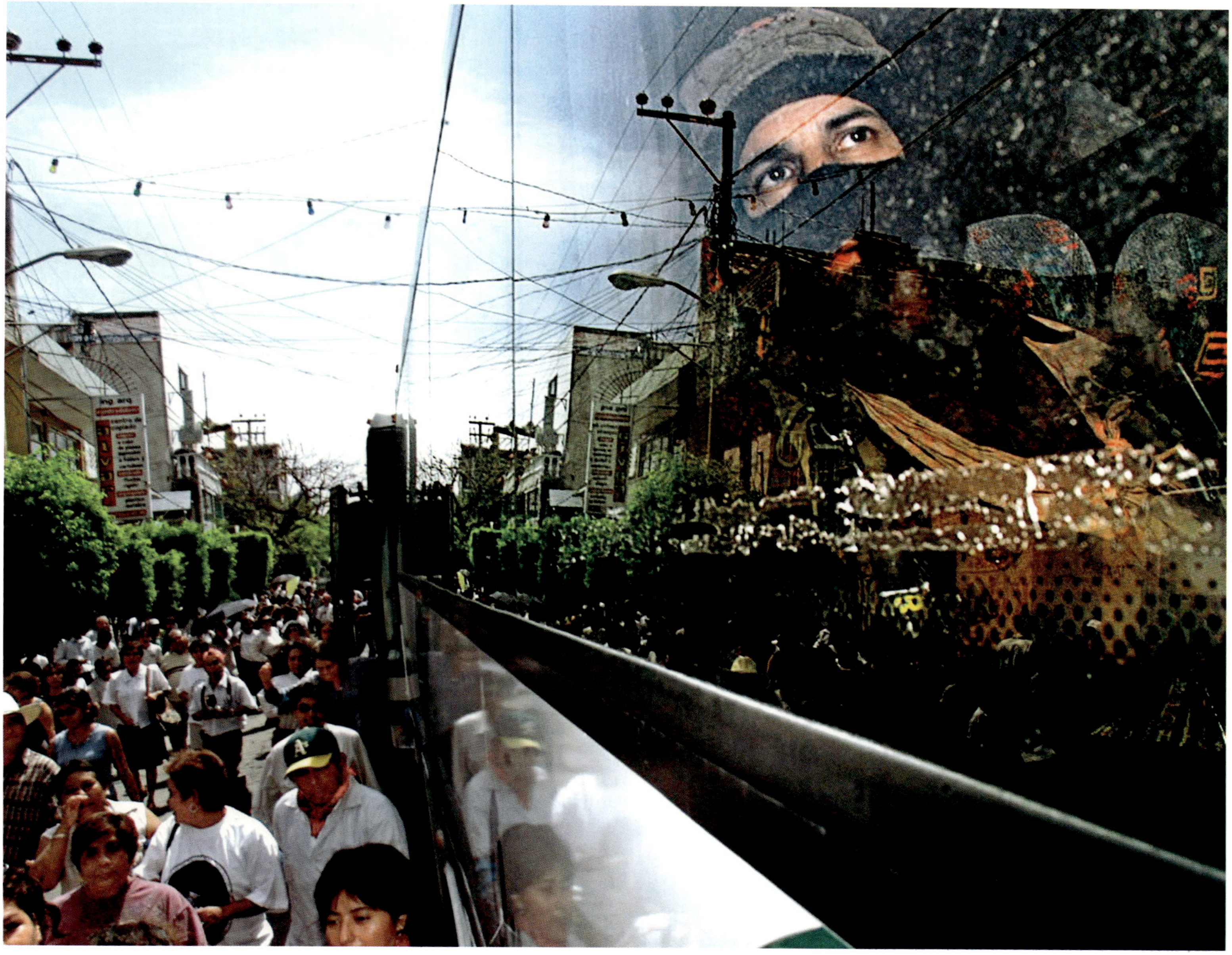

7TH MARCH 2001 – IGUALA, MEXICO – SUBCOMMANDANTE MARCOS, THE ZAPATISTA NATIONAL LIBERATION ARMY LEADER, ARRIVES IN GUERRERO STATE FOR A RALLY AS PART OF A NATIONWIDE CAMPAIGN IN SUPPORT OF A BILL OF RIGHTS FOR INDIGENOUS PEOPLE. (RAMON CAVALLO)

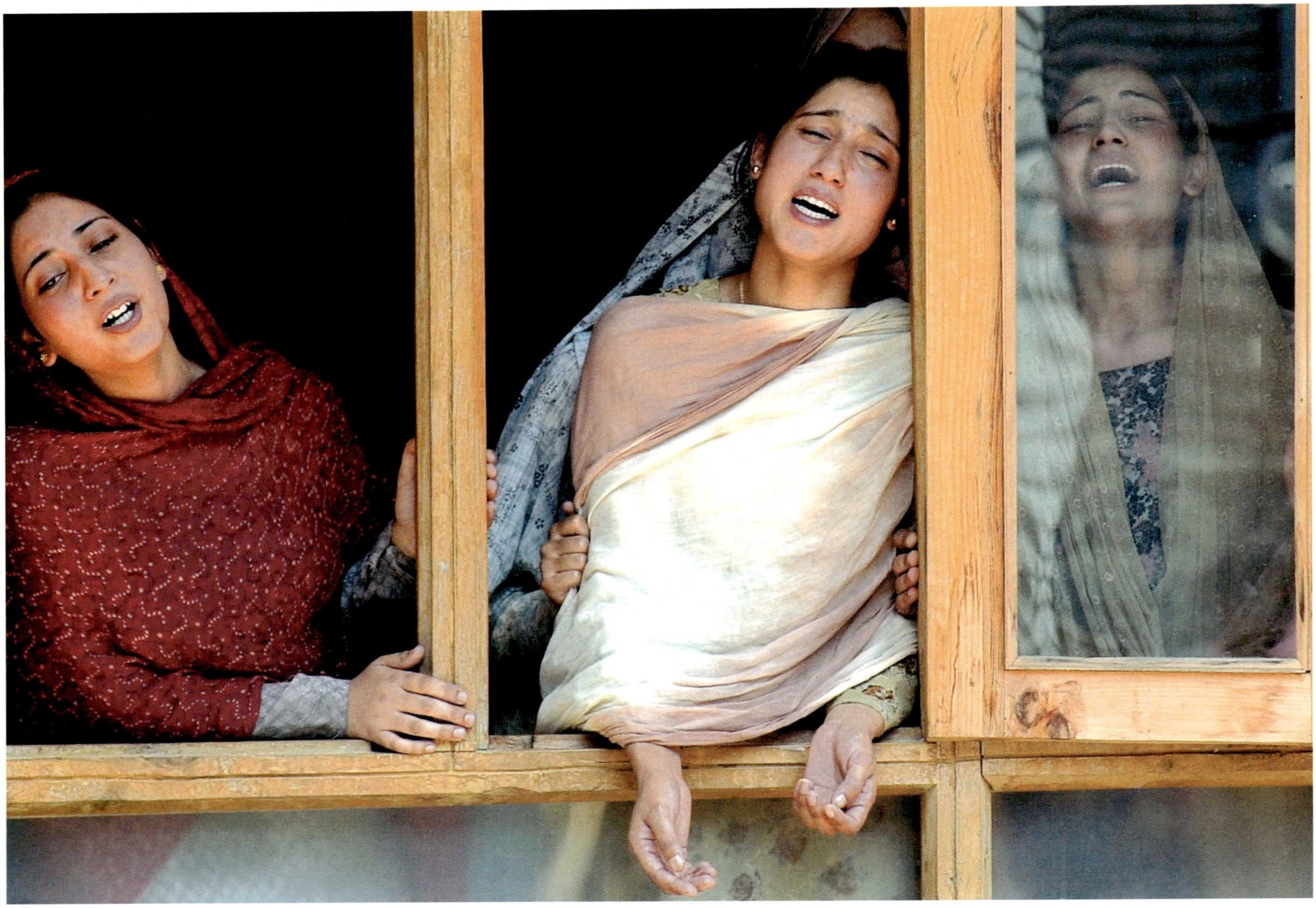

28TH AUGUST 2001 – SRINAGAR, INDIA – RELATIVES MOURN THE DEATH OF A KASHMIRI YOUTH KILLED BY INDIAN POLICE. (TAUSEEF MUSTAFA)

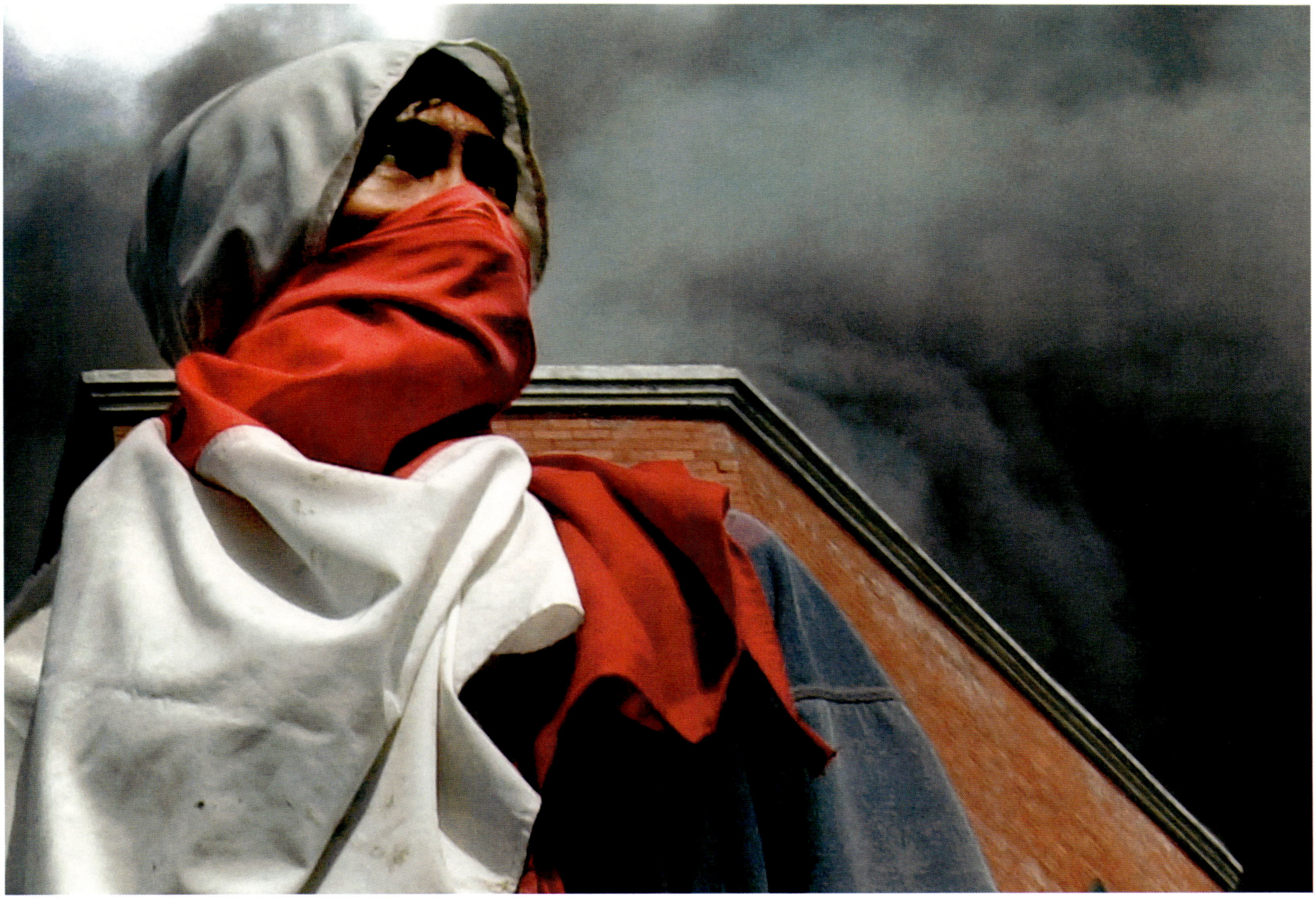

7TH FEBRUARY 2001 – SURABAYA, INDONESIA – A SUPPORTER OF PRESIDENT ABDURRAHMAN WAHID IN FRONT OF THE SMOKING REMAINS OF A DISTRICT OFFICE OF FORMER PRESIDENT SUHARTO'S GOLKAR PARTY. (WEDA)

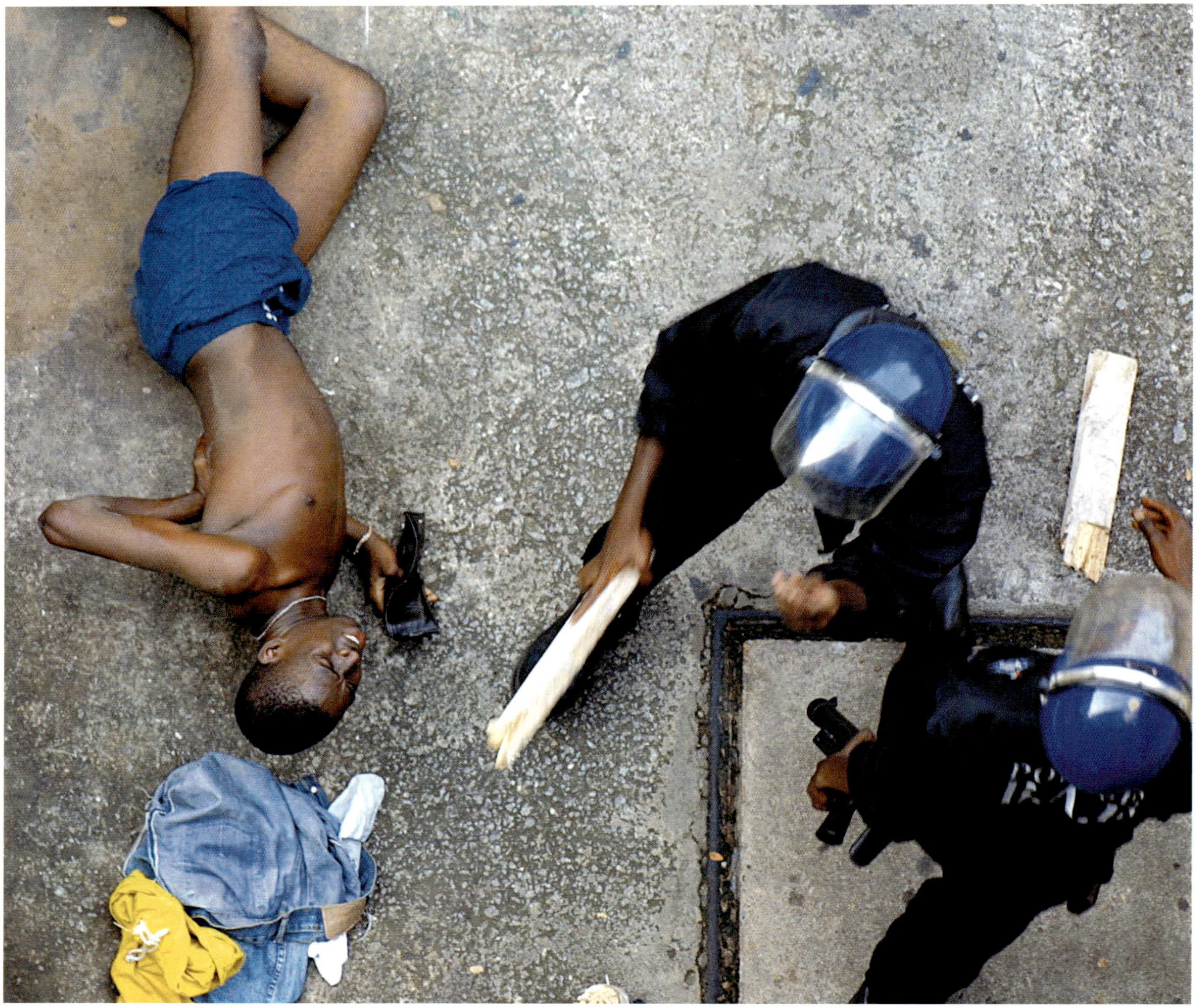

4TH DECEMBER 2000 – ABIDJAN, IVORY COAST – A SUPPORTER OF OPPOSITION LEADER ALASSANE OUATTARA IS BEATEN BY POLICE AFTER A DEMONSTRATION THROUGH THE STREETS OF THE CITY. (JEAN-PHILIPPE KSIAZEK)

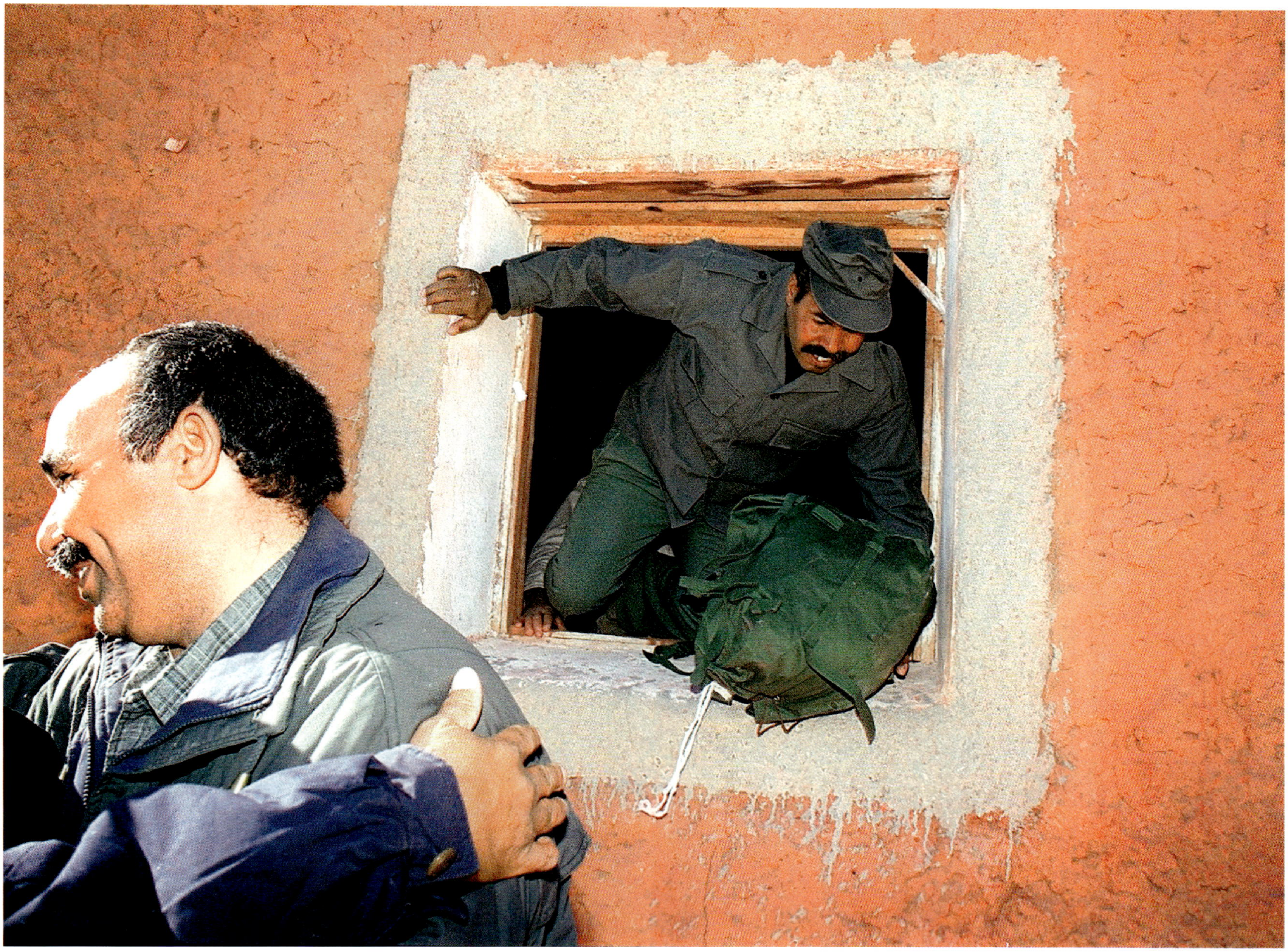

14TH DECEMBER 2000 – TINDOUF, ALGERIA – ONE OF TWO HUNDRED MOROCCAN PRISONERS OF WAR SET FREE BY THE POLISARIO FORCES AS A HUMANITARIAN GESTURE TO MARK THE HOLY MONTH OF RAMADAN LEAPS THROUGH A WINDOW TO FREEDOM. (HOCINE)

PORTRAITS

US-VOTE-RECOUNT
URGENT¥¥¥ GORE CAMPAIGN WAITS FOR RECOUNT RESULT FROM FLORIDA
NASHVILLE, TENNESSEE, NOV 8 (AFP) – THE AL GORE PRESIDENTIAL CAMPAIGN IS WAITING FOR RESULTS OF A VOTE RECOUNT IN FLORIDA, WHICH IS TRIGGERED AUTOMATICALLY WHEN THE MARGIN OF A CANDIDATE'S VICTORY IS LESS THAN FIVE PERCENT, MSNBC REPORTED CITING A CAMPAIGN SPOKESMAN.
MK/FGF

PHILIPPINES-ESTRADA-JAIL
URGENT¥¥¥ ESTRADA ARRESTED, LED TO JAIL
MANILA, APRIL 25 (AFP) – DISGRACED FORMER PHILIPPINE PRESIDENT JOSEPH ESTRADA WAS ARRESTED AT HIS HOME AND DRIVEN TO A NEARBY JAIL ON WEDNESDAY ON THE CHARGE OF ECONOMIC PLUNDER, WHICH IS PUNISHABLE BY DEATH, POLICE SAID.
CGM/PP/JIT

BRITAIN-VOTE,2ND LEAD
BLAIR WINS HISTORIC VICTORY IN BRITISH ELECTION
LONDON, JUNE 8 (AFP) - BRITISH PRIME MINISTER TONY BLAIR WON A LANDSLIDE GENERAL ELECTION VICTORY FRIDAY, RETURNING HIS RULING LABOUR PARTY TO POWER FOR A HISTORIC SECOND TERM.
PK/KM/BM

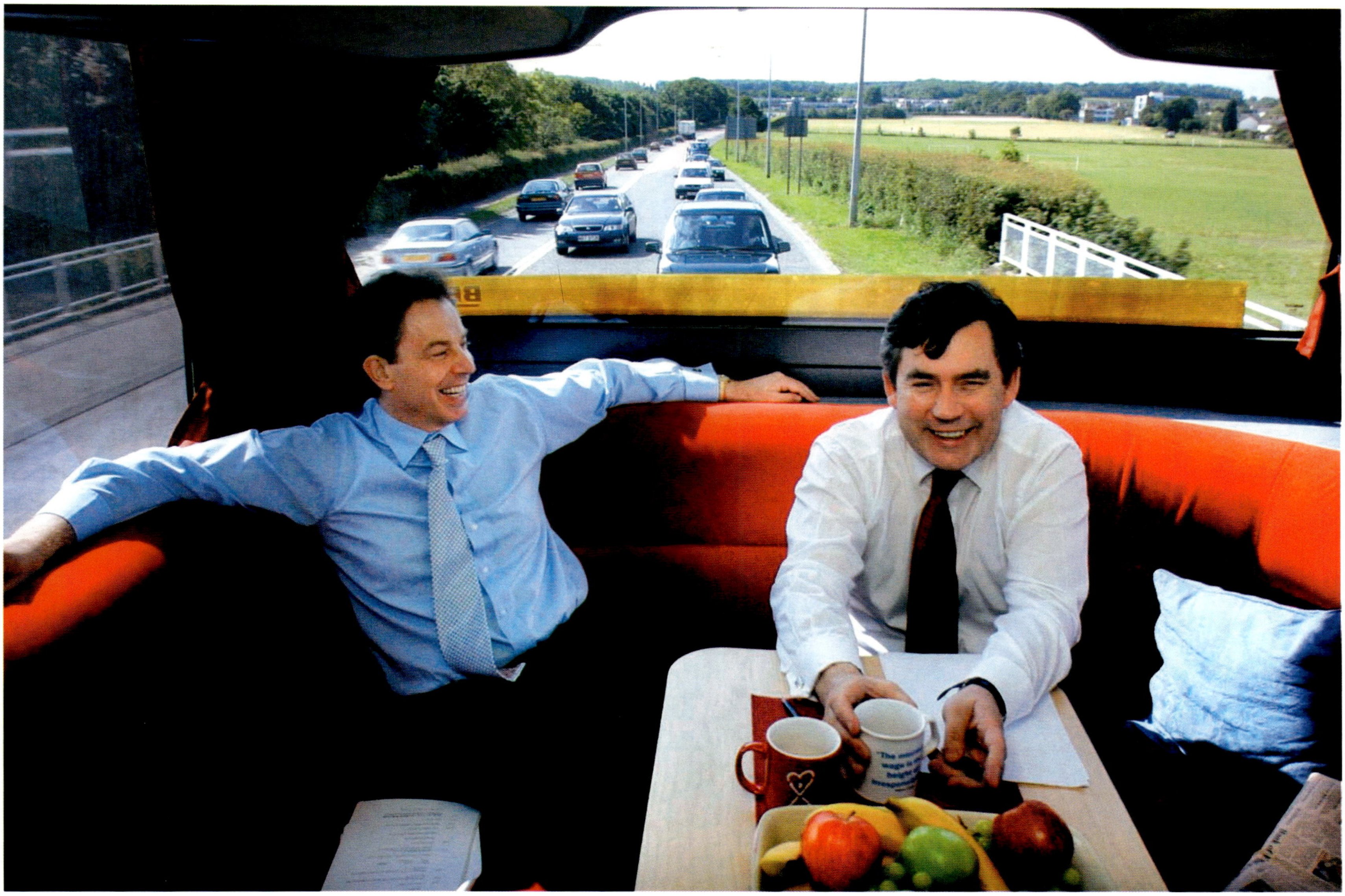

4TH JUNE 2001 – HARLOW, ENGLAND – BRITISH PRIME MINISTER TONY BLAIR (LEFT) AND CHANCELLOR OF THE EXCHEQUER GORDON BROWN ABOARD THE LABOUR PARTY CAMPAIGN BUS DURING THE GENERAL ELECTION CAMPAIGN. (ADRIAN DENNIS)

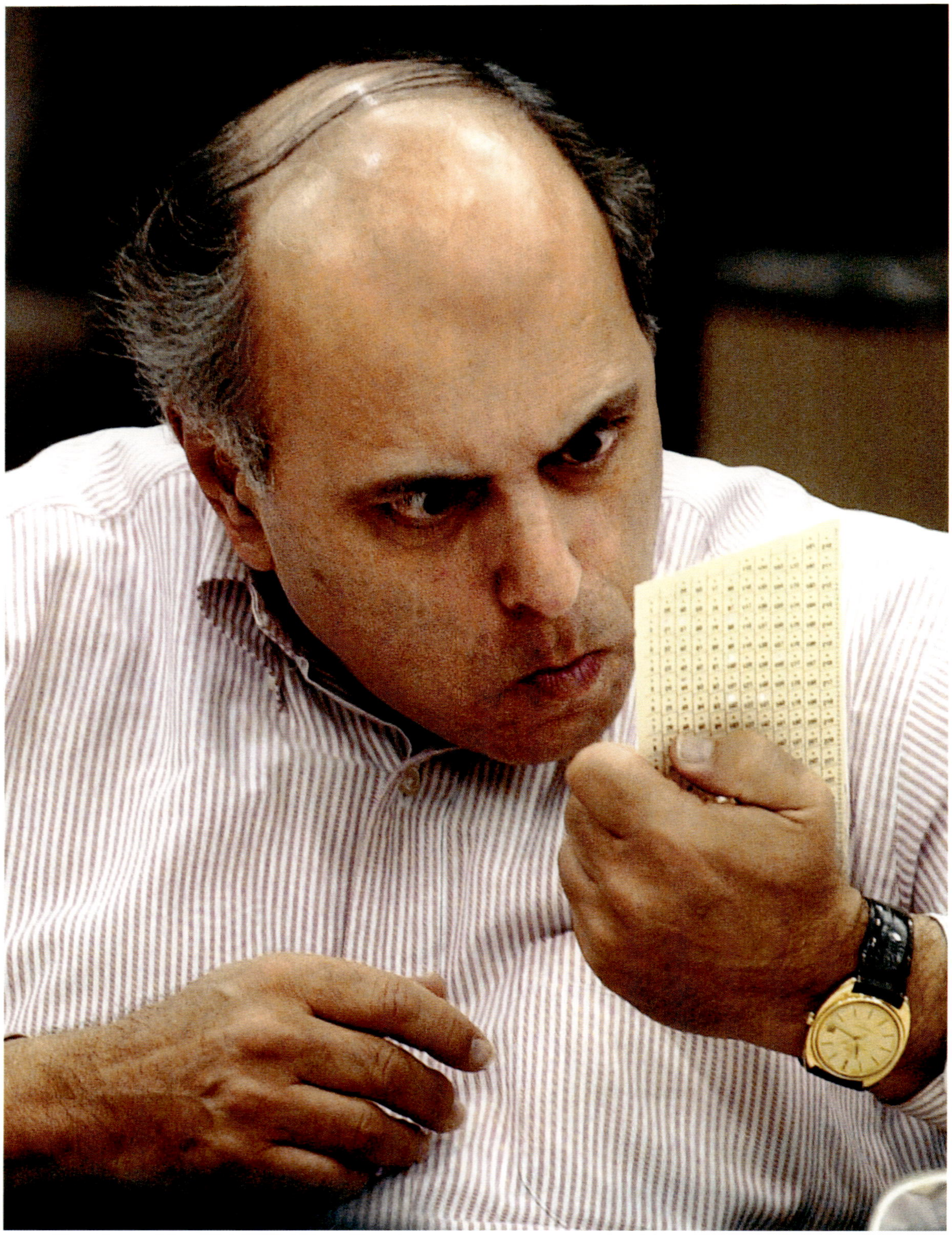

25TH NOVEMBER 2000 – FORT LAUDERDALE, USA – JUDGE ROBERT ROSENBERG INSPECTS A DOUBTFUL BALLOT PAPER IN HOWARD COUNTY RECOUNT WHICH EVENTUALLY GAVE GEORGE W. BUSH VICTORY OVER AL GORE IN THE US PRESIDENTIAL ELECTION. (RHONA WISE)

27TH SEPTEMBER 2000 – ALTOONA, USA – US PRESIDENTIAL CANDIDATE AL GORE DURING A MEET-THE-PEOPLE RALLY ON THE CAMPAIGN TRAIL IN IOWA. (LUKE FRAZZA)

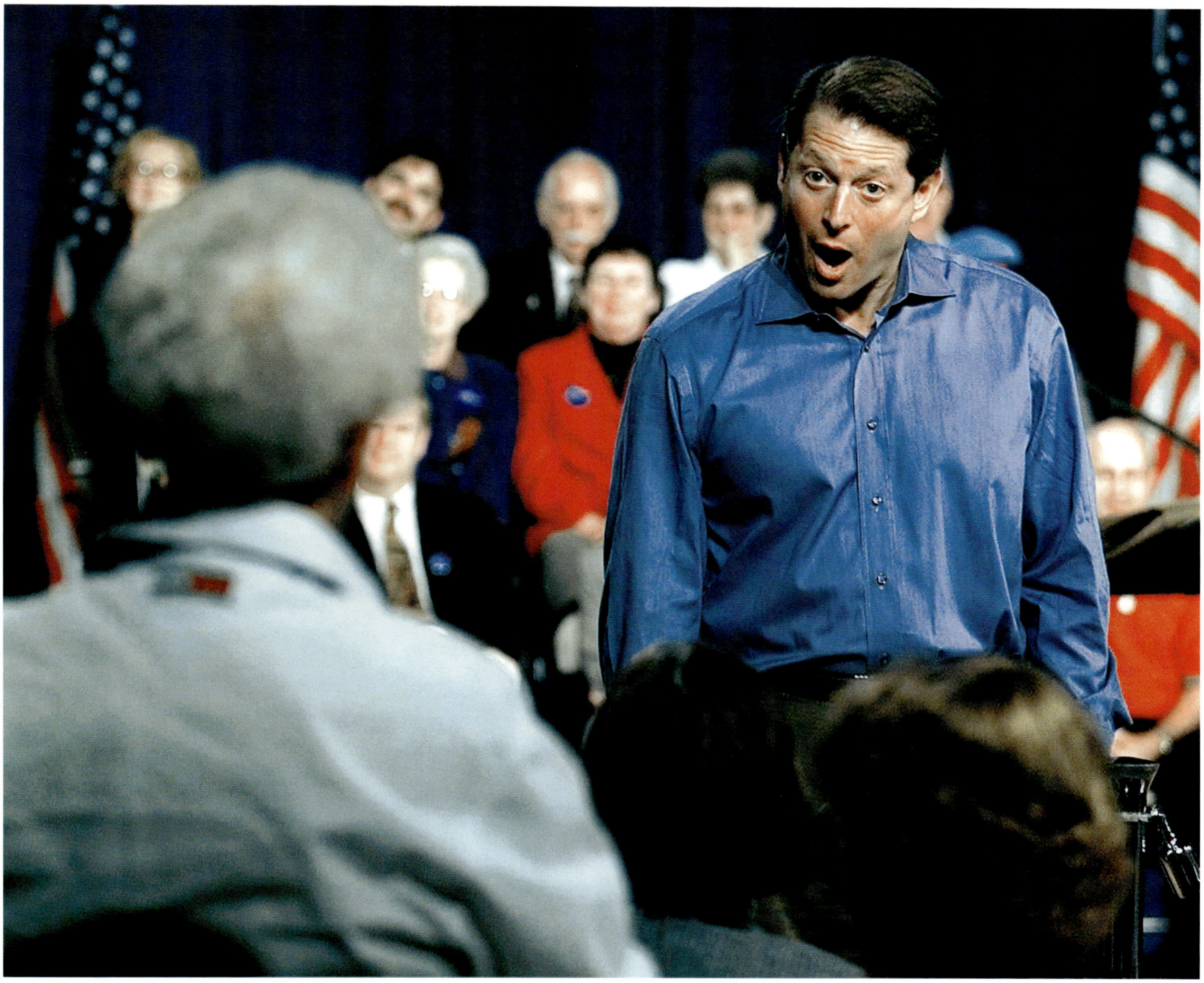

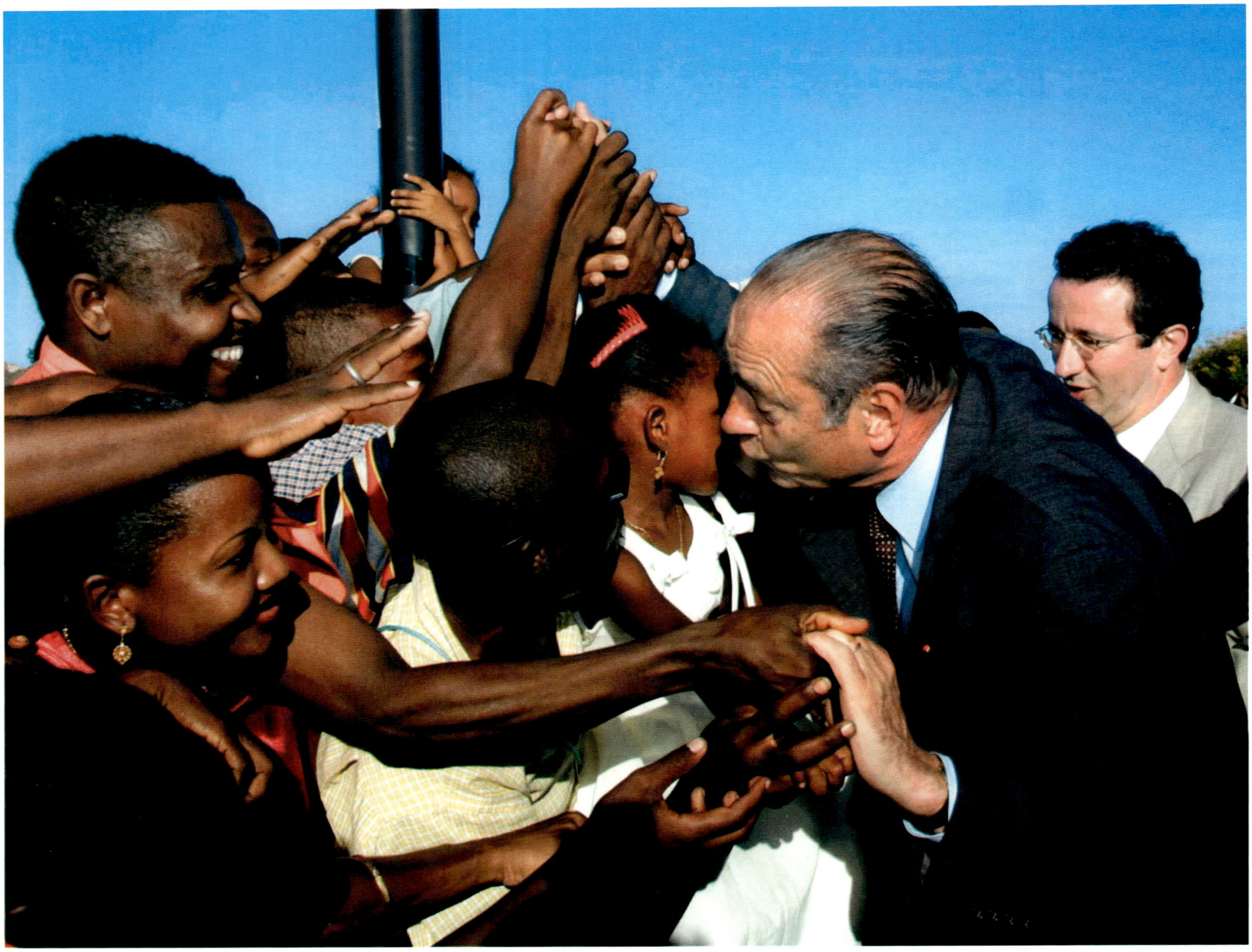

19TH MAY 2001 – PAMANDZI DZAOUDZI, MAYOTTE – FRENCH PRESIDENT JACQUES CHIRAC RECEIVES A WARM WELCOME ON HIS FIRST VISIT TO THE INDIAN OCEAN TERRITORY OF MAYOTTE. (PHILIPPE DESMAZES)

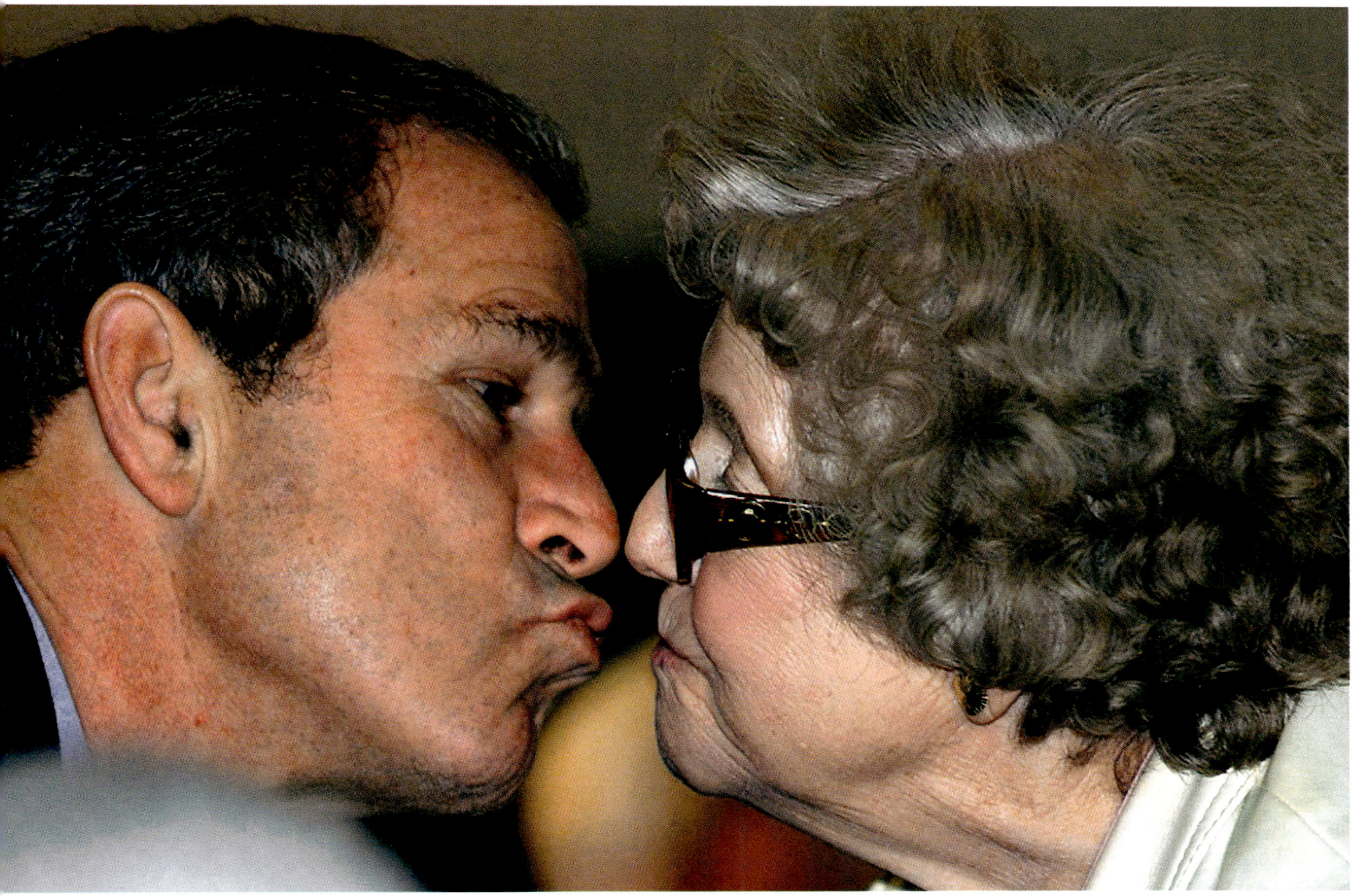

21ST MARCH 2001 – ORLANDO, USA – PRESIDENT GEORGE W. BUSH KISSES SENIOR CITIZEN ALMA PINELLO ON A VISIT TO FLORIDA. (LUKE FRAZZA)

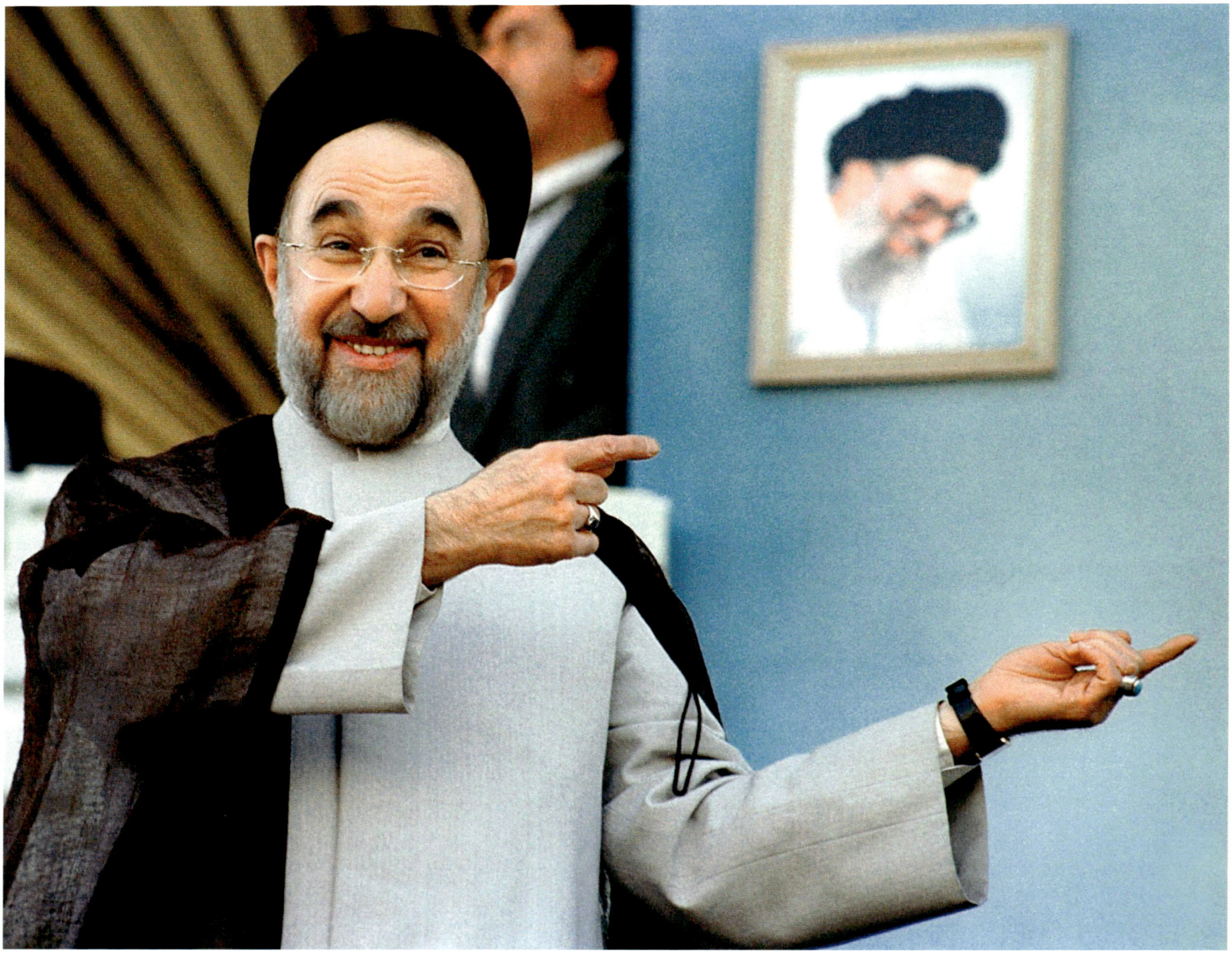

28TH MAY 2001 – TEHRAN, IRAN – PRESIDENT MOHAMMAD KHATAMI BEFORE A PUBLIC CAMPAIGN SPEECH AT THE TEHRAN STADIUM. (ATTA KENARE)

30TH MAY 2001 – TEHRAN, IRAN – IRANIAN WOMEN DEMONSTRATE IN SUPPORT OF PRESIDENT MOHAMMAD KHATAMI'S CALL FOR AN END TO DISCRIMINATION AGAINST WOMEN. (BEHROUZ MEHRI)

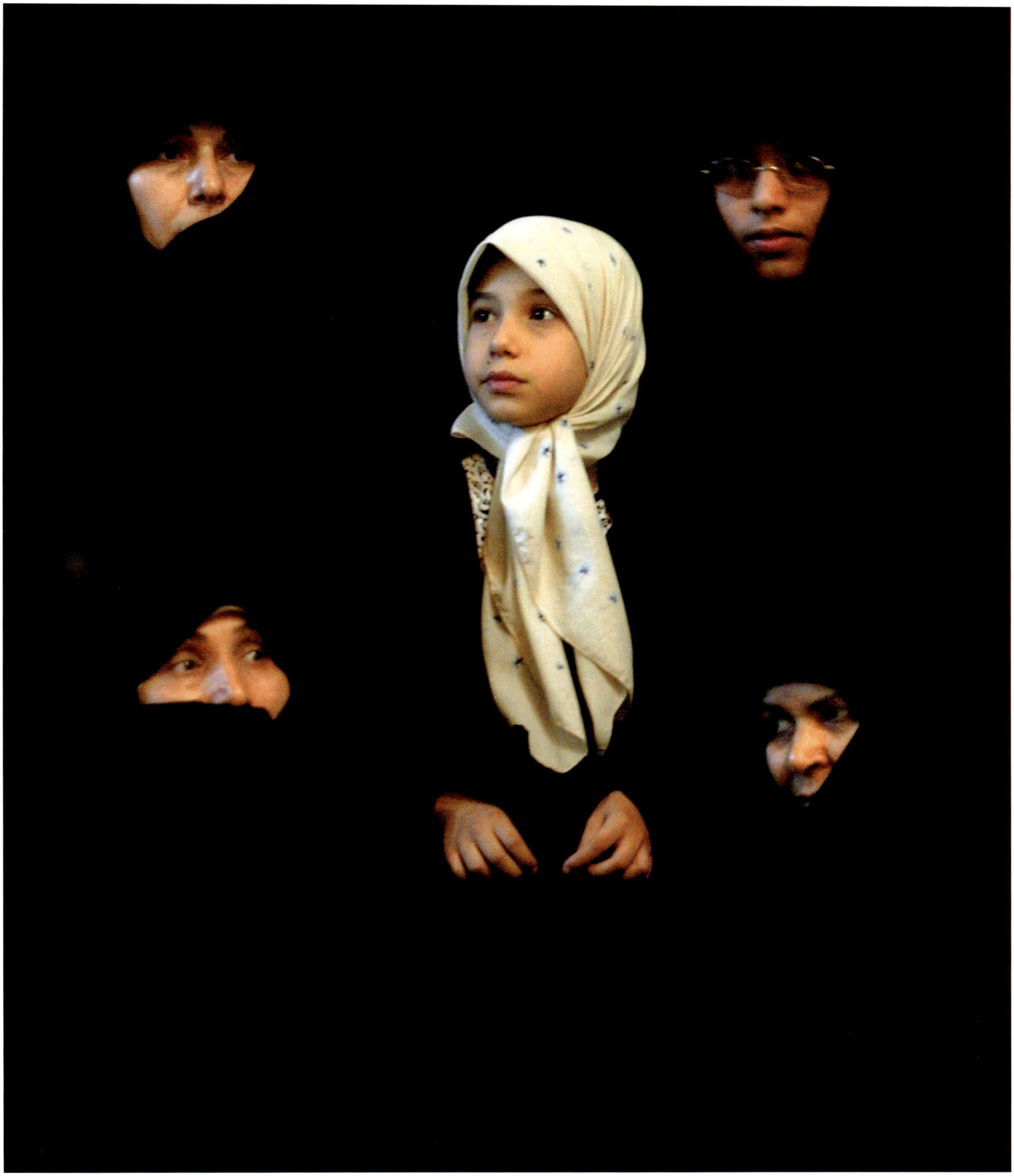

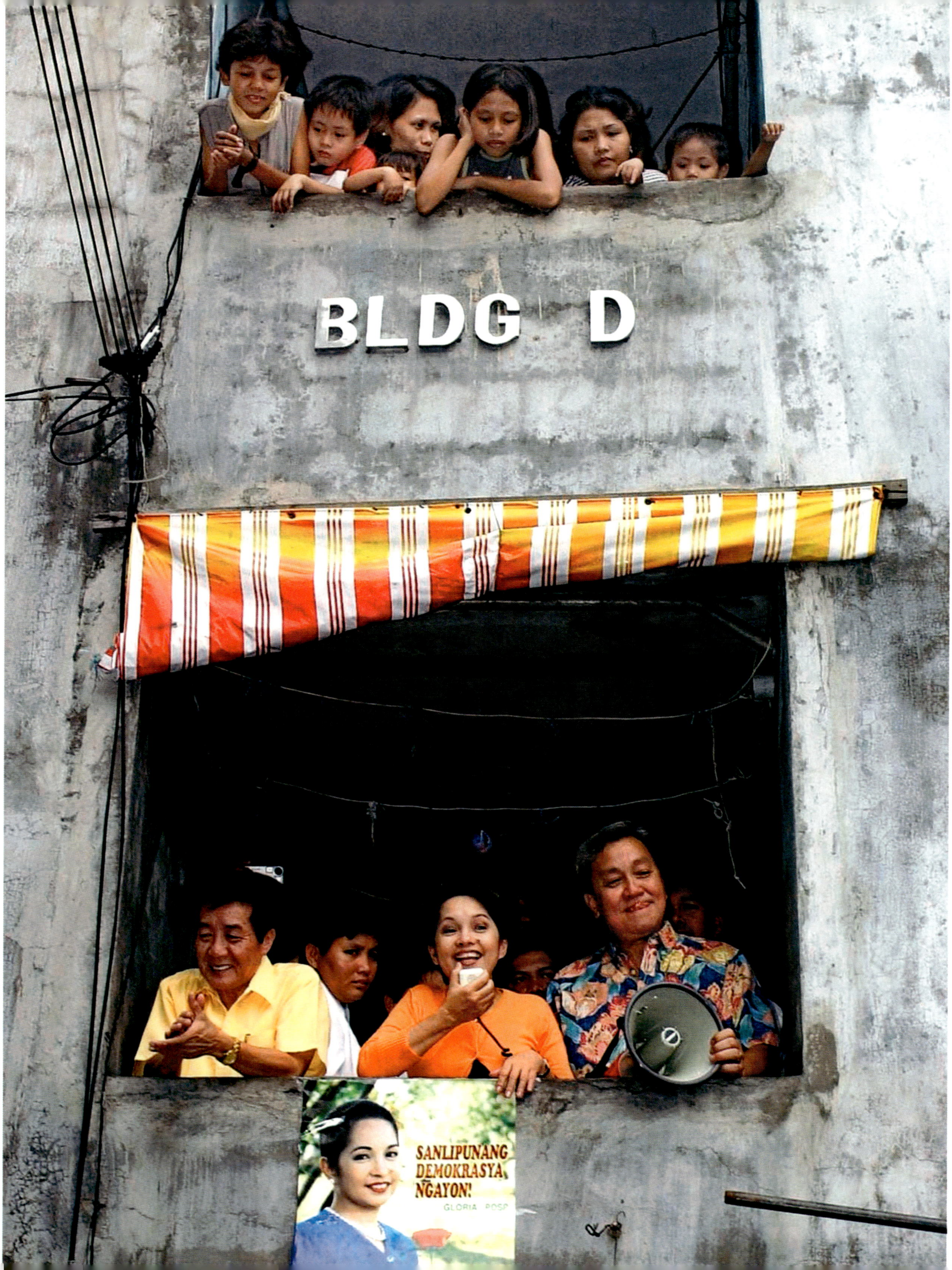
BLDG D
SANLIPUNANG
DEMOKRASYA
NGAYON!
GLORIA POSP

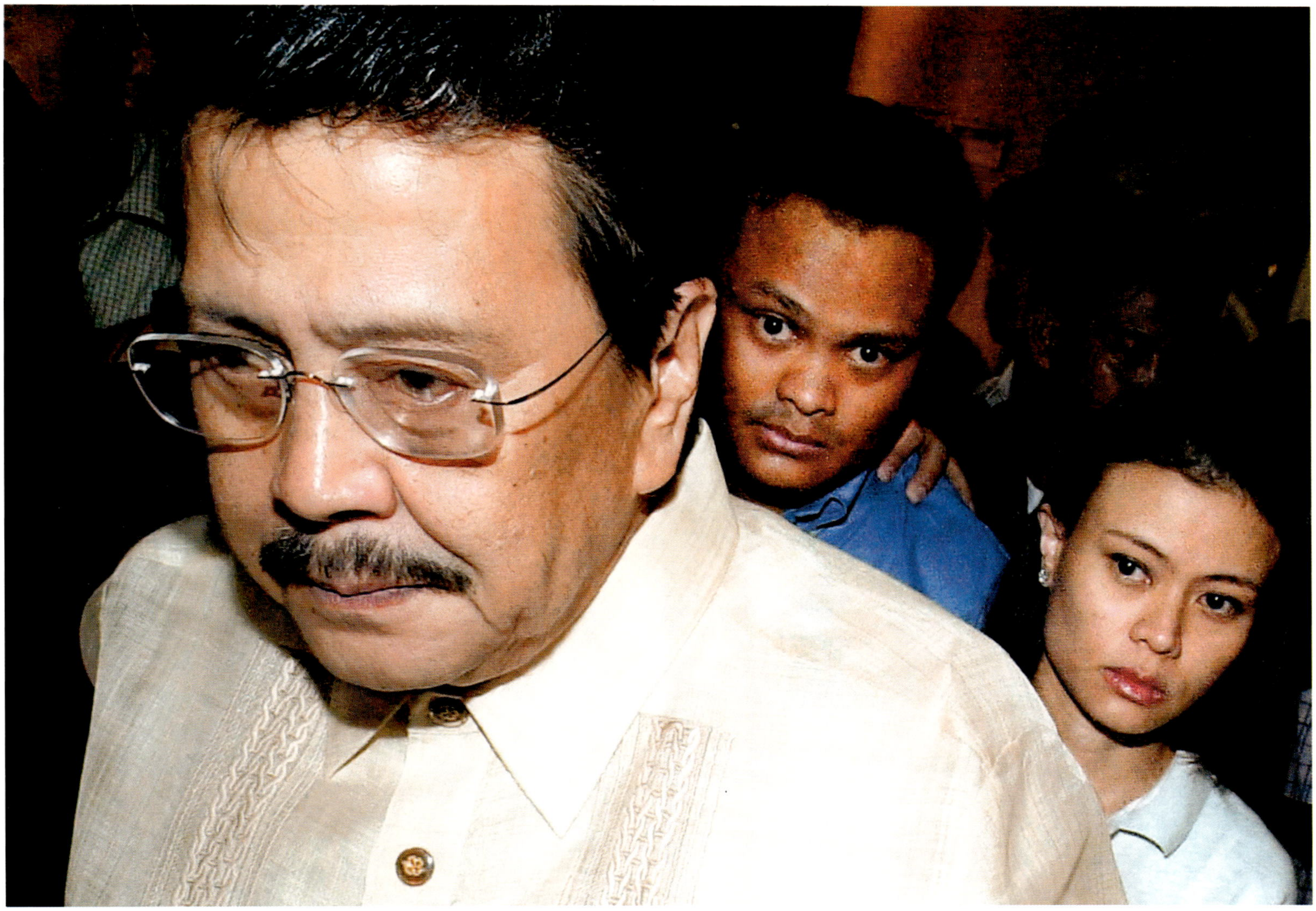

4TH OCTOBER 2001 – MANILA, PHILIPPINES – PRESIDENT GLORIA ARROYO (CENTRE, BOTTOM) ADDRESSES A CROWD FROM A MANILA SLUM BUILDING. (JOËL NITO)

17TH APRIL 2001 – MANILA, PHILIPPINES – DISGRACED FORMER PRESIDENT JOSEPH ESTRADA LEAVES COURT AFTER BEING RELEASED ON BAIL OVER CORRUPTION CHARGES. (JAY DIRECTO)

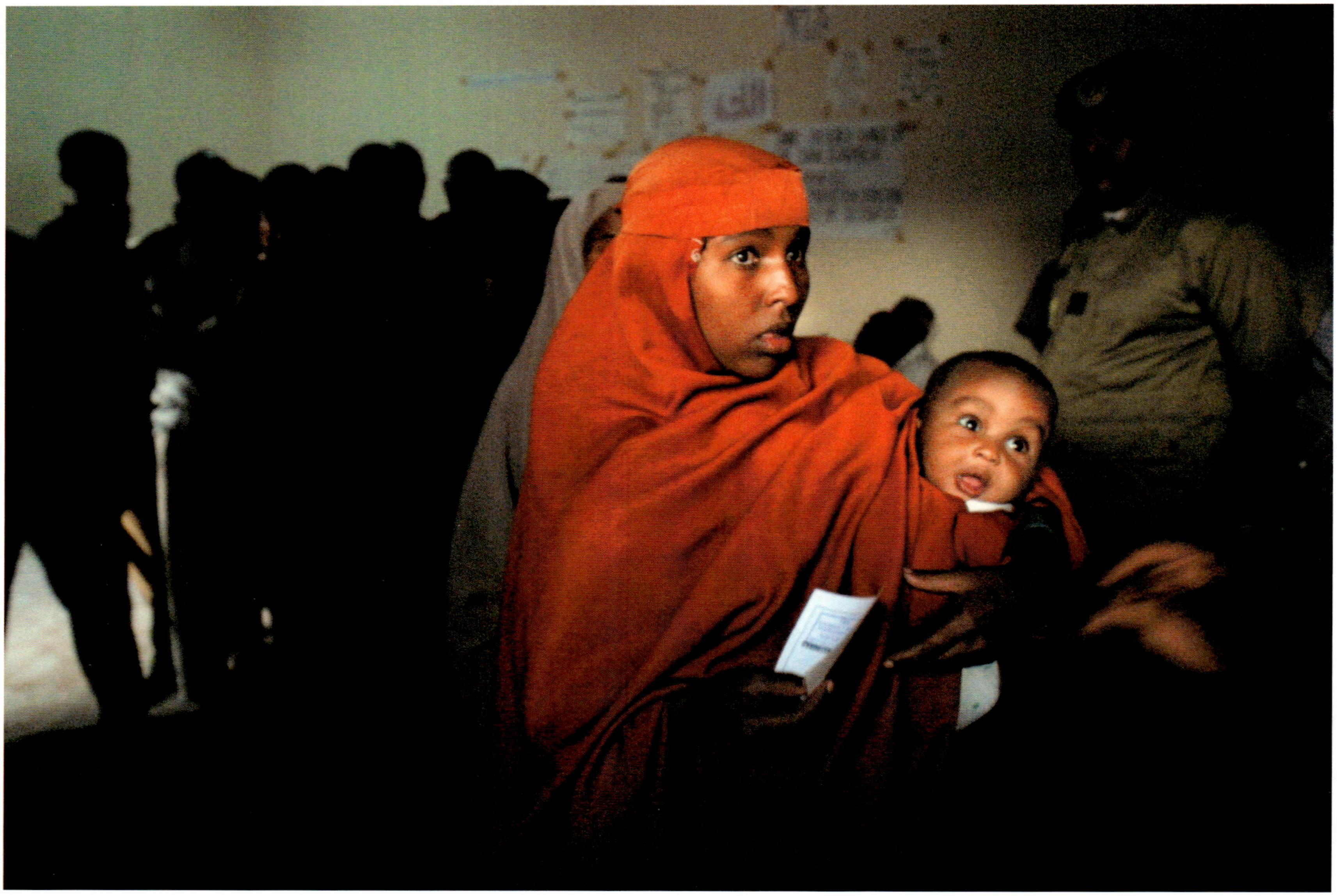

31ST MAY 2001 – HARGEISA, SOMALIA – A WOMAN IN SOMALILAND CASTS HER BALLOT IN A CONSTITUTIONAL REFERENDUM 10 YEARS AFTER THE REGION UNILATERALLY SECEDED FROM SOMALIA. (PEDRO UGARTE)

A SHRINKING PLANET AND A WORLD OF DANGER

EU-SUMMIT-DEMOS-SHOT,4TH LEAD
URGENT¥¥¥ THREE ADMITTED TO GOTHENBURG HOSPITAL WITH GUNSHOT WOUNDS
GOTHENBURG, SWEDEN, JUNE 15 (AFP) – THREE PEOPLE WERE ADMITTED
TO GOTHENBURG'S SAHLGRENSKA HOSPITAL WITH GUNSHOT WOUNDS AS
DEMONSTRATORS PROTESTED AT AN EU SUMMIT HERE, HOSPITAL OFFICIALS TOLD AFP.
PO/CCR

G8-PROTEST-INJURE
URGENT¥¥¥ PROTESTER SHOT DEAD AT G8 SUMMIT: WITNESSES
GENOA, JULY 20 (AFP) – AN ANTI-GLOBALISATION PROTESTER WAS SHOT DEAD DURING
DEMONSTRATIONS AGAINST THE G8 SUMMIT FRIDAY, WITNESSES SAID.
BUR/CCR

FRANCE-BLAST,3RD LEAD
URGENT¥¥¥ MANY HURT, PROBABLY DEATHS IN CHEMICAL PLANT BLAST
TOULOUSE, FRANCE, SEPT 21 (AFP) – MANY PEOPLE WERE HURT AND FATALITIES LIKELY
IN A HUGE EXPLOSION AT A PETROCHEMICAL PLANT IN THIS SOUTHWESTERN FRENCH
CITY FRIDAY, RESCUE WORKERS SAID.
POLICE SAID THE BLAST TOOK PLACE AT THE AZF PETROCHEMICAL PLANT, CAUSING
MAJOR DAMAGE.
PA/JZ/NS

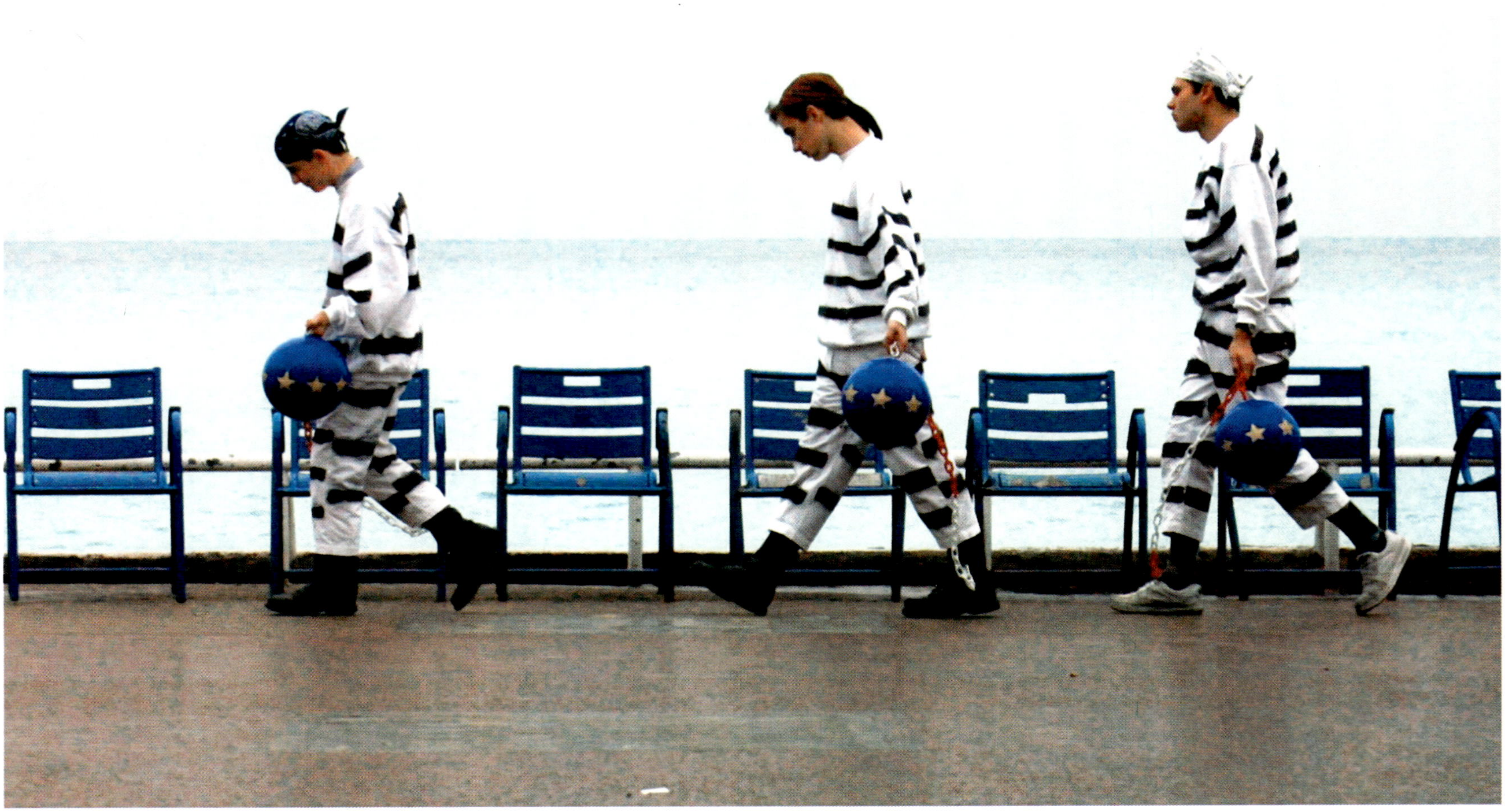

8TH DECEMBER 2000 – NICE, FRANCE – THREE MEN IN PRISON UNIFORM CARRY BALLS-AND-CHAINS IN THE COLOURS OF THE EUROPEAN FLAG TO PROTEST AT THE EUROPEAN UNION SUMMIT. (PATRICE LAPOIRIE)

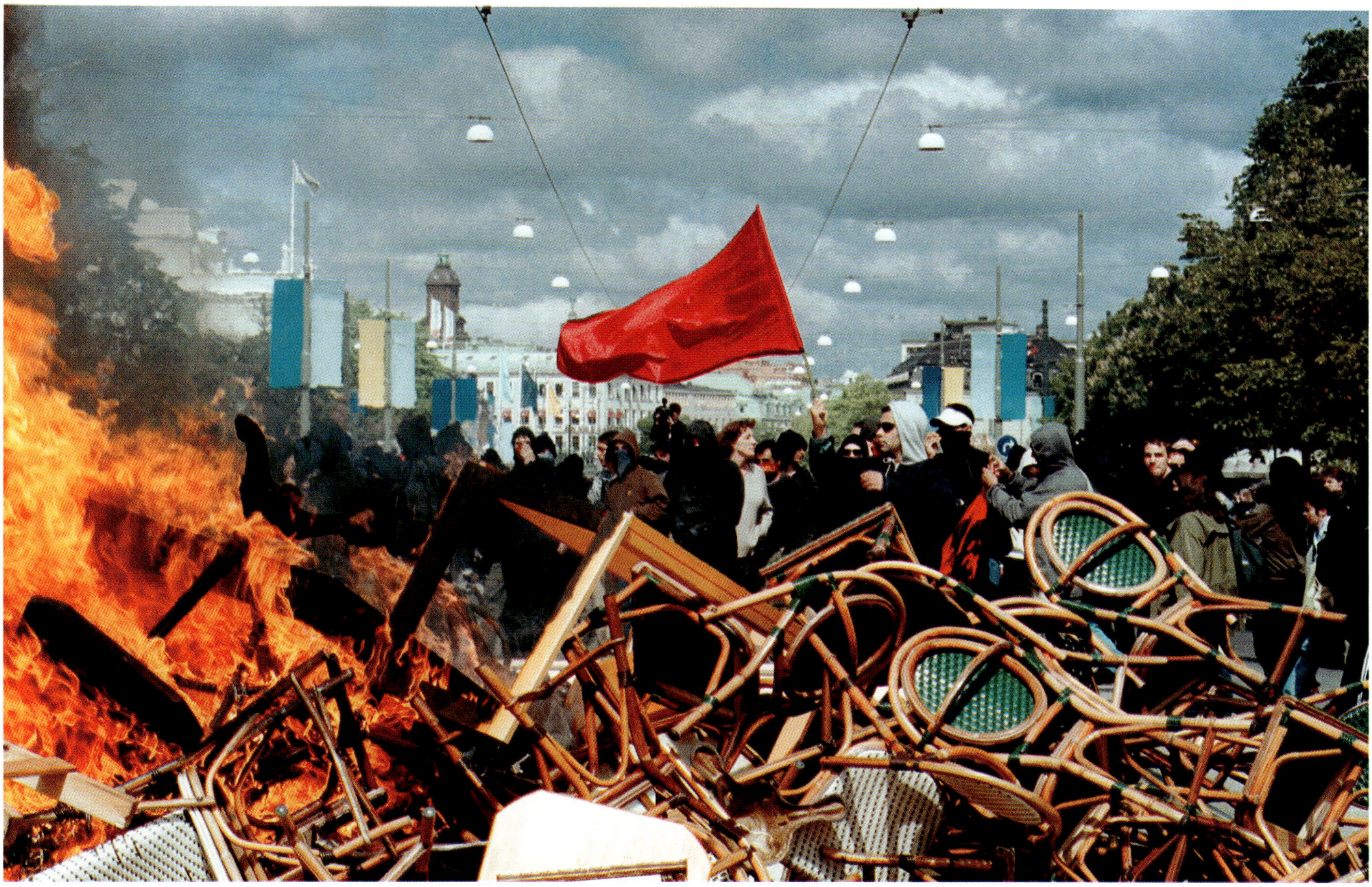

15TH JUNE 2001 – GOTHENBURG, SWEDEN – A BARRICADE SET UP WITH CHAIRS AND TABLES FROM CAFES BURNS DURING AN ANTI-EUROPEAN SUMMIT DEMONSTRATION. (JOAN FRAMST/PRESSENS BILD)

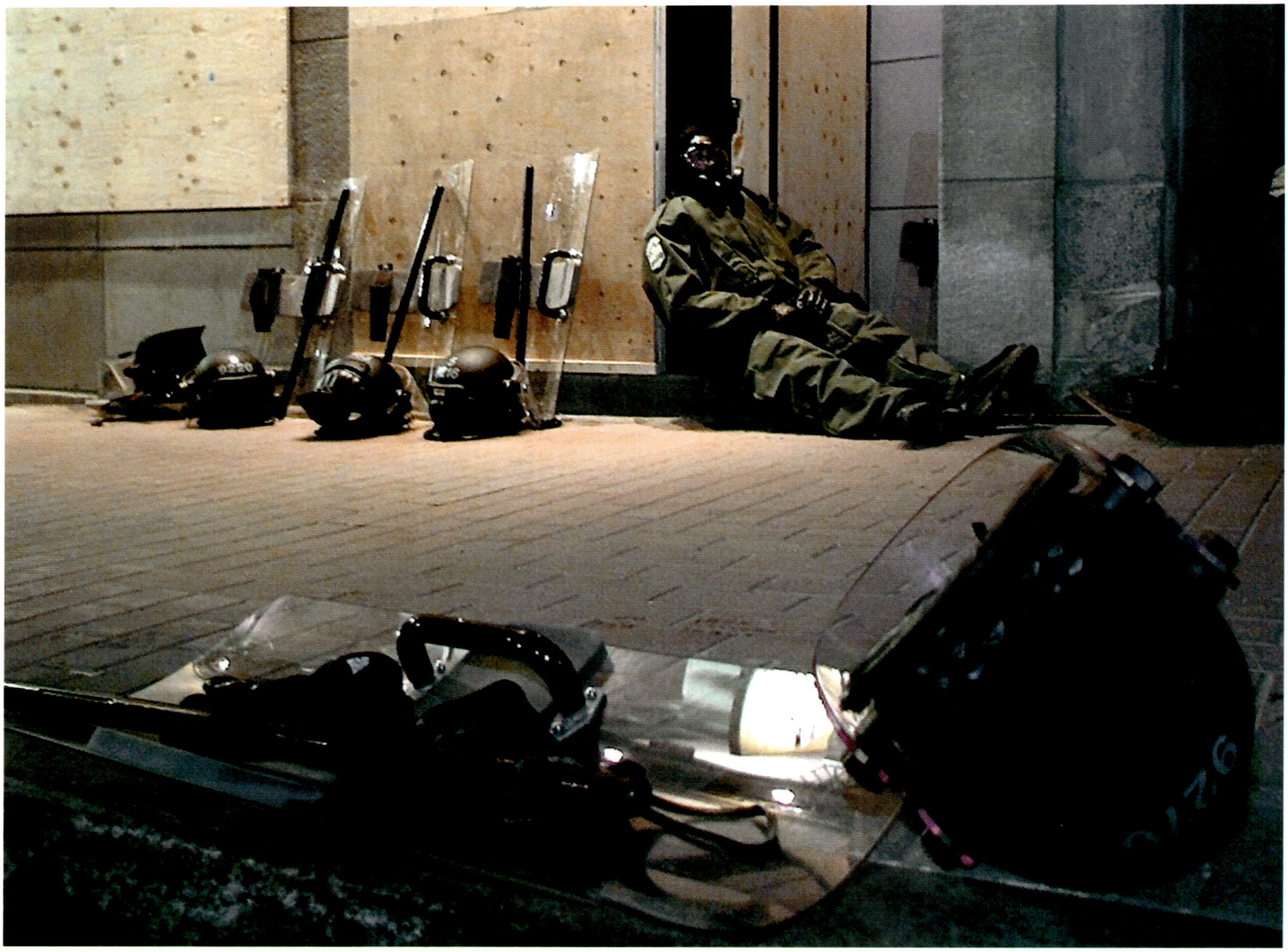

20TH APRIL 2001 – QUEBEC CITY, CANADA – A POLICE OFFICER TAKES A REST AFTER A LONG SHIFT DEALING WITH PROTESTORS AT THE THIRD SUMMIT OF THE AMERICAS. (PAUL J. RICHARDS)

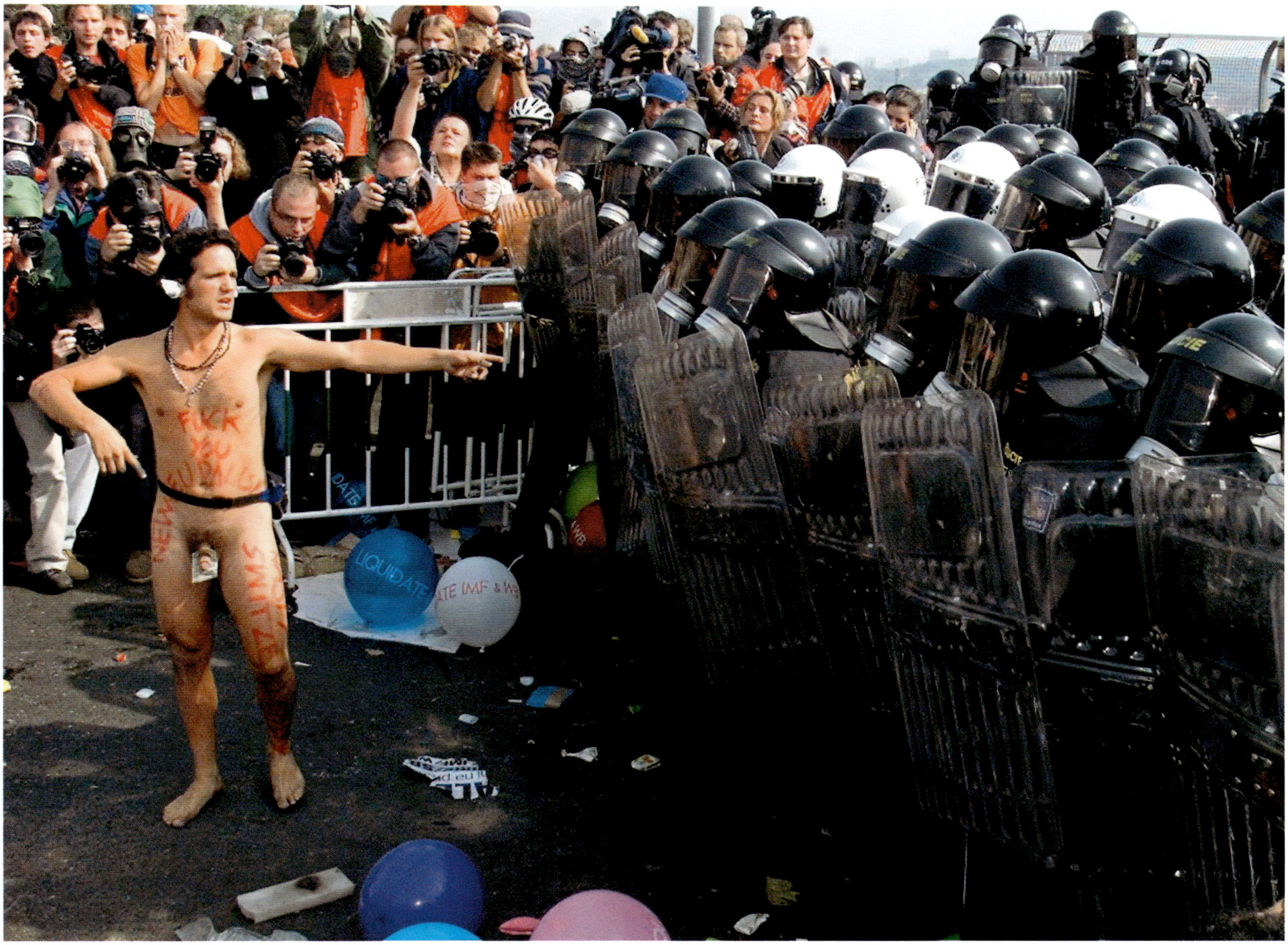

26TH SEPTEMBER 2000 – PRAGUE, CZECH REPUBLIC – AN ANTI-GLOBALISATION PROTESTOR, WITH OBSCENE REMARKS WRITTEN ON HIS CHEST, CONFRONTS RIOT POLICE DURING THE IMF/WORLD BANK ANNUAL PLENARY MEETING. (JACK GUEZ)

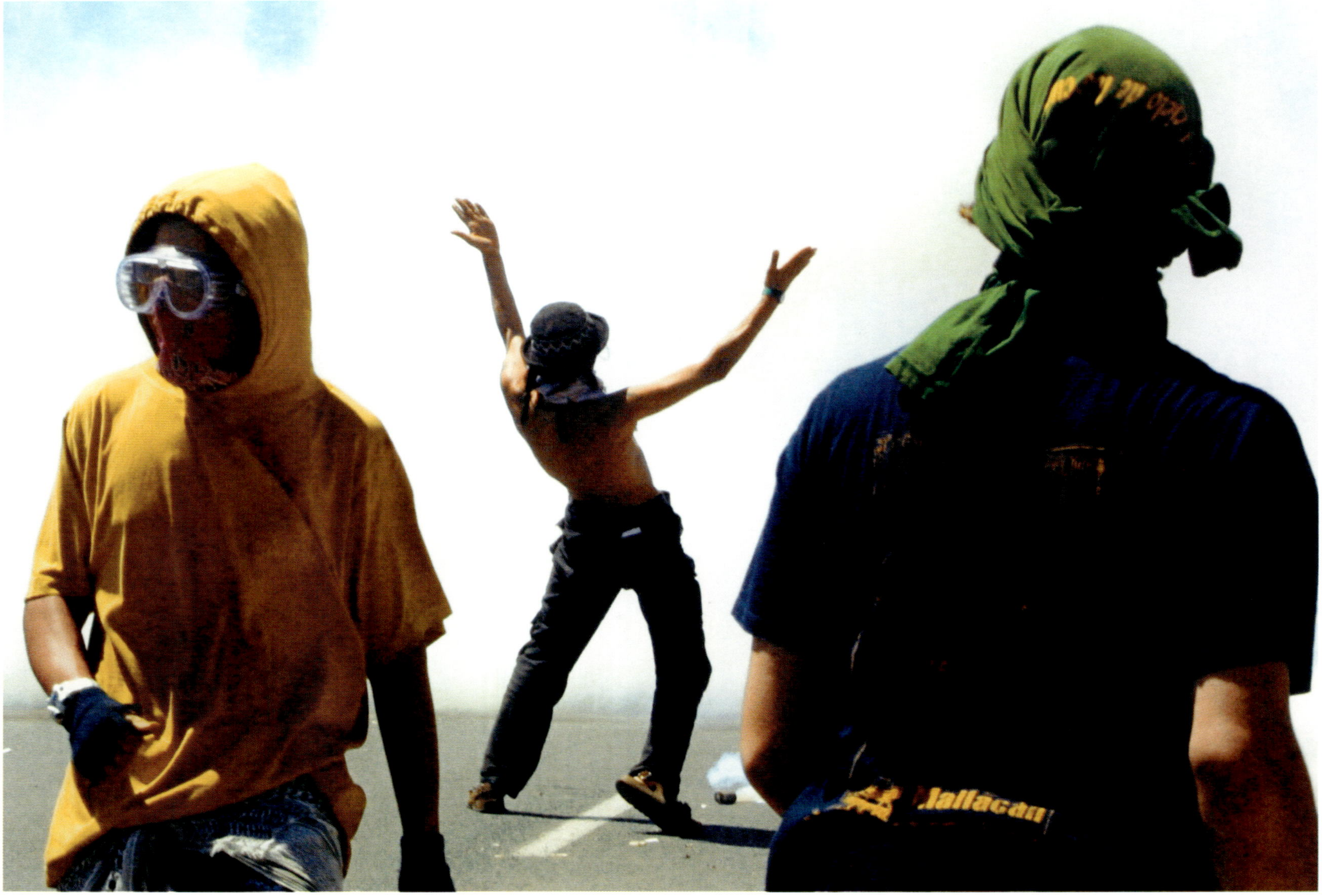

21ST JULY 2001 – GENOA, ITALY – ANTI-GLOBALISATION DEMONSTRATORS PROVOKE THE POLICE DURING THE G8 SUMMIT MEETING. (GABRIEL BOUYS)

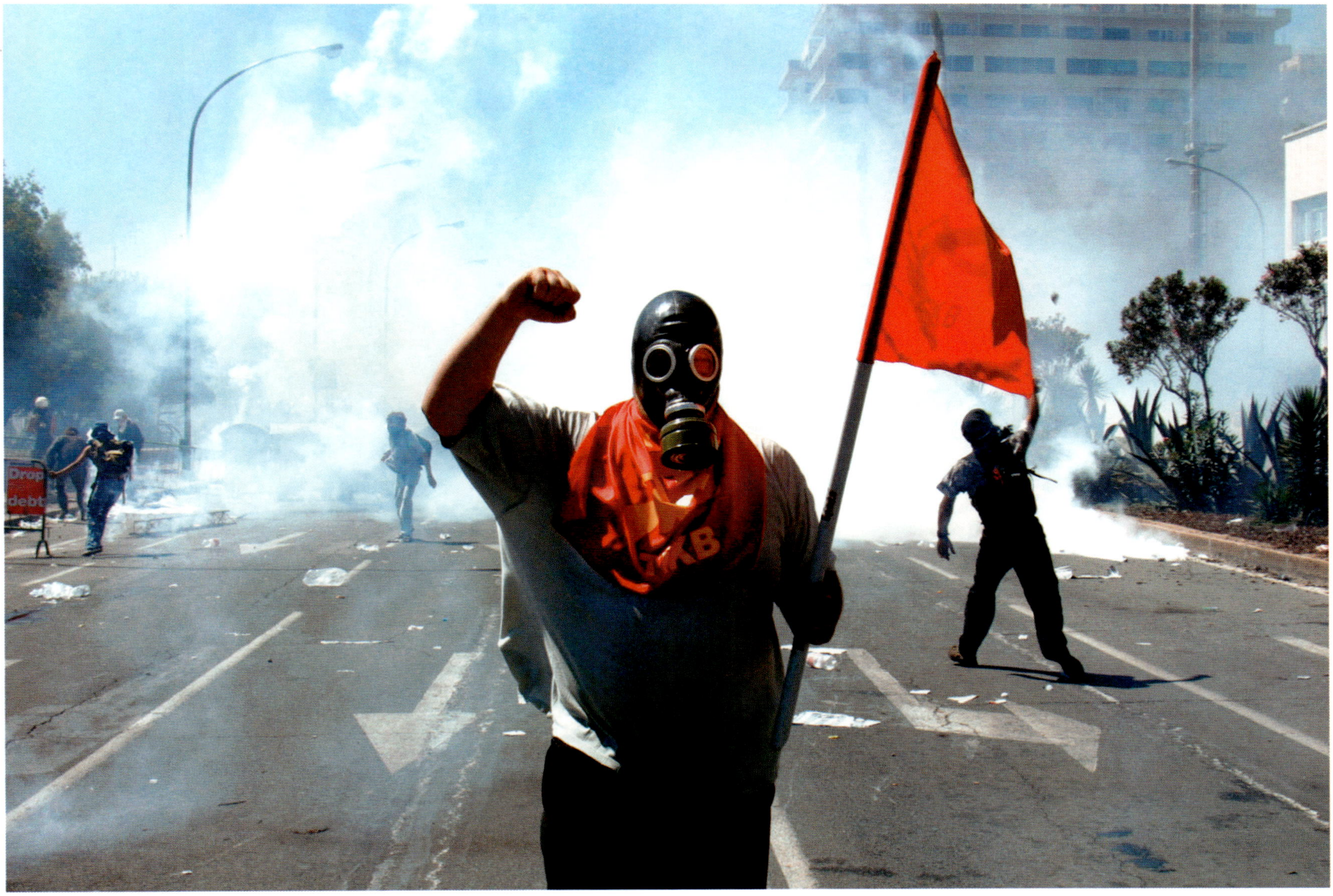

21ST JULY 2001 – GENOA, ITALY – AN ANTI-GLOBALISATION DEMONSTRATOR DURING THE G8 SUMMIT MEETING. (PHILIPPE DESMAZES)

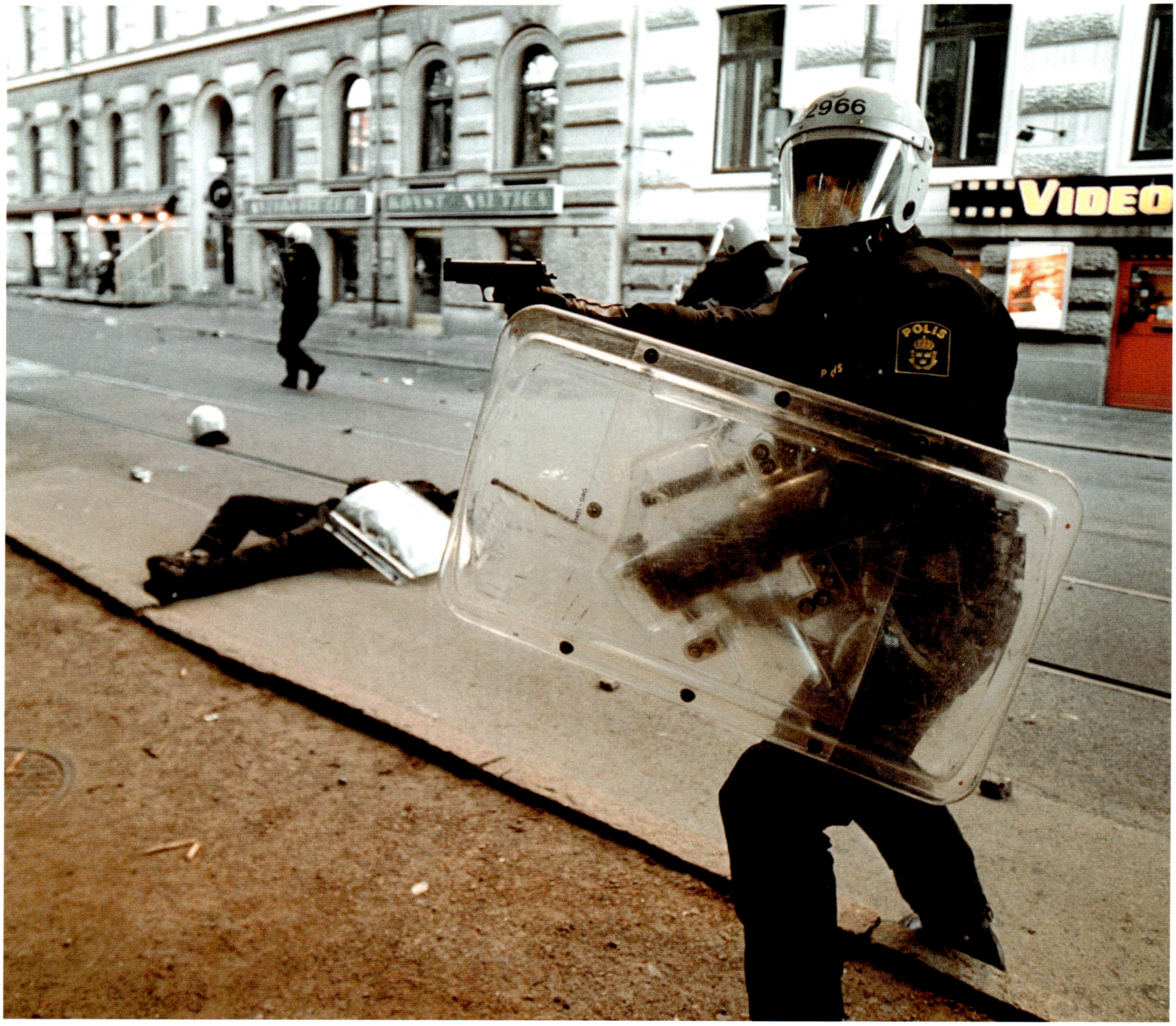

15TH JUNE 2001 – GOTHENBURG, SWEDEN – A POLICEMAN FIRES GUNSHOTS TOWARDS ANTI-EUROPEAN SUMMIT ACTIVISTS AFTER HIS COLLEAGUE, LYING ON THE GROUND, WAS HIT BY STONES. (LARSERIC LINDEN/PRESSENS BILD)

20TH JULY 2001 – GENOA, ITALY – POLICEMEN STAND BY THE CORPSE OF CARLO GIULIANI WHO WAS KILLED DURING ANTI-G8 SUMMIT DEMONSTRATIONS. (ZENNARO/ANSA)

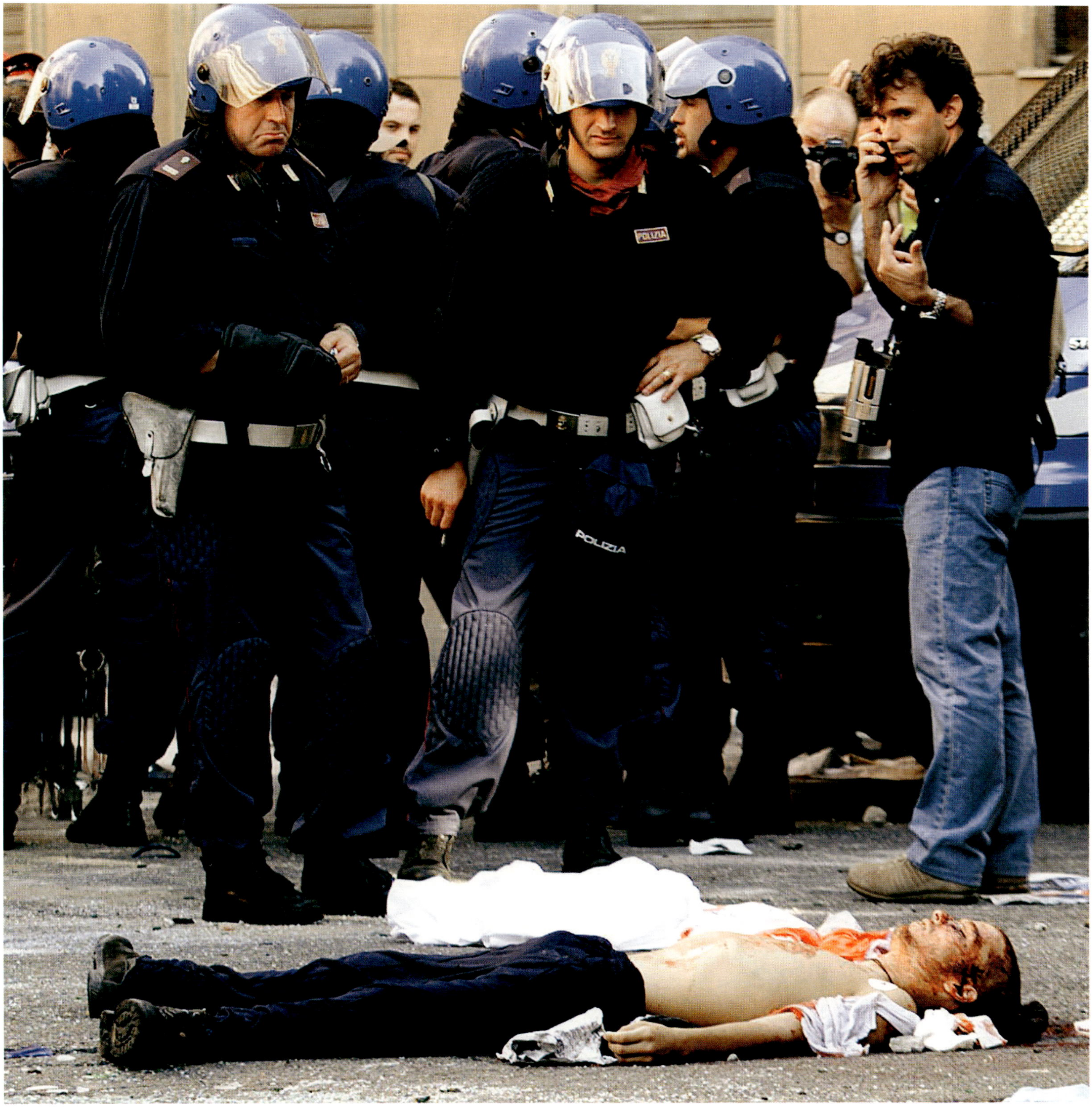
POLIZIA
POLIZIA

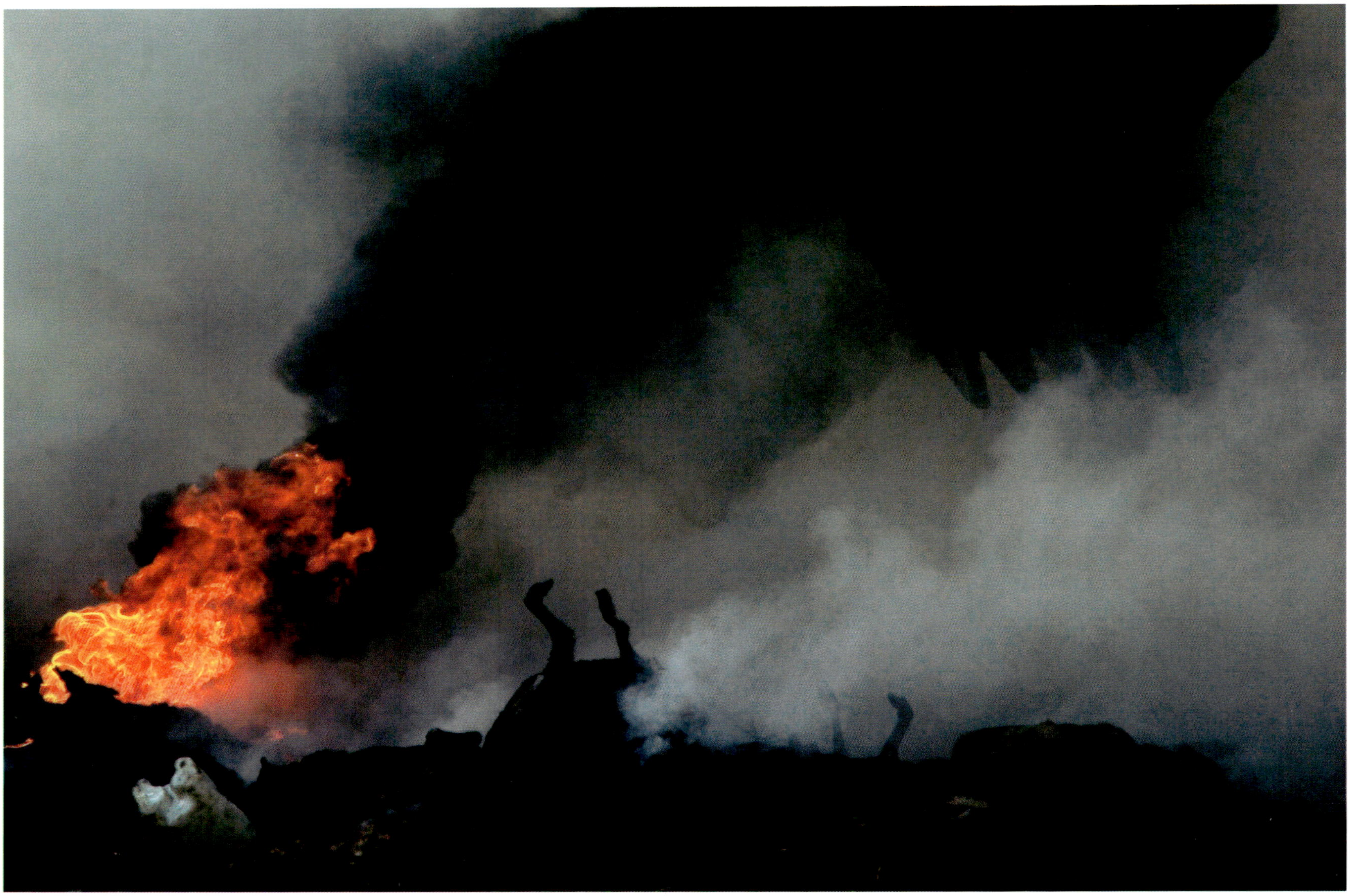

15TH MARCH 2001 – PRESSAGNY-L'ORGUEILLEUX, FRANCE – THE CARCASSES OF SHEEP ARE BURNED IN AN EFFORT TO HALT THE SPREAD OF FOOT-AND-MOUTH DISEASE. (MEDHI FEDOUACH)

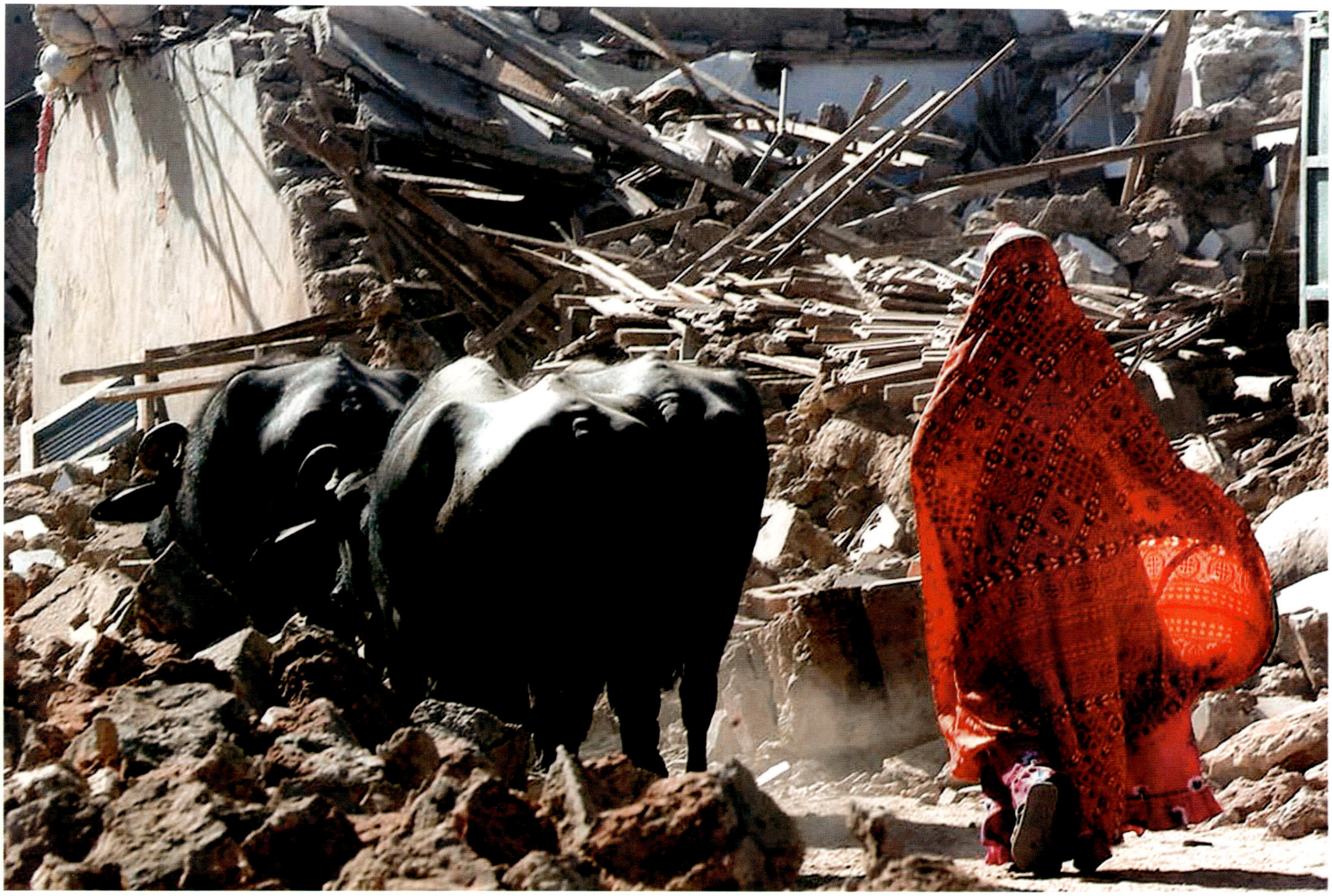

3RD FEBRUARY 2001 – VONDH, INDIA – A WOMAN LEADS HER BUFFALO THROUGH THE DEVASTATED VILLAGE OF VONDH, EPICENTRE OF A HUGE EARTHQUAKE. (EMMANUEL DUNAND)

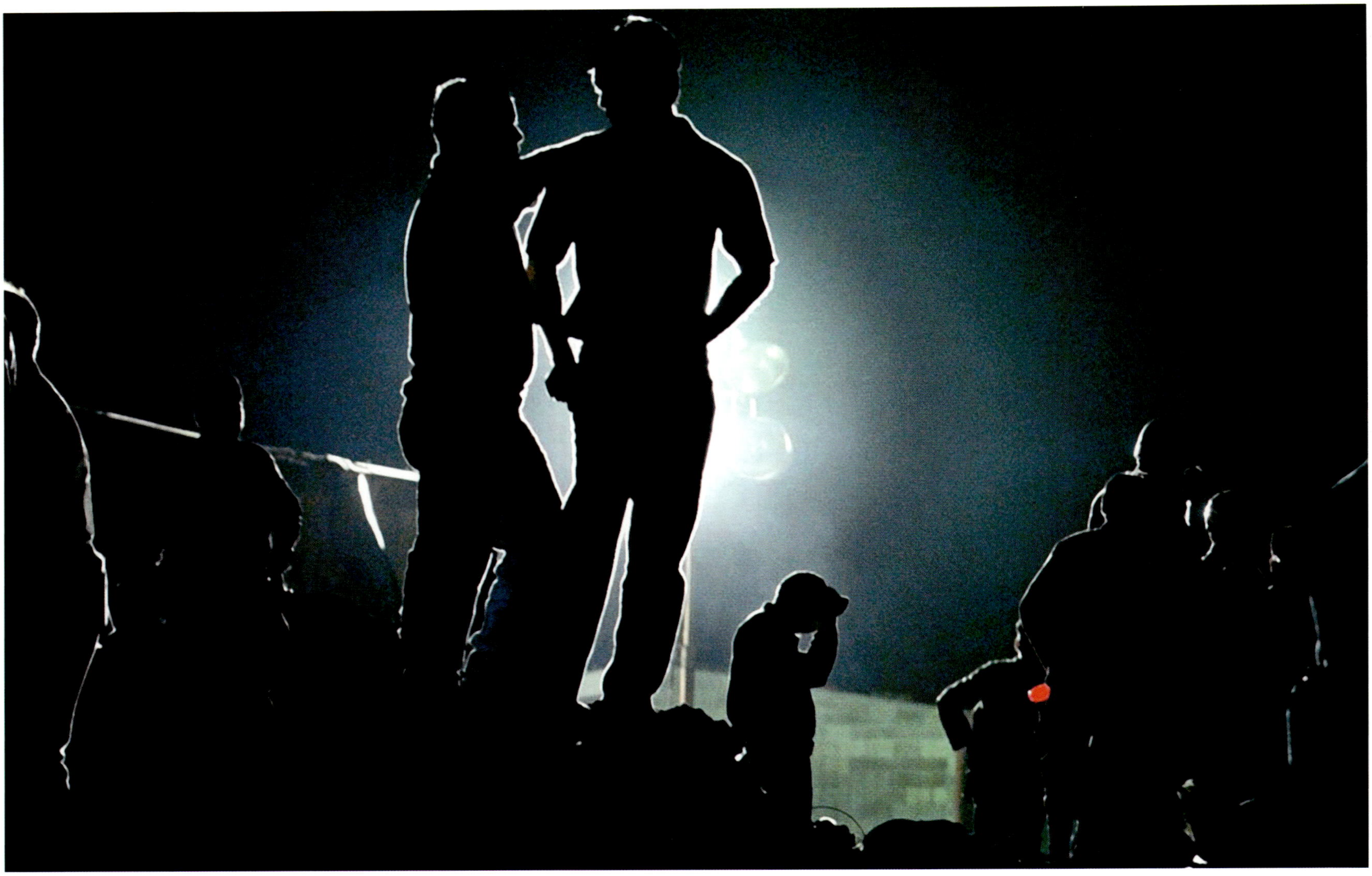

14TH JANUARY 2001
– SAN SALVADOR, EL SALVADOR –
RESCUE WORKERS SURVEY
THE SCENE OF THE MASSIVE
EARTHQUAKE WHICH MEASURED
7.9 ON THE RICHTER SCALE AND
ROCKED THE LAS COLINAS AREA
OF THE CITY. (JORGE UZON)

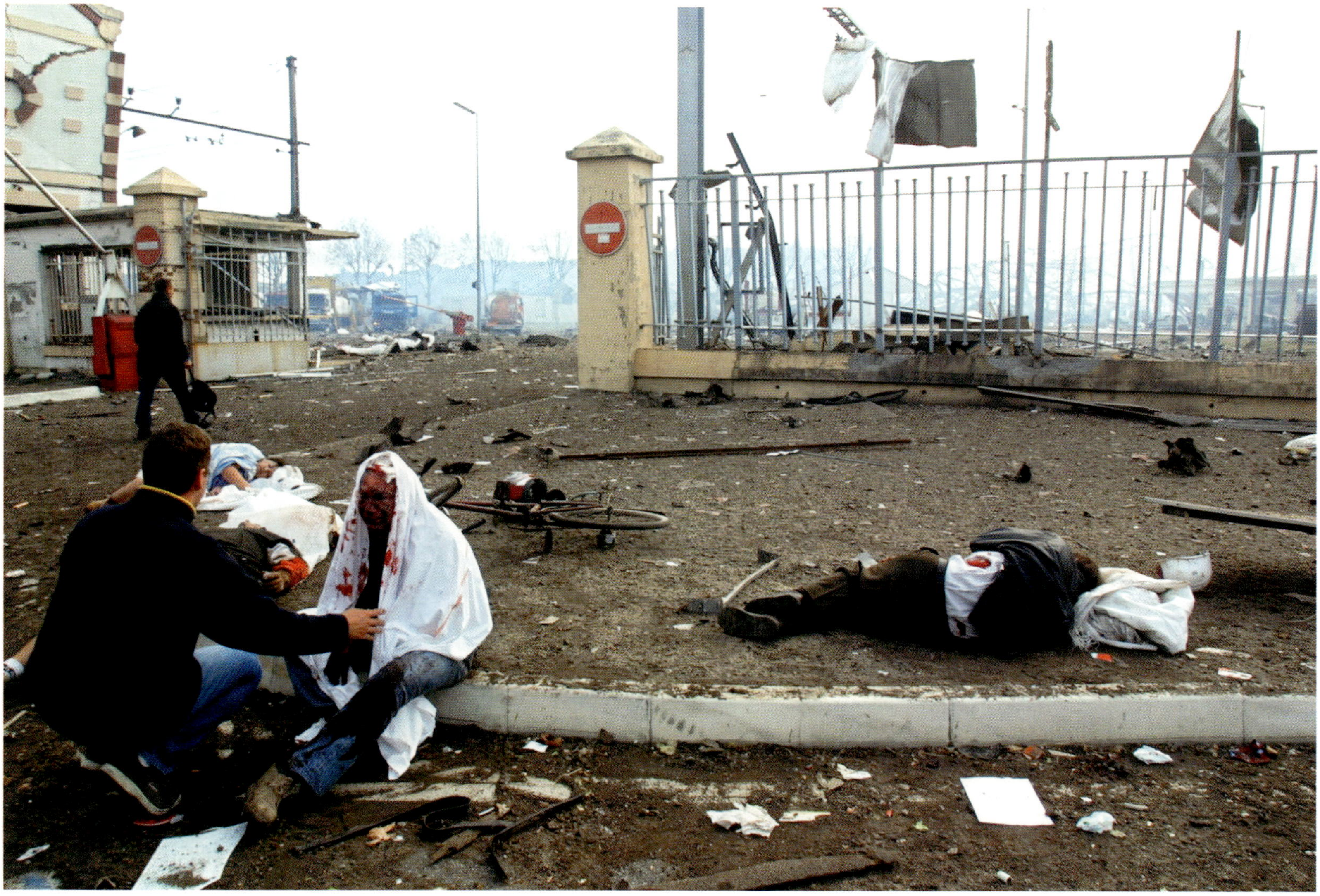

21ST SEPTEMBER 2001 – TOULOUSE, FRANCE – IN THE AFTERMATH OF THE EXPLOSION AT THE AZF PETROCHEMICAL FACTORY, SOME OF THE INJURED AWAIT MEDICAL ATTENTION. (ÉRIC CABANIS)

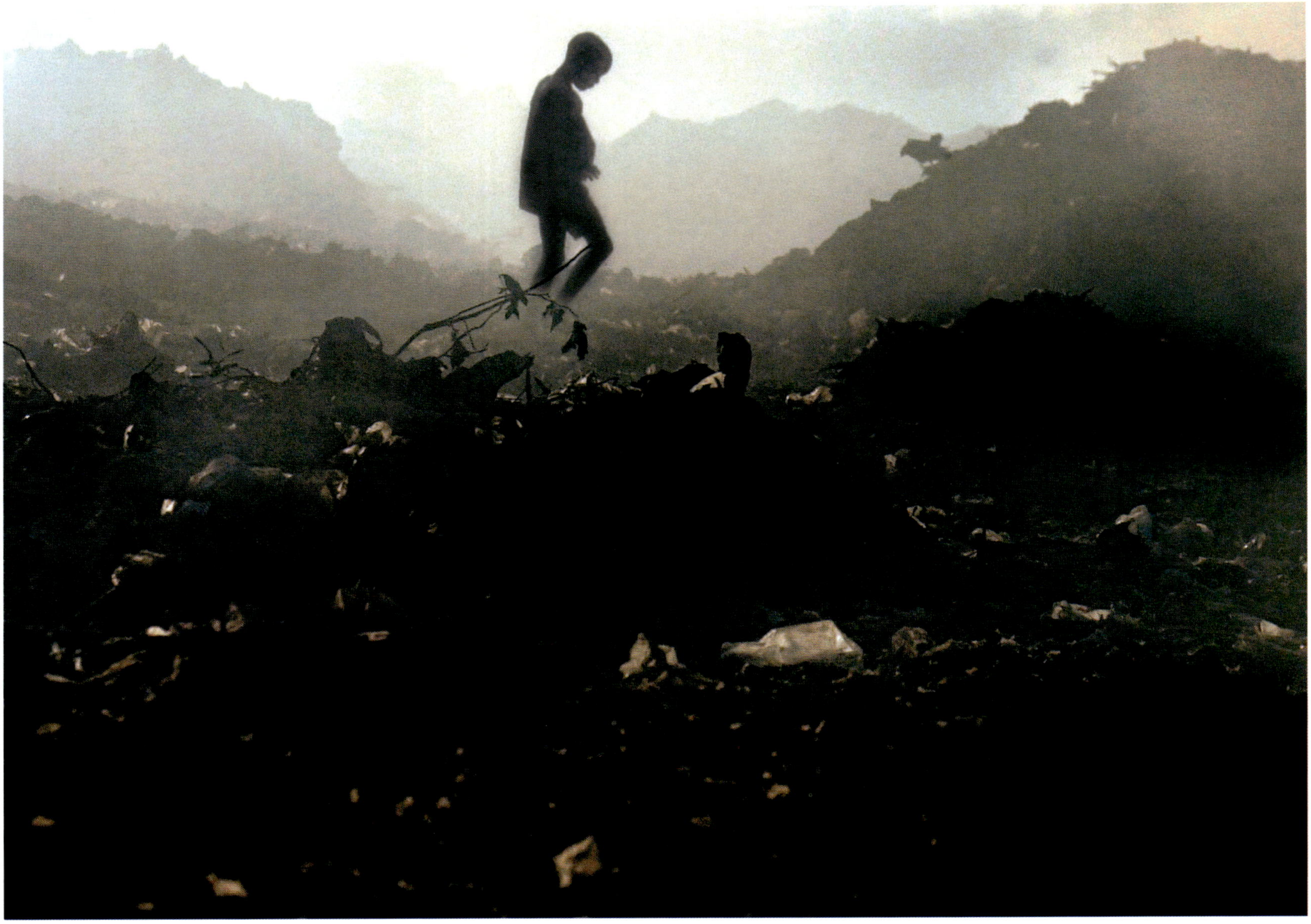

23TH NOVEMBER 2000
– PORT-AU-PRINCE, HAITI –
A BOY SCOURS A RUBBISH DUMP
FOR ANYTHING HE CAN SALVAGE
AND RE-SELL. (ROBERTO SCHMIDT)

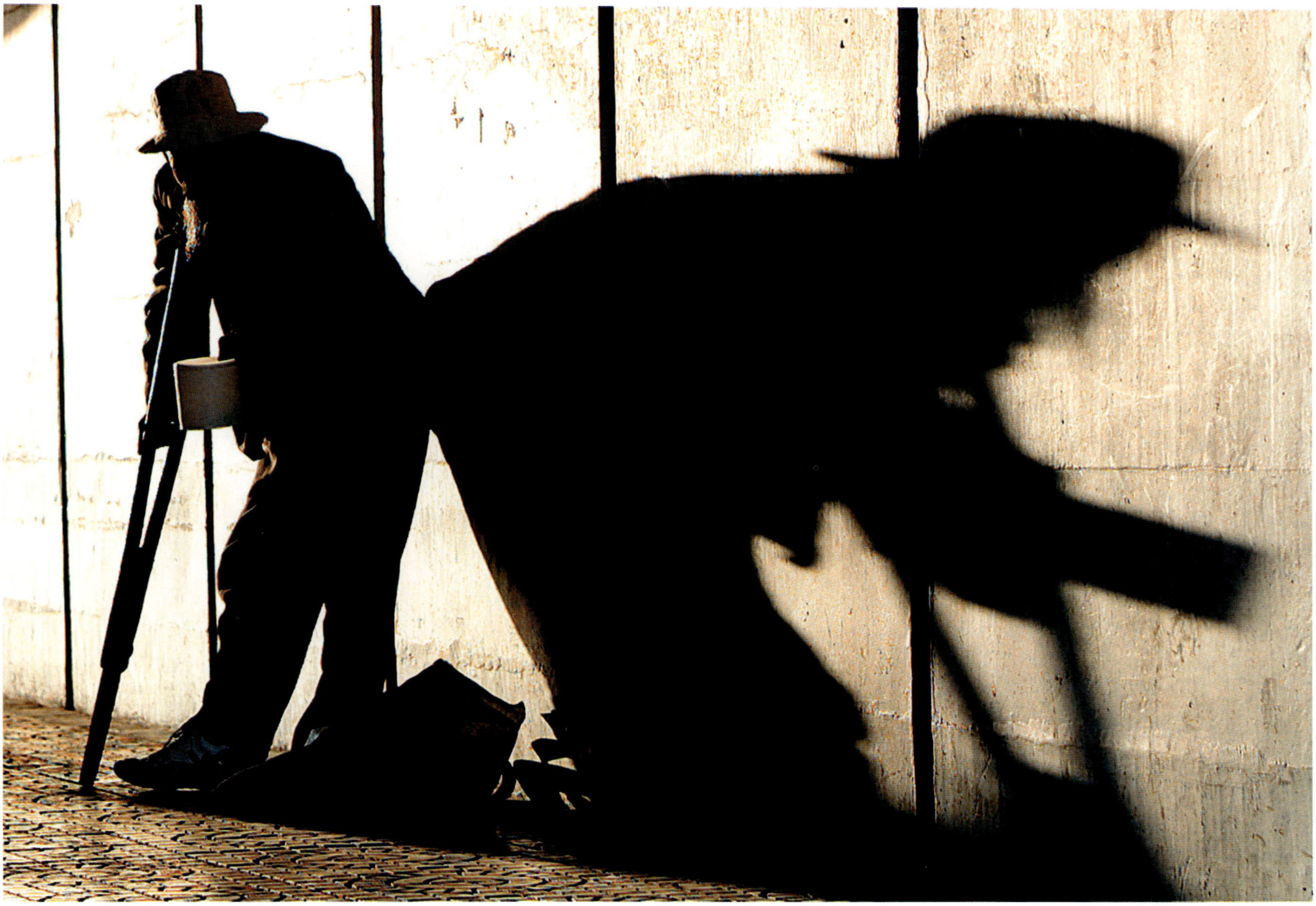

4TH OCTOBER 2001 – BEIJING, CHINA – A BEGGAR CASTS A LONG SHADOW IN A BEIJING UNDERPASS. (FREDERIC J. BROWN)

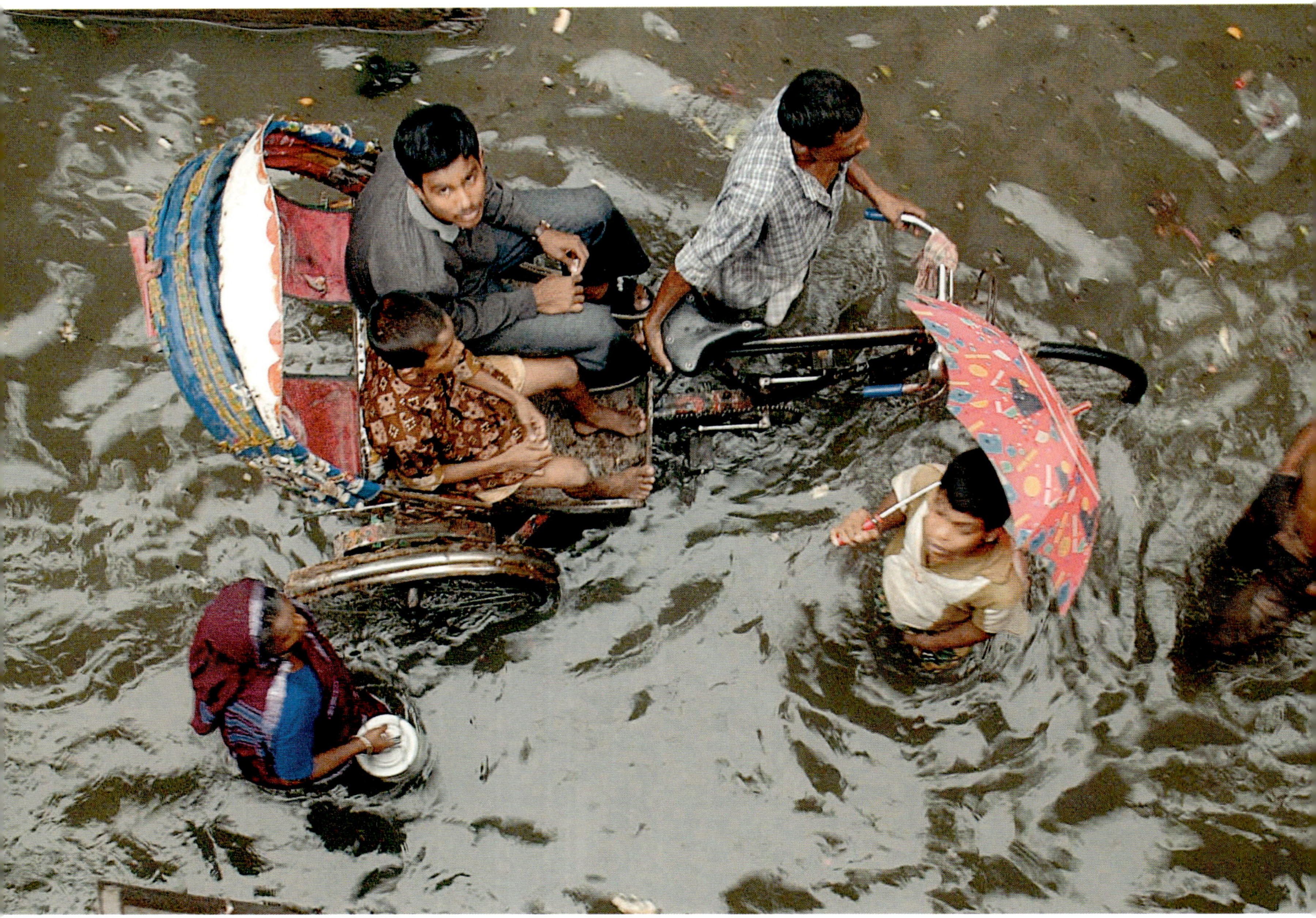

9TH MAY 2001 – DHAKA, BANGLADESH – RESIDENTS WADE THROUGH A FLOODED STREET AFTER RAINSTORMS SWEPT THROUGH THE BANGLADESHI CAPITAL. (JEWEL SAMAD)

26TH JULY 2001 – ETNA, ITALY – A TORRENT OF LAVA IS HURLED INTO THE AIR AS MOUNT ETNA, EUROPE'S MOST ACTIVE VOLCANO, ERUPTS AGAIN. (GABRIEL BOUYS)

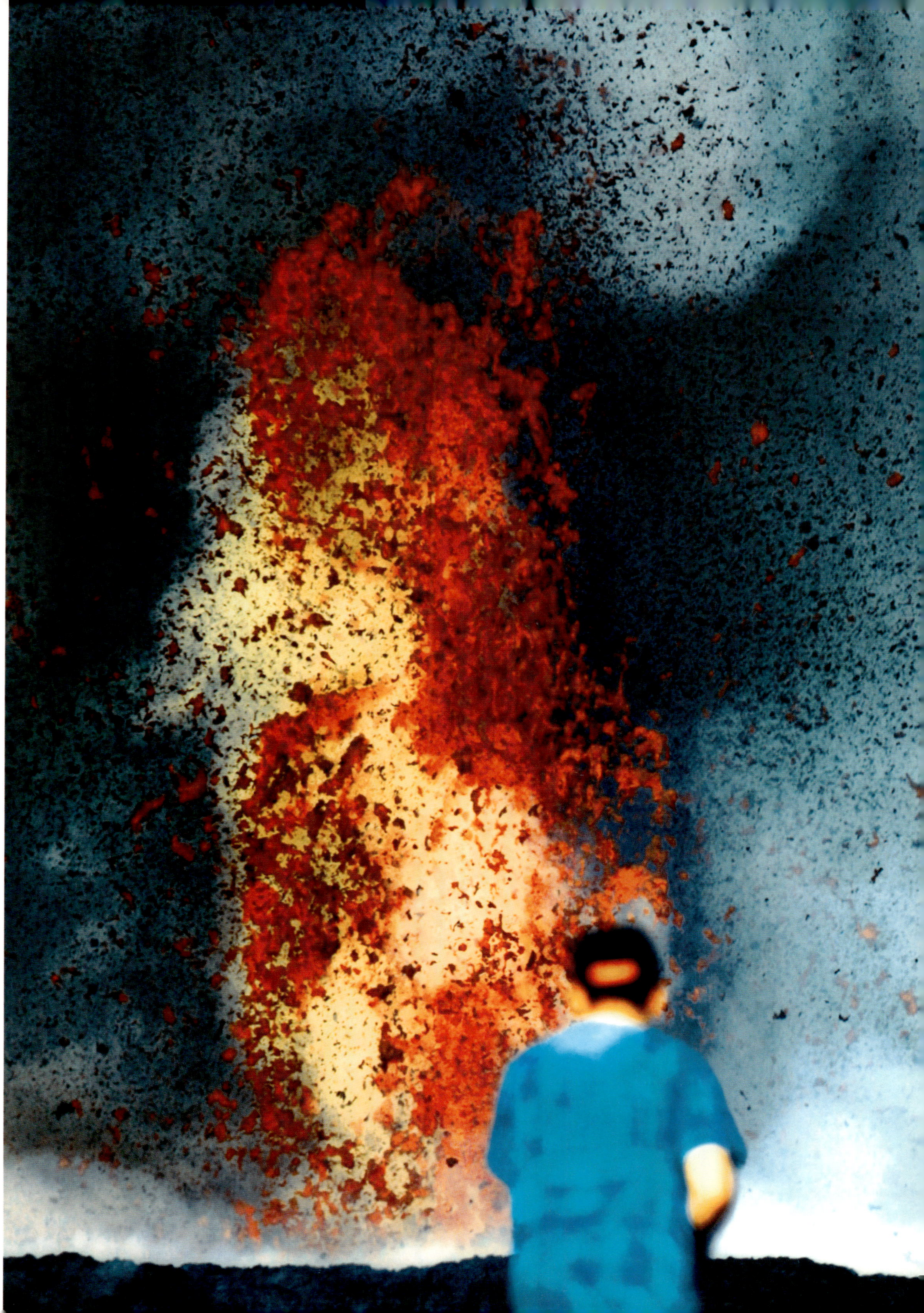

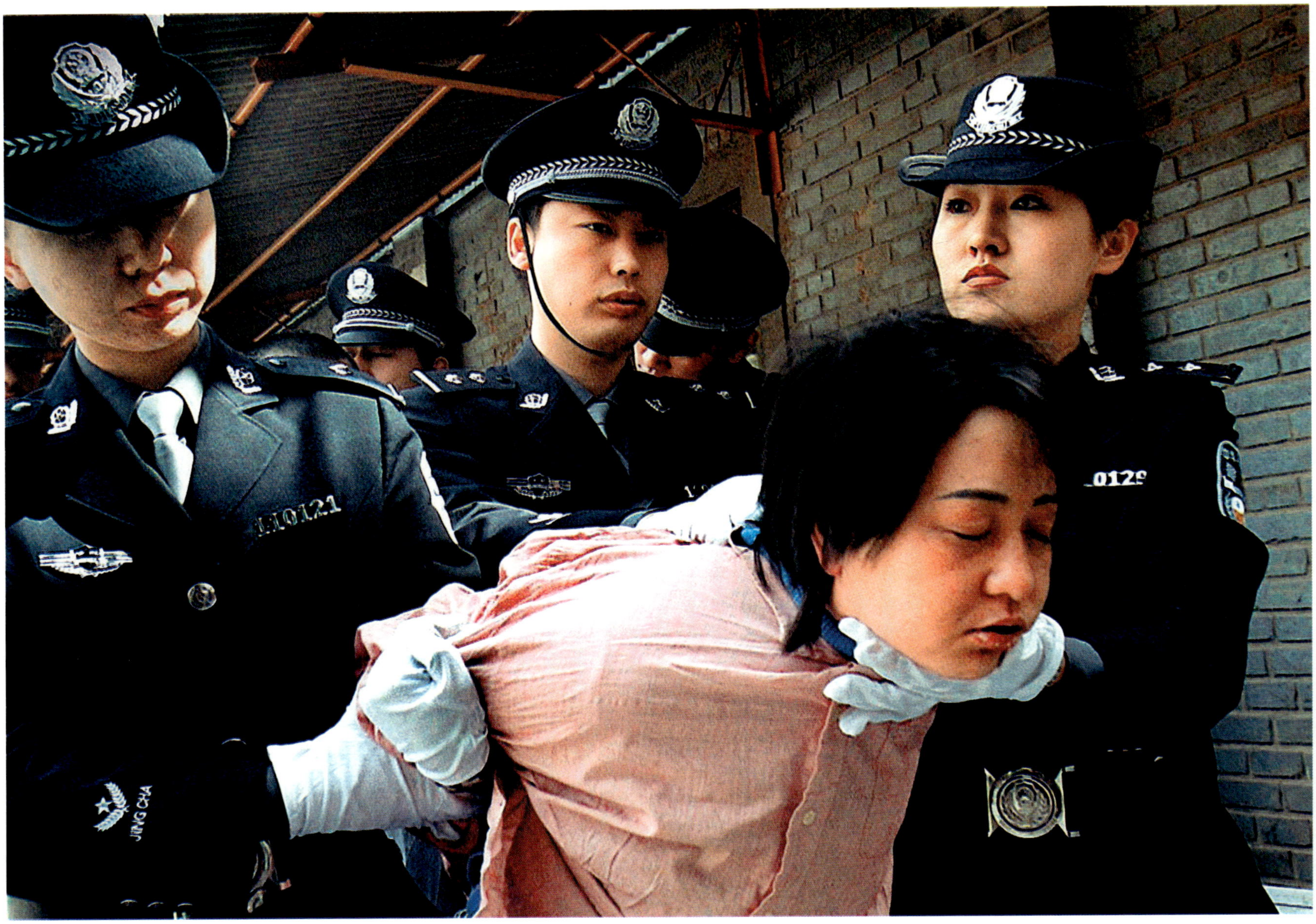

20TH APRIL 2001 – BEIJING, CHINA – A WOMAN IS TAKEN AWAY FOR EXECUTION AFTER BEING ONE OF SIXTEEN PEOPLE CONDEMNED AT A SENTENCING RALLY IN THE CHINESE CAPITAL AS PART OF A NATIONWIDE "STRIKE BLACKNESS AND WIPE OUT EVIL" CAMPAIGN.

RENDEZ-VOUS WITH GOD

AFGHAN-HERITAGE
AFGHAN TALIBAN BEGIN DESTRUCTION OF ANCIENT BUDDHA STATUES
KABUL, MARCH 1 (AFP) – IGNORING AN INTERNATIONAL OUTCRY, AFGHANISTAN'S PURITANICAL TALIBAN ISLAMIC MILITIA BEGAN DEMOLISHING STATUES ACROSS THE COUNTRY ON THURSDAY, INCLUDING TWO TOWERING ANCIENT STONE BUDDHAS.
MBR-SMC/BEN

INDIA-PILGRIMAGE
INDIA BRACES FOR THE GREATEST GATHERING ON EARTH
ALLAHABAD, INDIA, JAN 3 (AFP) – TENS OF MILLIONS OF HINDU PILGRIMS WILL BEGIN CONVERGING ON THE NORTHERN INDIA CITY OF ALLAHABAD NEXT WEEK FOR WHAT IS BEING TOUTED AS THE WORLD'S GREATEST GATHERING OF MASS HUMANITY.
AT ITS PEAK, THE 42-DAY MAHA (GREAT) KUMBH MELA, WHICH BEGINS JANUARY 19, IS EXPECTED TO BRING TOGETHER UPWARDS OF 30 MILLION PILGRIMS TO THE CITY WHERE THE HOLY GANGES AND YAMUNA RIVERS MEET.
SM

URGENT GIANT MONDAROM STATUE BLOWN UP
CASTELLANE, FRANCE, SEPT 6 (AFP) – DEMOLITION WORKERS BLEW UP THE GIANT STATUE OF MONDAROM IN THE SECT'S SO-CALLED "HOLY CITY" HERE ON FRIDAY, AFP WITNESSED.
PR-LAL/JPB

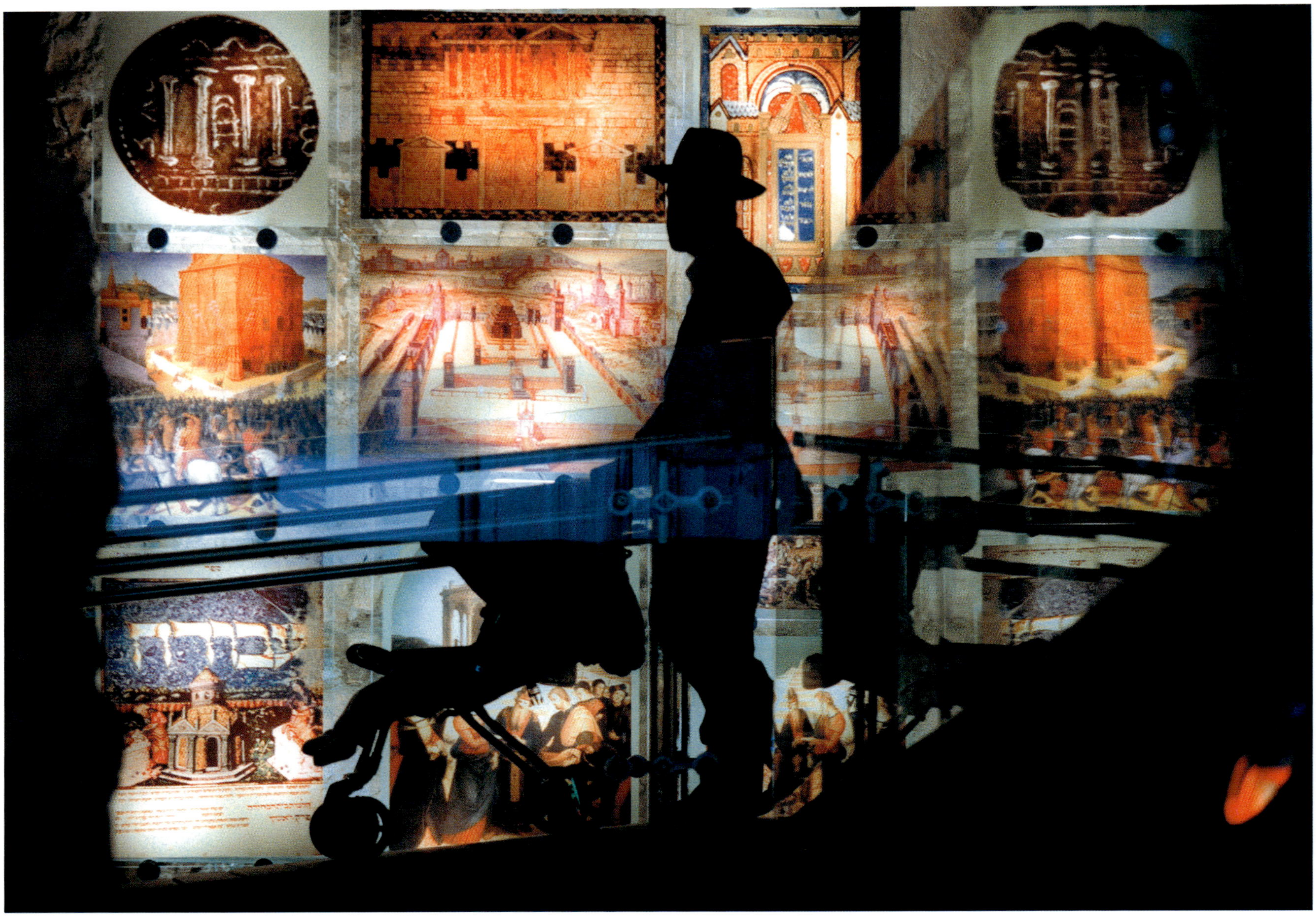

19TH APRIL 2001 – JERUSALEM – AN ULTRA-ORTHODOX JEW VIEWS A REPRESENTATION OF ANCIENT ICONS FROM THE SECOND TEMPLE IN THE HIGH-TECH INTERACTIVE JEWISH MUSEUM IN JERUSALEM'S OLD CITY. (MENAHEM KAHANA)

22ND DECEMBER 2000 – DHAKA, BANGLADESH – AN EIGHT-YEAR-OLD WORKING BOY PRAYING ON THE STREET AT THE END OF THE HOLY MONTH OF RAMADAN. (JEWEL SAMAD)

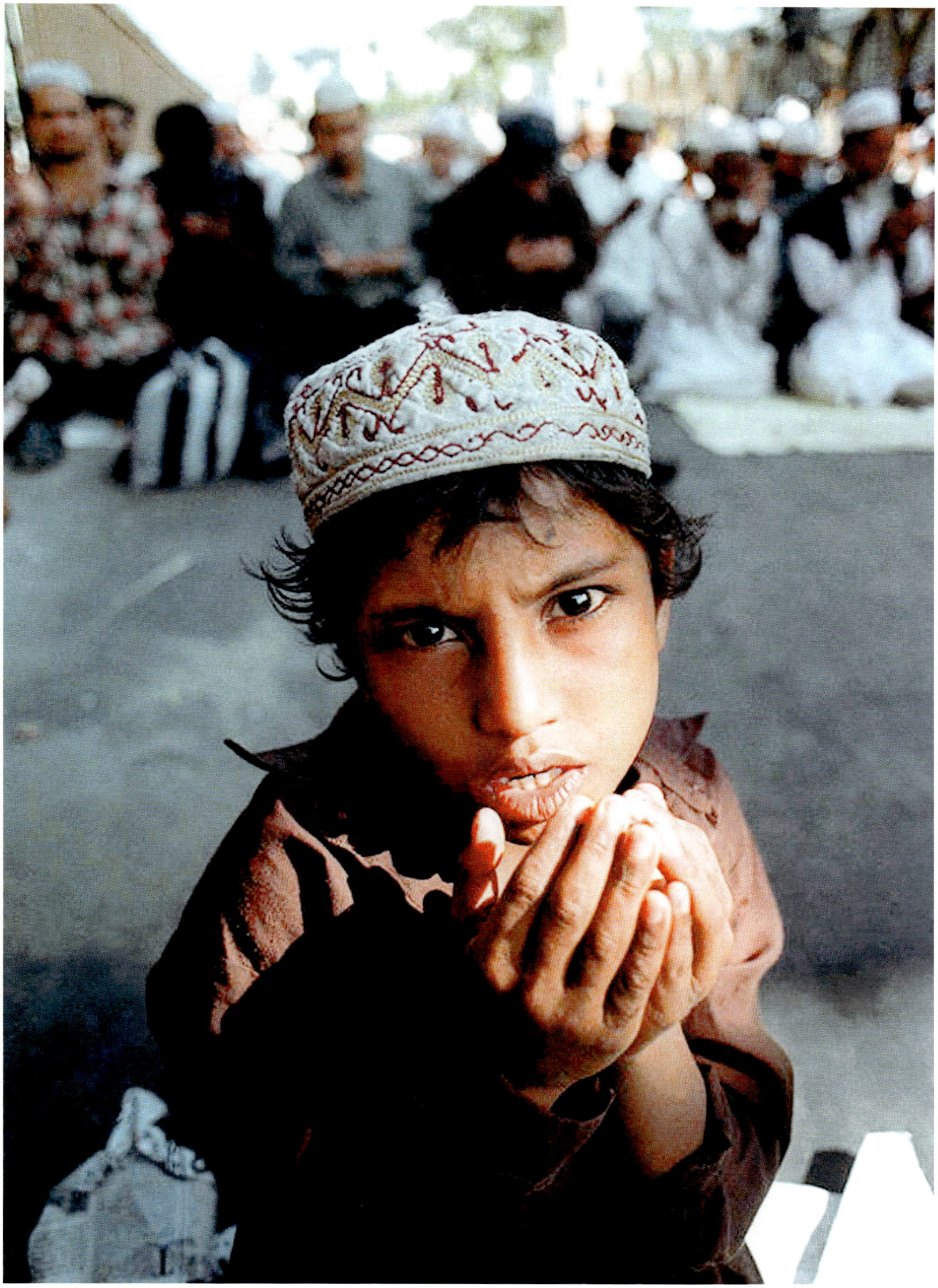

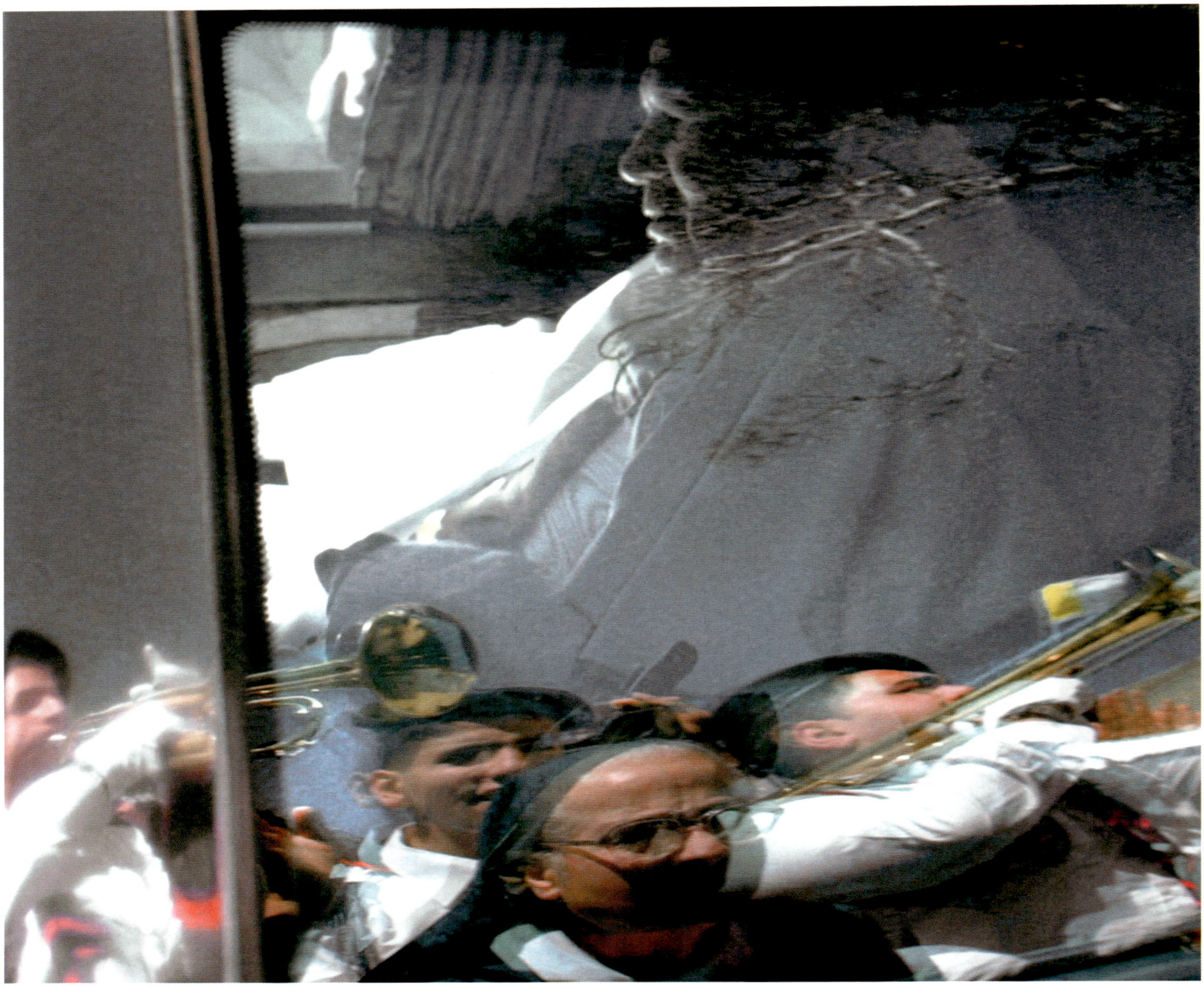

7TH MAY 2001 – DAMASCUS, SYRIA – POPE JOHN PAUL II ARRIVES FOR A PRIVATE MASS IN THE SYRIAN CAPITAL INSIDE A BULLET-PROOF LIMOUSINE. (GABRIEL BOUYS)

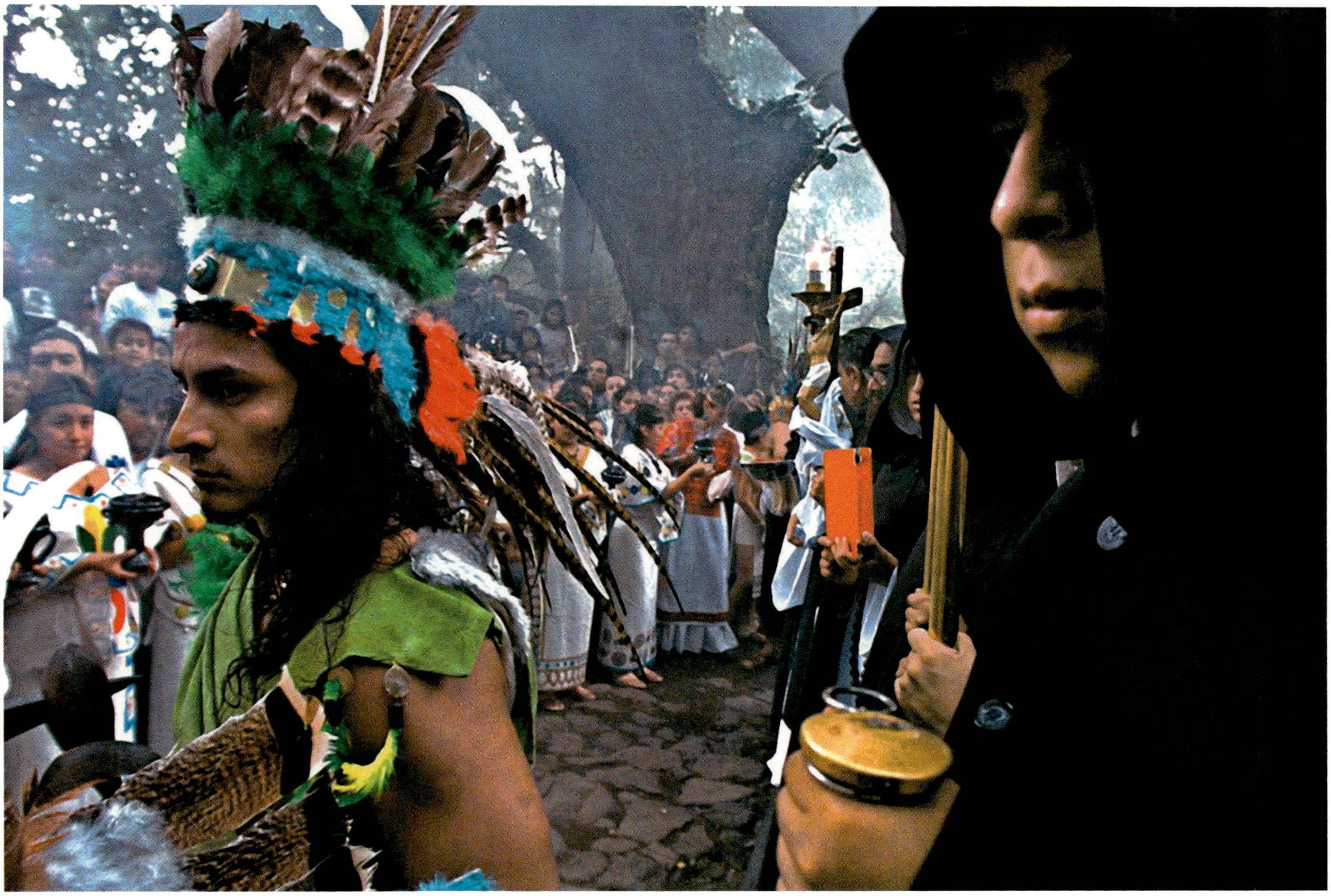

7TH SEPTEMBER 2001
– TEPOZTLAN, MEXICO –
A SCENE FROM THE CEREMONY HELD TO COMMEMORATE THE CONVERSION TO CHRISTIANITY AND BAPTISM OF LOCAL KING TEPUZLTECATL. (JORGE UZON)

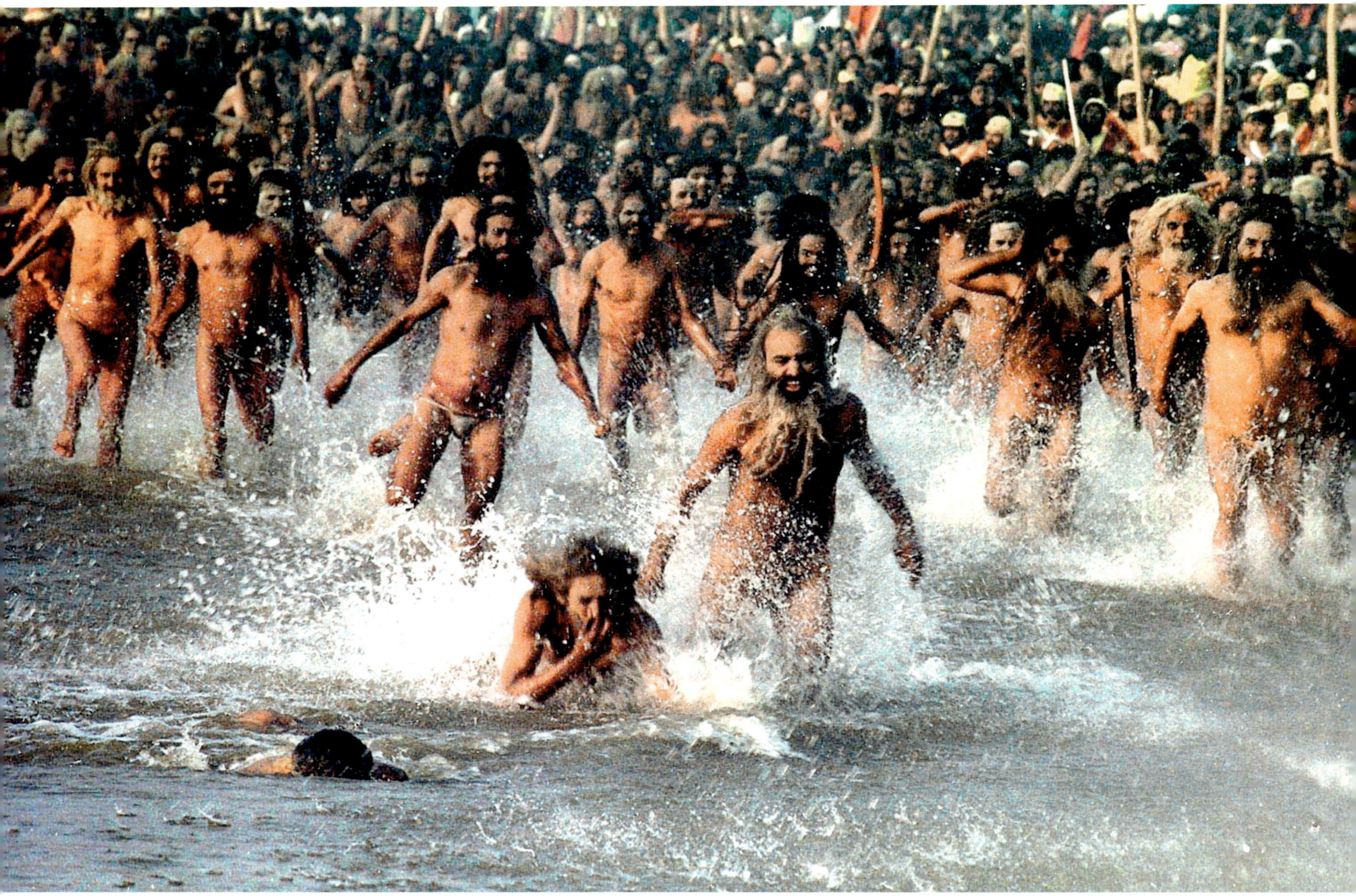

14TH JANUARY 2001 – ALLAHABAD, INDIA – HINDU SADHUS RUN TO THE CONFLUENCE OF THE THREE RIVERS, GANGA, YAMUNA AND THE MYTHICAL SWARASWATI TO BATHE ON THE AUSPICIOUS DAY OF MAKAR SANKR SANKRANTI. (DESHAKALYAN CHOWDHURY)

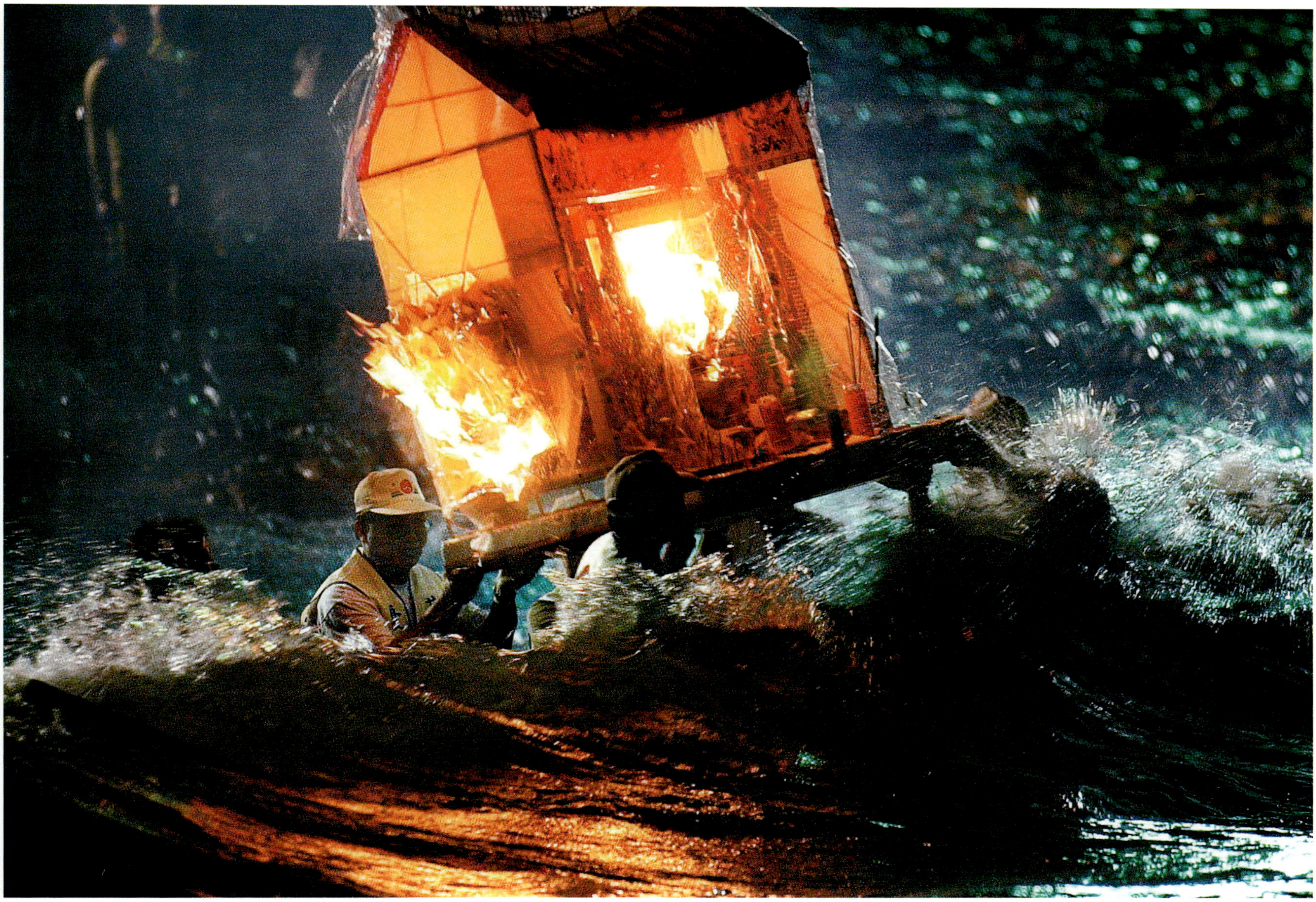

2ND SEPTEMBER 2001 – KEELUNG, TAIWAN – A BURNING LANTERN IS CARRIED OUT INTO THE SEA DURING GHOST MONTH, WHEN IT IS BELIEVED THAT LANTERNS COMFORT THE SPIRITS AND BRING GOOD FORTUNE.

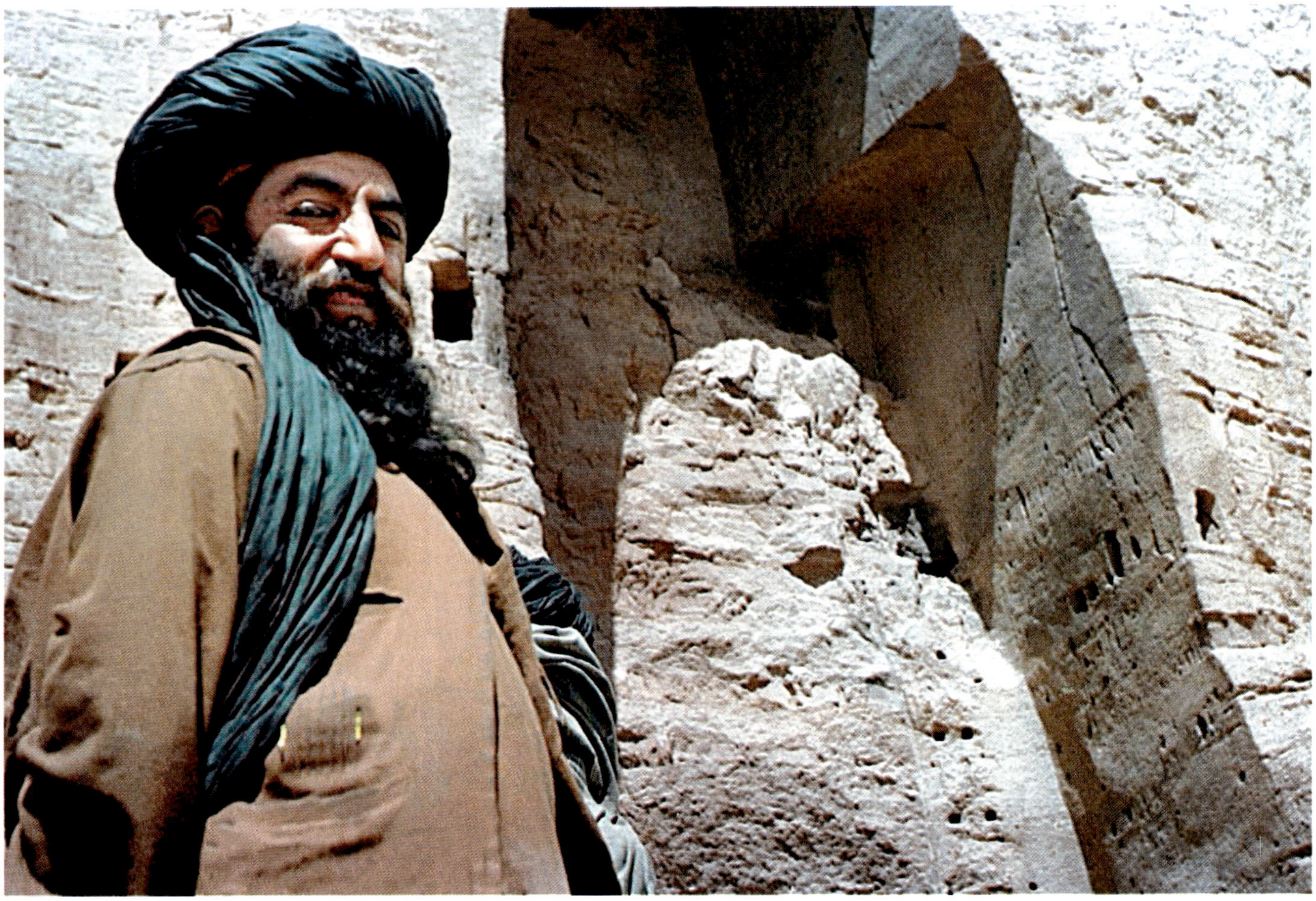

26TH MARCH 2001 – BAMIYAN, AFGHANISTAN – A MEMBER OF THE RULING TALIBAN MILITIA AND THE REMNANTS OF ONE OF THE TWO GIANT STATUES OF BUDDHA DESTROYED BY THE REGIME. (SAEED KHAN)

26TH FEBRUARY 2001 – BAMIYAN, AFGHANISTAN – THE WORLD'S TALLEST STANDING STATUE OF BUDDHA BEFORE ITS DESTRUCTION BY THE RULING TALIBAN AS PART OF A PURGE AGAINST ALL NON-ISLAMIC WORKS IN THE COUNTRY. (JEAN-CLAUDE CHAPON)

FOLLOWING PAGE:
6TH SEPTEMBER 2001 – CASTELLANE, FRANCE – THE GIANT STATUE OF SELF-STYLED "COSMOPLANETARY MESSIAH" GILBERT BOURDIN, FOUNDER OF THE OBSCURE MANDAROM SECT, IS DEMOLISHED ON THE ORDERS OF A FRENCH COURT. (BORIS HORVAT)

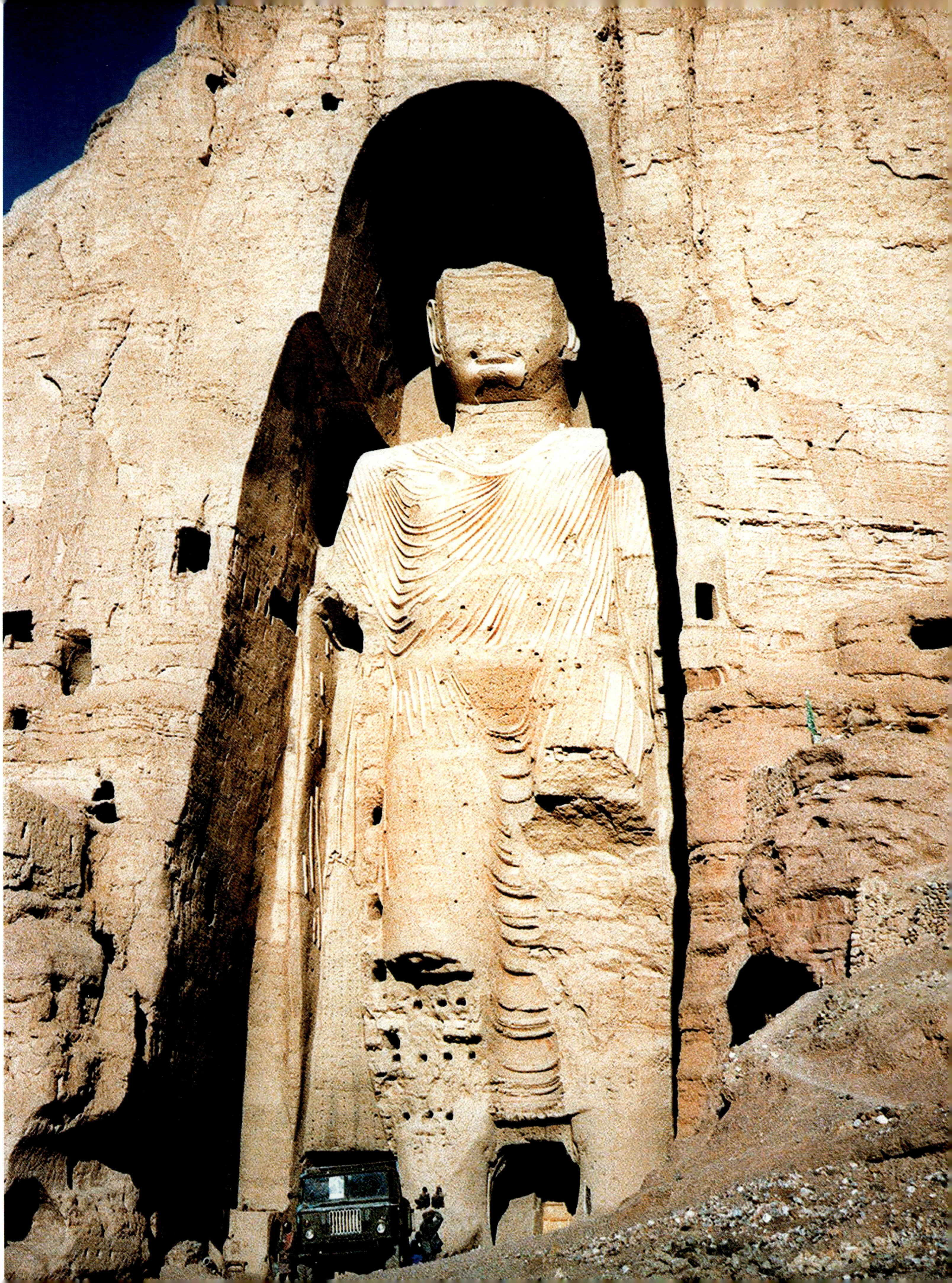

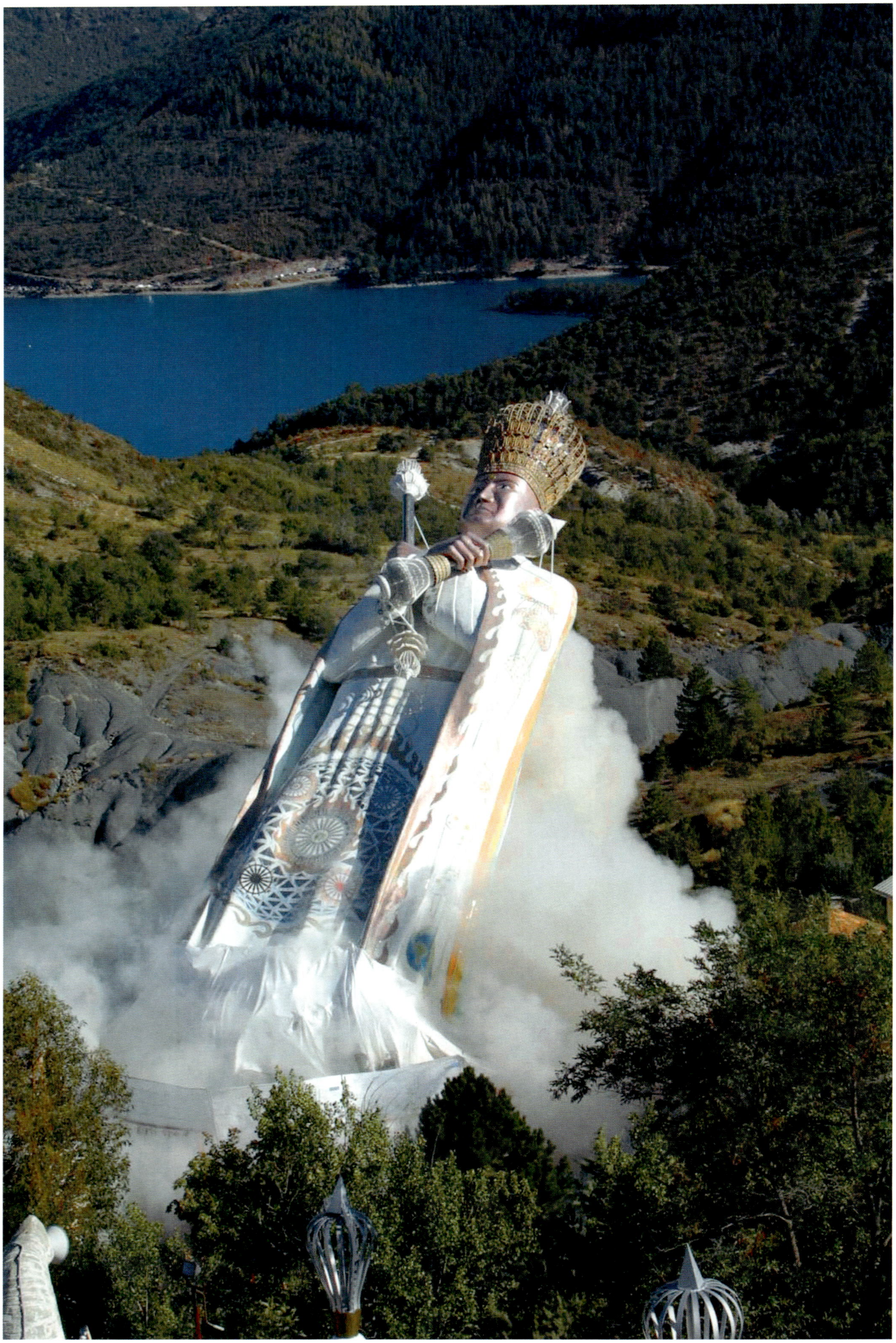

BLINK OF AN EYE

US-MORMON-POLYGAMIST
JURY SELECTION BEGINS IN MORMON MAN ACCUSED OF POLYGAMY
PROVO, UTAH, MAY 14 (AFP) – JURY SELECTION BEGAN MONDAY IN THE TRIAL OF AVOWED POLYGAMIST TOM GREEN, A MEMBER OF A FUNDAMENTALIST MORMON SECT THAT ACCEPTS THE PRACTICE.
GREEN'S FIVE WIVES – THREE OF THEM PREGNANT – AND 11 OF HIS 29 CHILDREN WERE IN THE COURTROOM FOR THE TRIAL, EXPECTED TO FOCUS ATTENTION ON THE PRACTICE ABANDONED BY MAINSTREAM MORMONS A CENTURY AGO AS A CONDITION OF UTAH STATEHOOD.
STR/LHK/MAC

RUSSIA-US-SPACE,2NDLEAD
TOURIST TITO TAKES UP QUARTERS IN SPACE
MOSCOW, APRIL 30 (AFP) – PIONEERING SPACE TOURIST DENNIS TITO CLAMBERED ABOARD THE INTERNATIONAL SPACE STATION HUNDREDS OF MILES ABOVE THE EARTH MONDAY AND TOLD RUSSIAN MISSION CONTROLLERS ON THE GROUND: "I LOVE SPACE".
THE 60-YEAR-OLD MULTIMILLIONAIRE FLOATED THROUGH THE AIR HATCHES AND ONTO THE SPACE PLATFORM AT 0931 GMT TO BE GREETED BY ISS CREWMEMBERS, A SPOKESMAN FOR THE MISSION CONTROL CENTRE (TSUP) NEAR MOSCOW, NIKOLAI KRYUCHKOV, SAID.
BB/DM

CANADA-PHOTO-NAKED
2,000 MONTREALERS BARE IT ALL FOR US PHOTOG
MONTREAL, MAY 26 (AFP) – SOME 2,000 PEOPLE OF ALL AGES, SHAPES AND SIZES TOOK TO THE STREETS OF DOWNTOWN MONTREAL SATURDAY TO BARE IT ALL FOR ENFANT TERRIBLE PHOTOGRAPHER SPENCER TUNICK.
TUNICK, WHO WAS RECENTLY AWARDED 33,000 DOLLARS IN A NEW YORK FEDERAL COURT FOR HAVING BEEN UNJUSTLY HINDERED BY THE CITY, HAS ALSO CAPTURED MODELS IN THEIR BIRTHDAY SUITS ON FILM IN SAN FRANCISCO, JERUSALEM, ROME AND LONDON.
CHC/LG

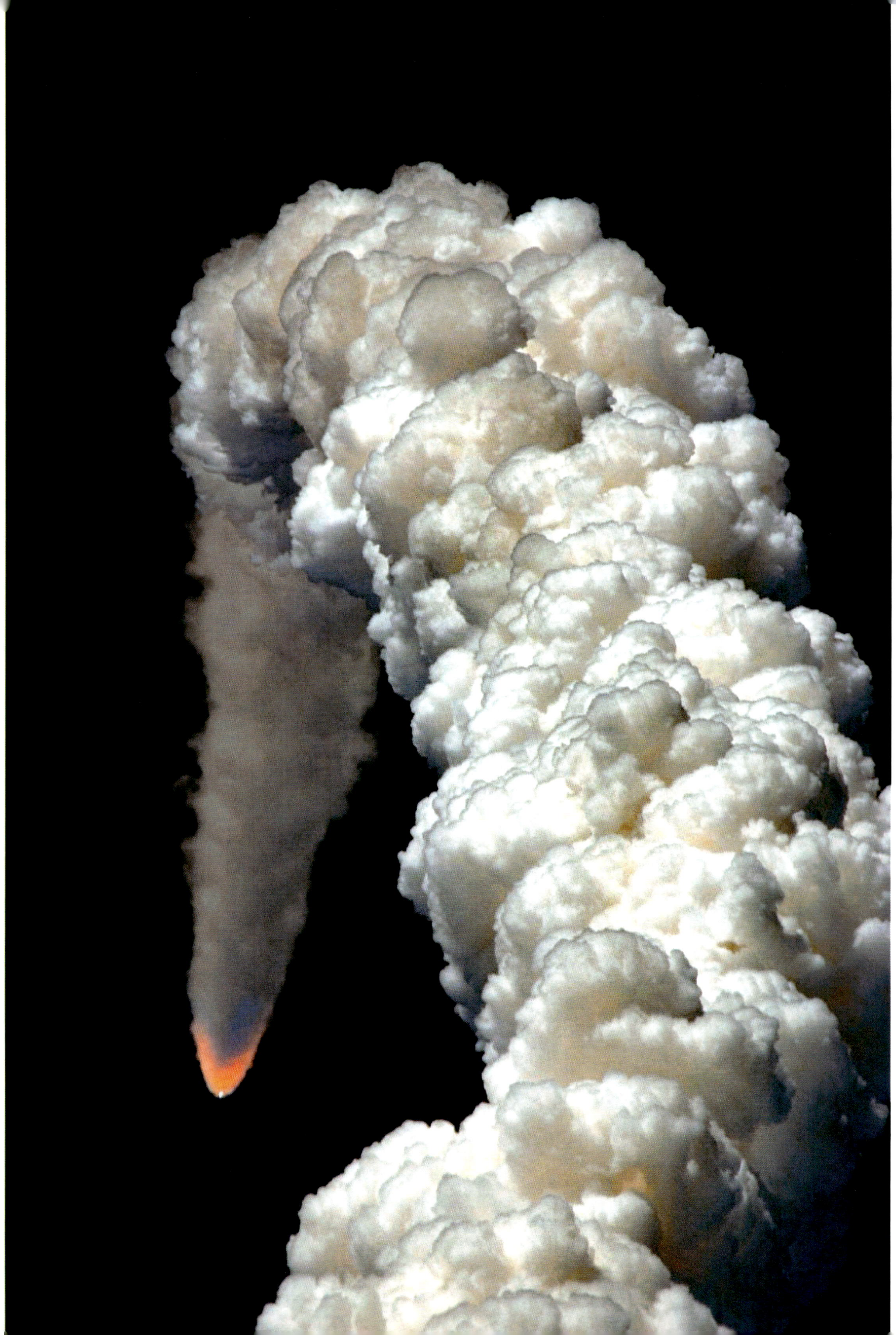

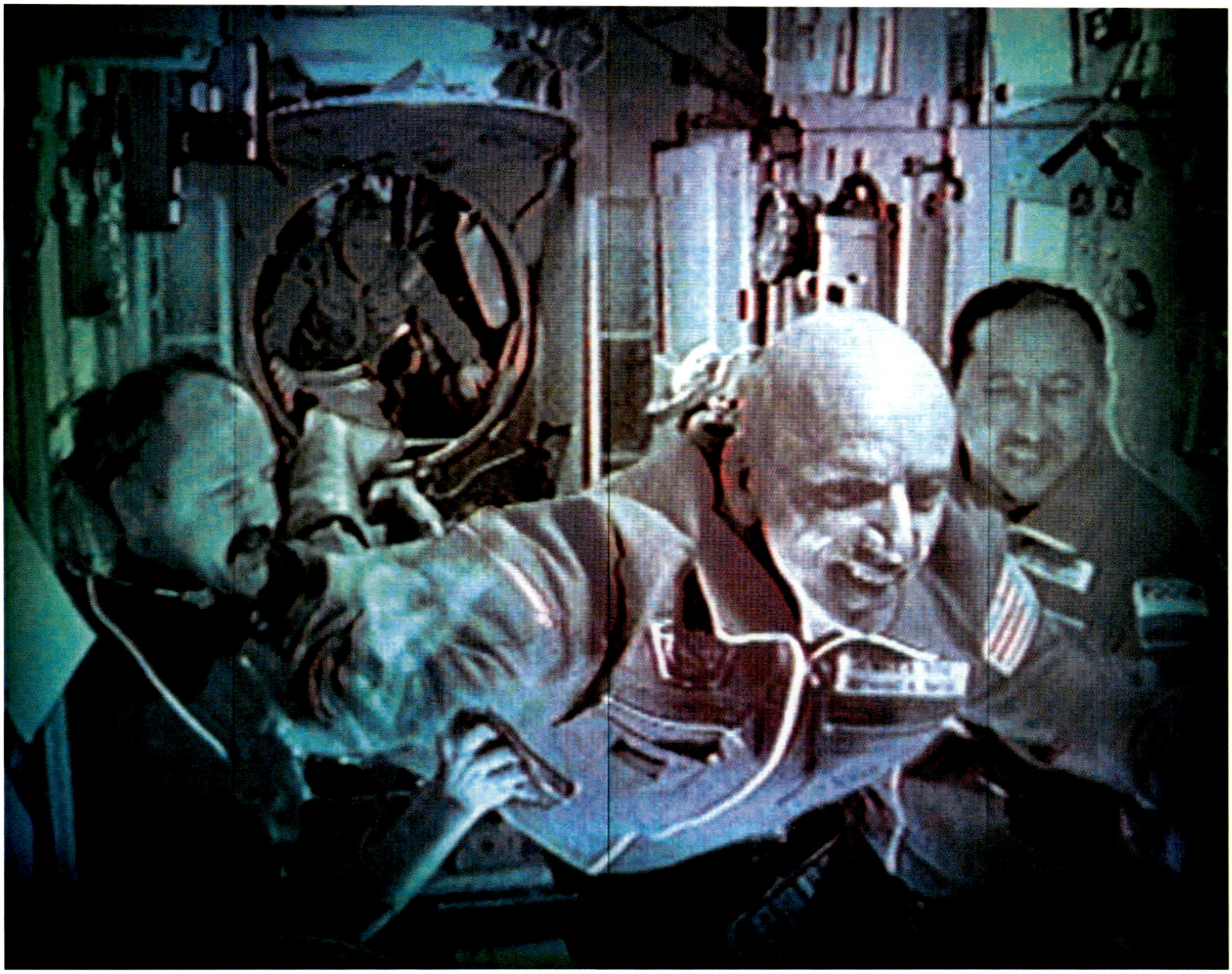

10TH AUGUST 2001 – KENNEDY SPACE CENTER, USA – THE SPACE SHUTTLE DISCOVERY HEADS FOR ORBIT WITH A REPLACEMENT CREW FOR THE INTERNATIONAL SPACE STATION AFTER ITS LAUNCH IN FLORIDA. (BRUCE WEAVER)

30TH APRIL 2001 – KOROLYOV, KAZAKHSTAN – A TELEVISION PICTURE OF AMERICAN BILLIONAIRE DENNIS TITO, THE FIRST "SPACE TOURIST" BEING HELPED TO ENTER THE INTERNATIONAL SPACE STATION AFTER THE RUSSIAN SOYUZ SPACESHIP HAS SAFELY DOCKED. (YURI KADOBNOV/EPA)

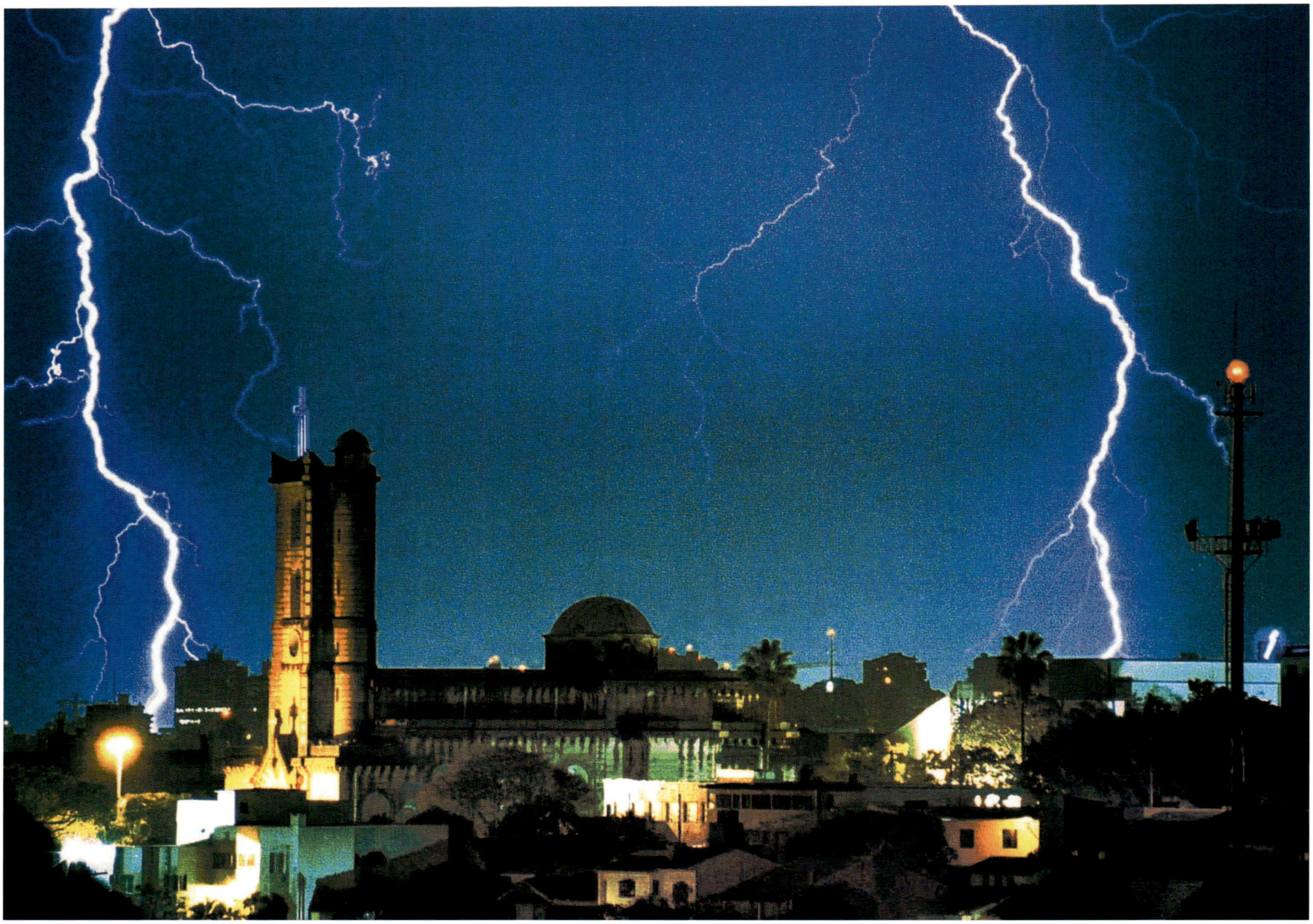

20TH JULY 2001 – PORTO ALEGRE, BRAZIL – LIGHTNING LIGHTS UP THE NIGHT SKY DURING A VIOLENT STORM. (NABOR GOULART)

1ST AUGUST 2001 – OHRID, MACEDONIA – AN OLD MAN FISHING IN THE RIVER VARDAR WHILE OLD CARS BURN CLOSE TO THE SITE OF PEACE TALKS BETWEEN MACEDONIAN AND ALBANIAN LEADERS. (SASA STANKOVIC/EPA)

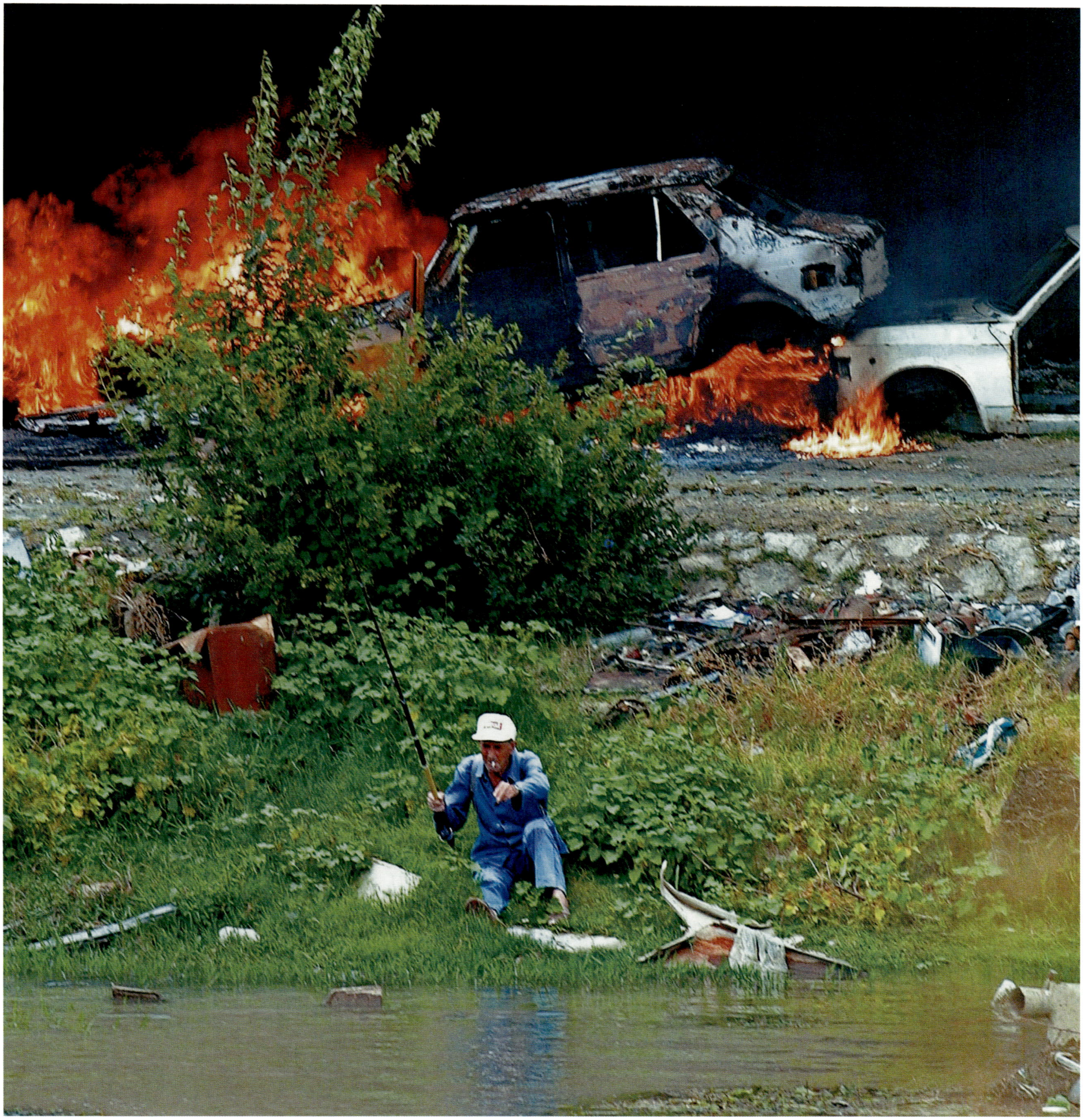

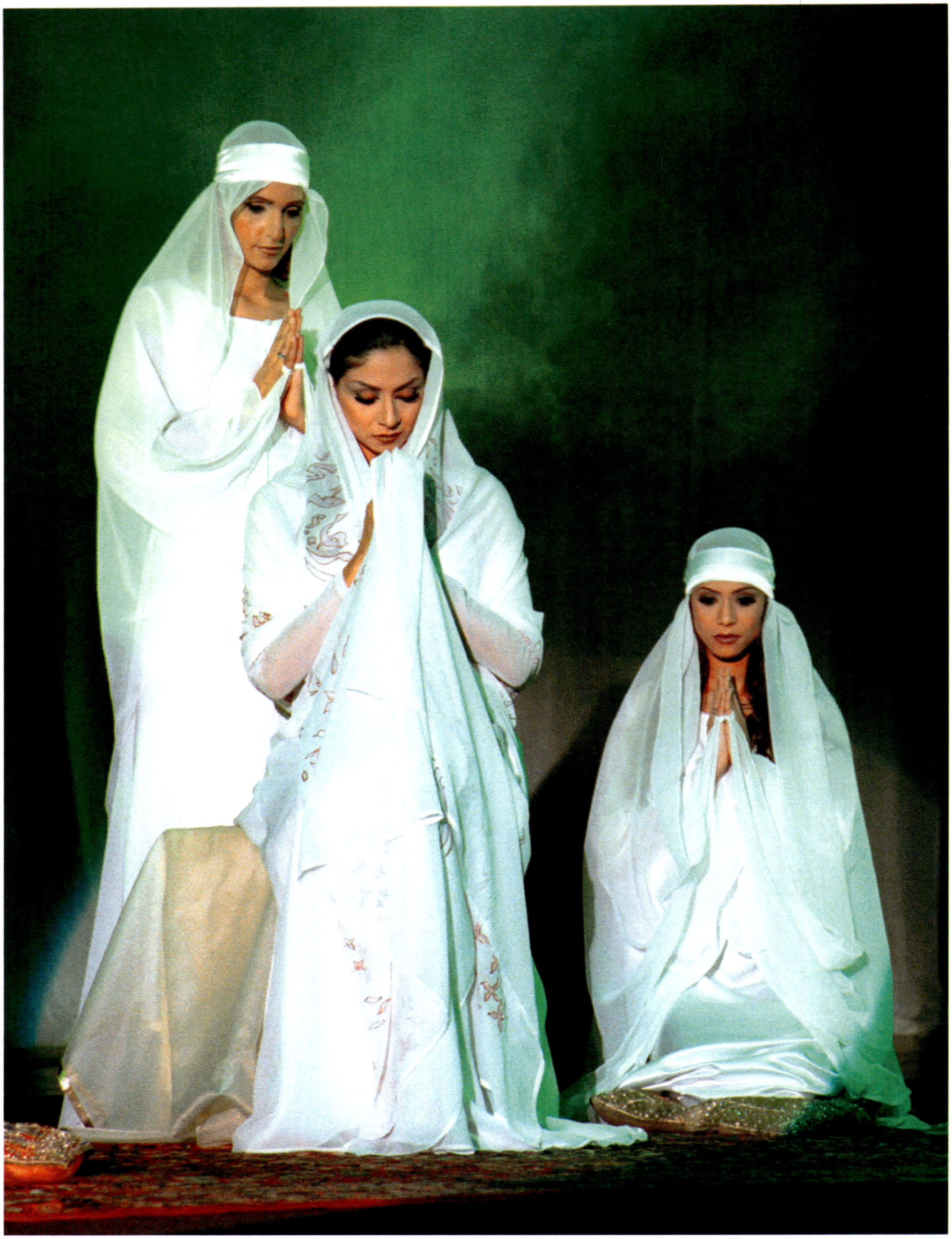

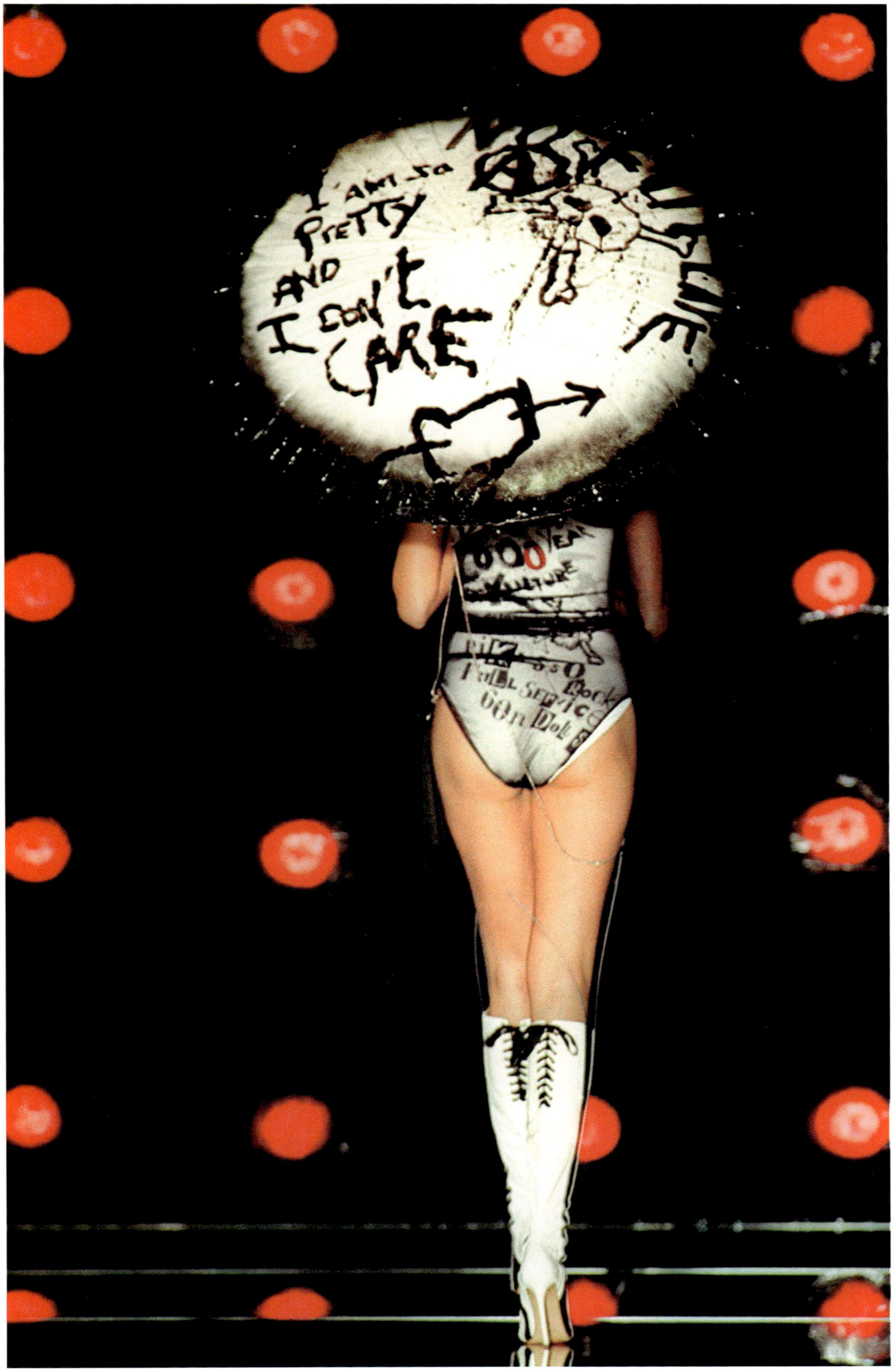

24TH JANUARY 2001 – MUSCAT, OMAN – SILK GOWNS INSPIRED BY TRADITIONAL SUFI DESIGNS FROM THE EARLY ISLAMIC PERIOD IN A FASHION SHOW BY IRAQI DESIGNER NIRAN SAMARAEE. (MOHAMED MAHJOUB)

12TH OCTOBER 2000 – PARIS, FRANCE – A SEXY ENSEMBLE WITH PARASOL AND TONGUE-IN-CHEEK GRAFFITI BY BRITISH DESIGNER JOHN GALLIANO FOR HIS SPRING-SUMMER READY-TO-WEAR COLLECTION. (JEAN-PIERRE MULLER)

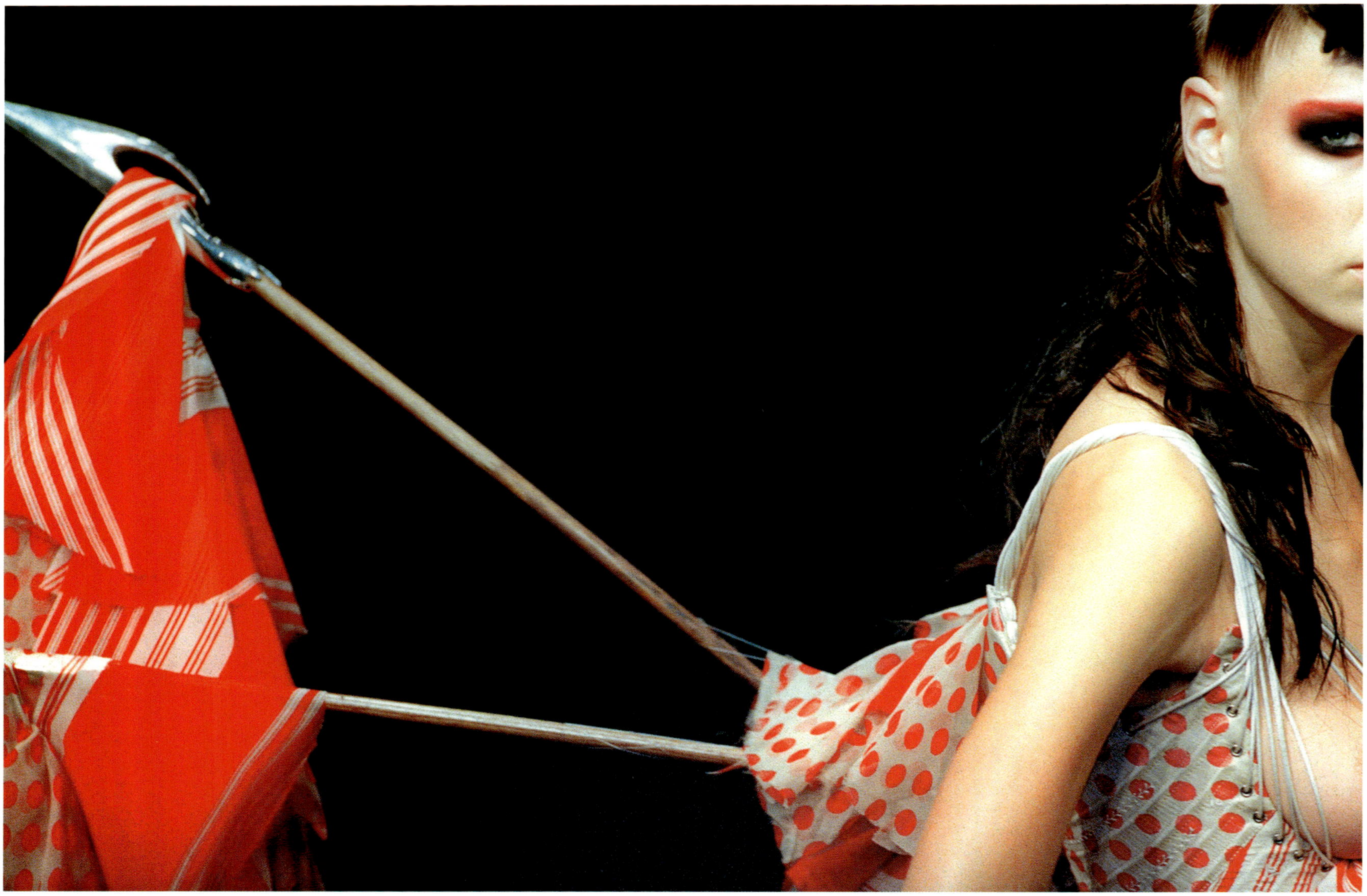

6TH OCTOBER 2001 – PARIS, FRANCE – ONE OF THE CREATIONS FROM BRITISH DESIGNER ALEXANDER MCQUEEN'S SPRING-SUMMER READY-TO-WEAR COLLECTION. (PIERRE VERDY)

22ND JANUARY 2001 – PARIS, FRANCE – A MODEL PRESENTS A HAND-PAINTED SILK ORGANZA DRESS FOR BRITISH DESIGNER JOHN GALLIANO'S SPRING-SUMMER HAUTE COUTURE COLLECTION FOR THE HOUSE OF CHRISTIAN DIOR. (JEAN-PIERRE MULLER)

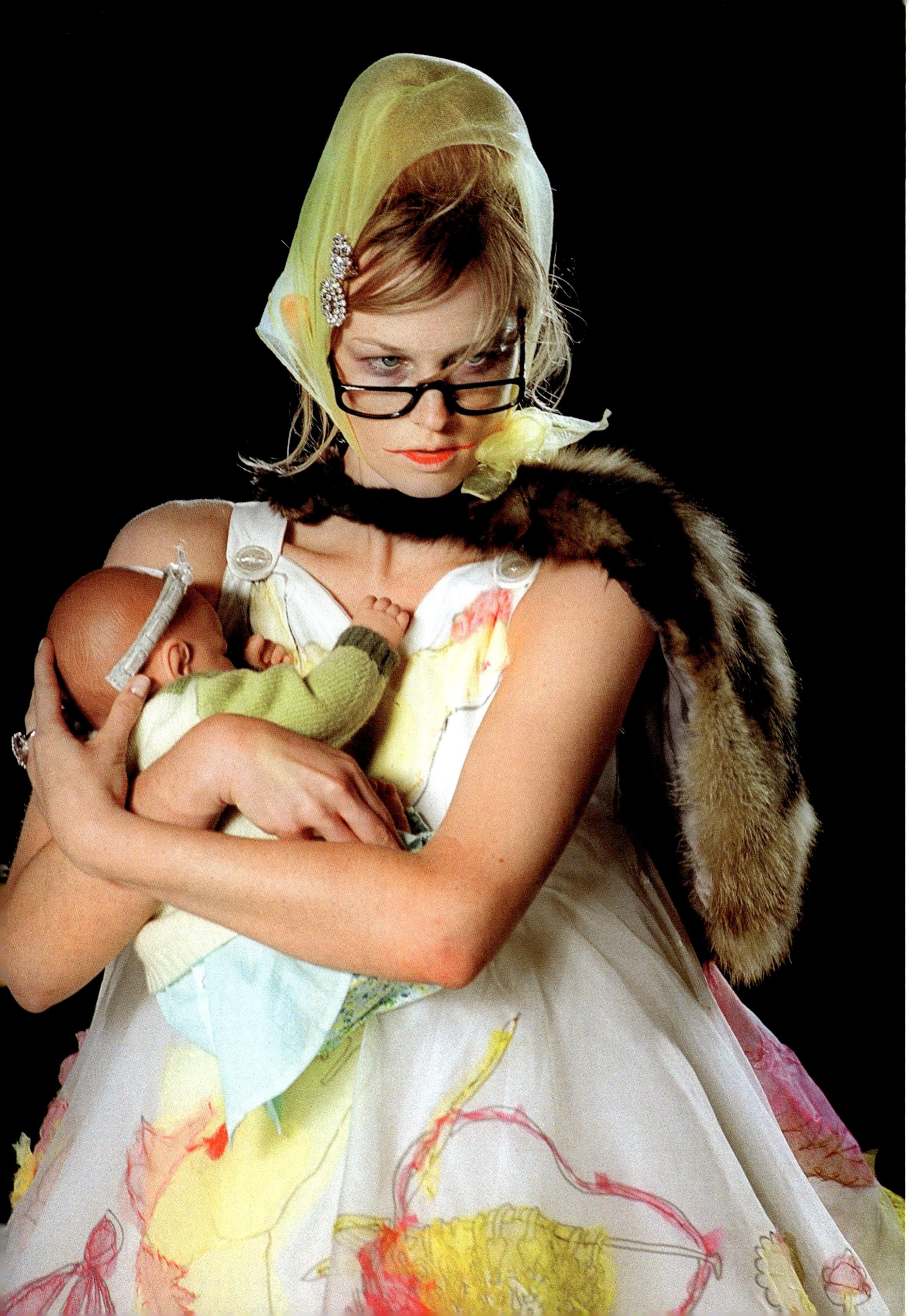

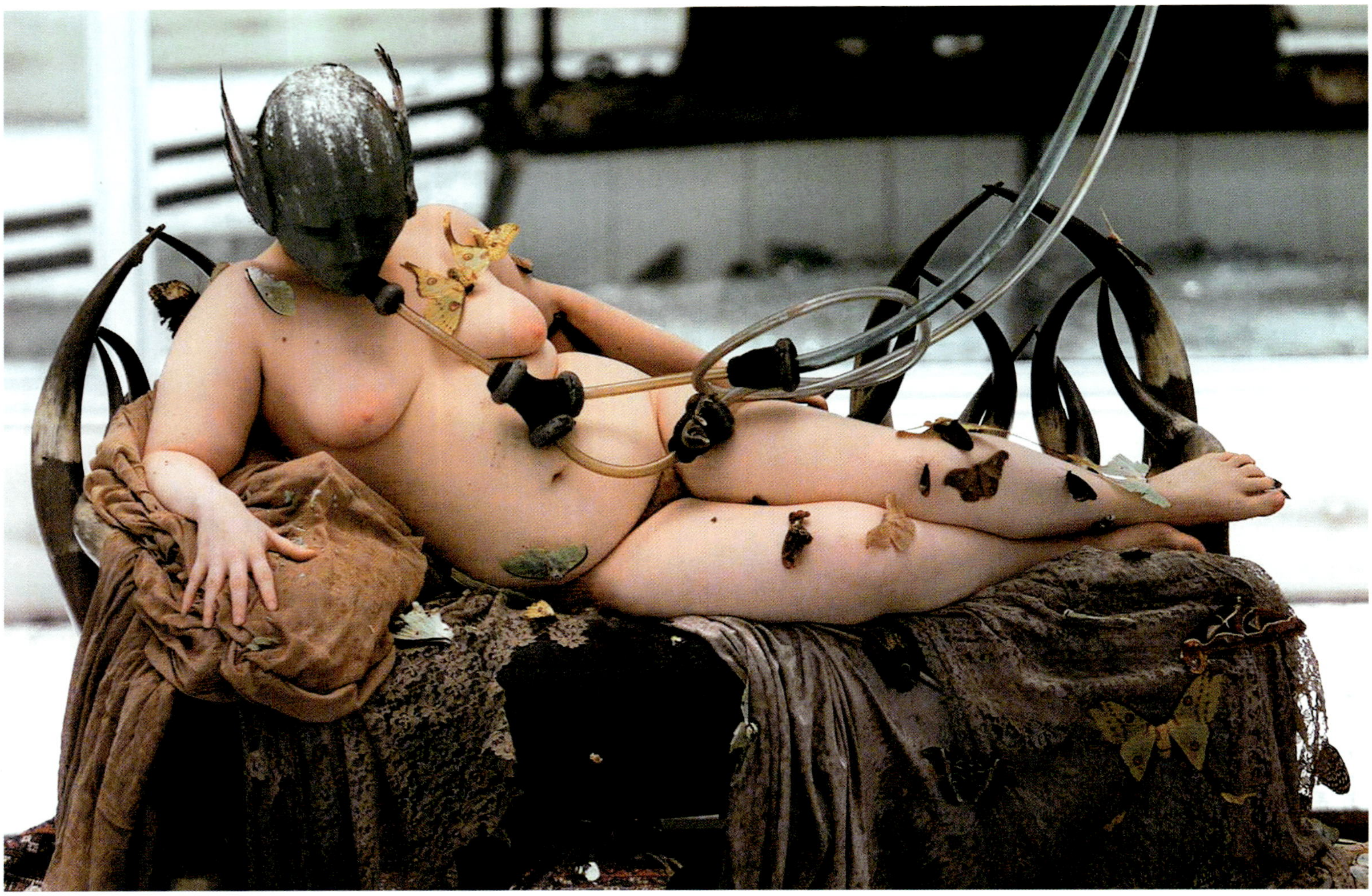

26TH SEPTEMBER 2000 – LONDON, ENGLAND – ONE OF THE CREATIONS BY ALEXANDER MCQUEEN FOR HIS SPRING-SUMMER COLLECTION PRESENTED DURING LONDON FASHION WEEK. (HUGO PHILPOTT)

26TH MAY 2001 – MONTREAL, CANADA – SOME OF THE 1,000 PEOPLE WHO VOLUNTEERED TO POSE NAKED FOR AMERICAN PHOTOGRAPHER SPENCER TUNICK AS PART OF HIS PROJECT TO PHOTOGRAPH NUDE CROWDS AROUND THE WORLD. (ANDRÉ FORGET)

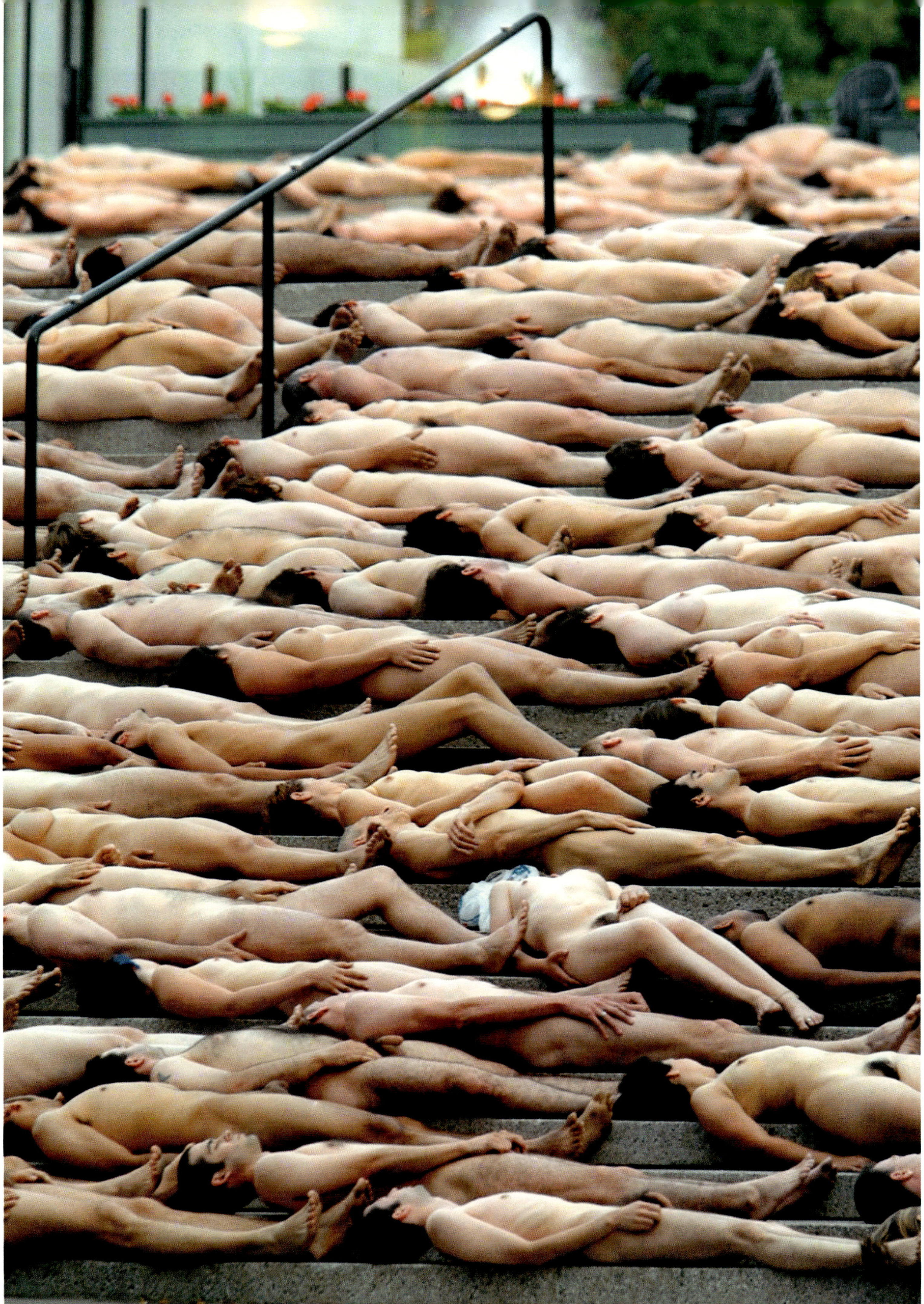

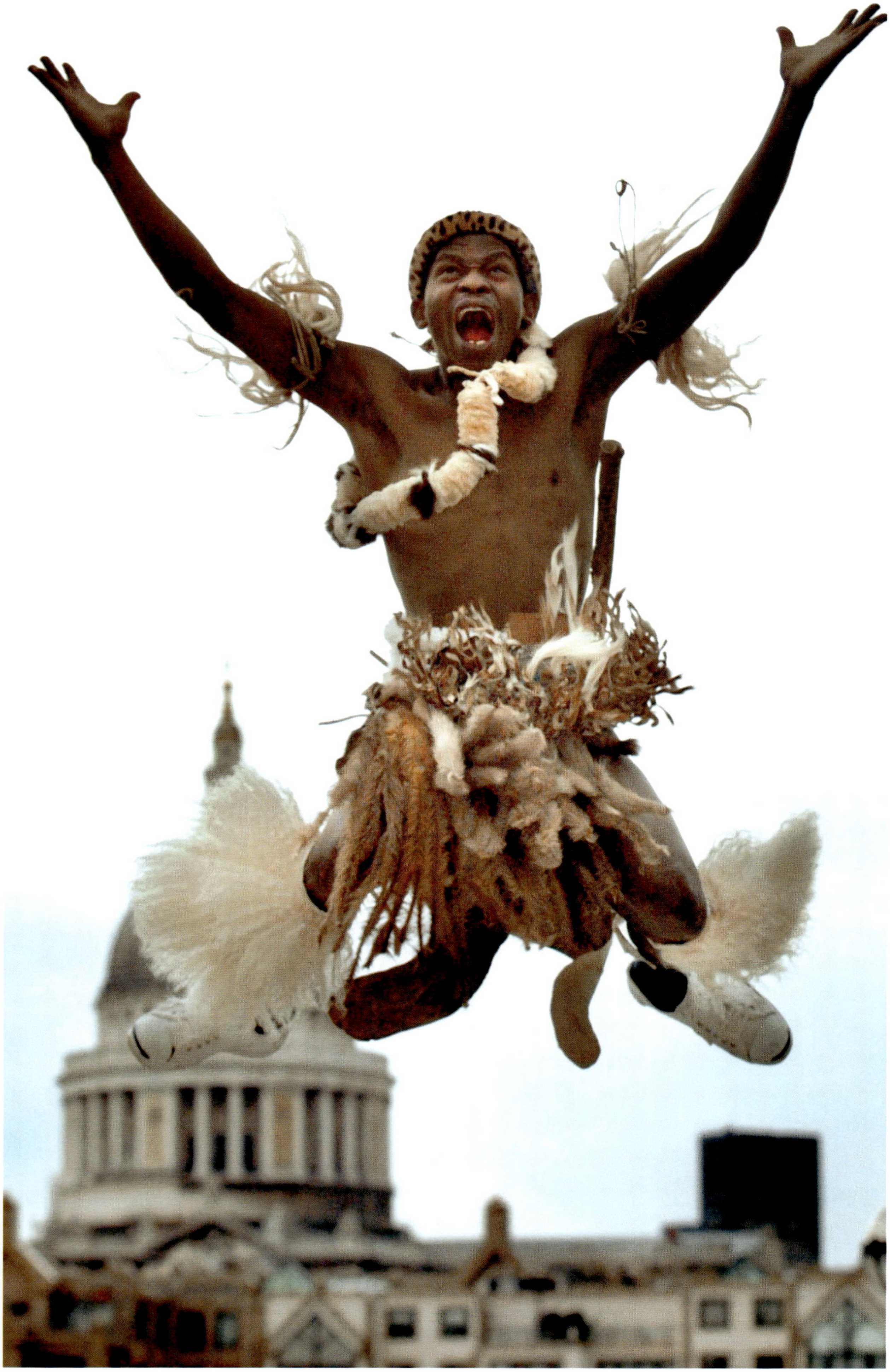

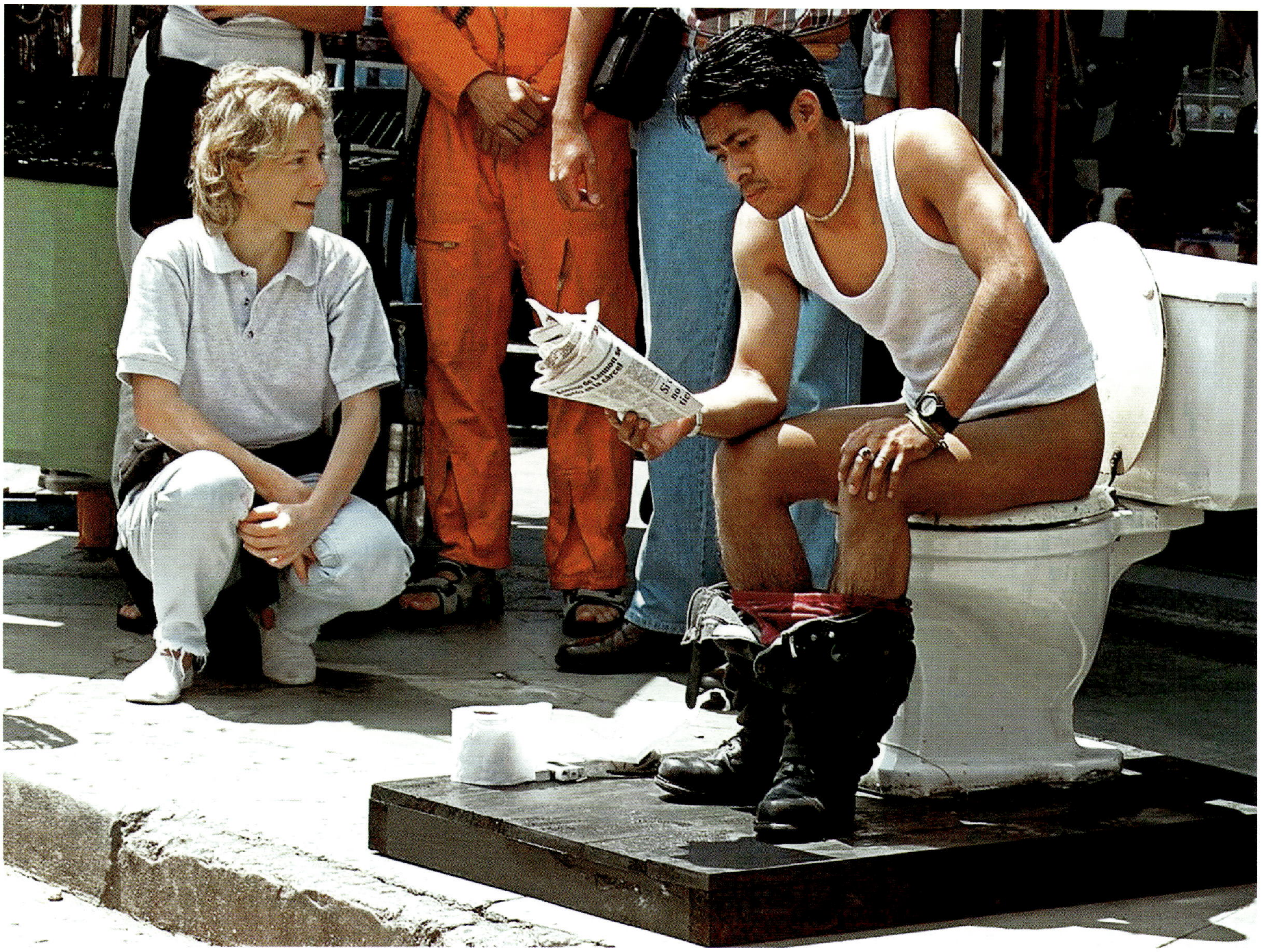

18TH APRIL 2001 – LONDON, ENGLAND – PATRICK TSHANINI OF THE TOURING UMABATHA COMPANY PERFORMING A ZULU VERSION OF MACBETH OUTSIDE THE SHAKESPEAREAN GLOBE THEATRE WITH SAINT PAUL'S CATHEDRAL IN THE BACKGROUND. (ADRIAN DENNIS)

4TH OCTOBER 2000 – CIUDAD DE GUATEMALA, GUATEMALA – PERFORMANCE ARTIST TOMMY GARCIA IN HIS OWN STREET-THEATRE PRODUCTION "THE TOILET". (JORGE UZON)

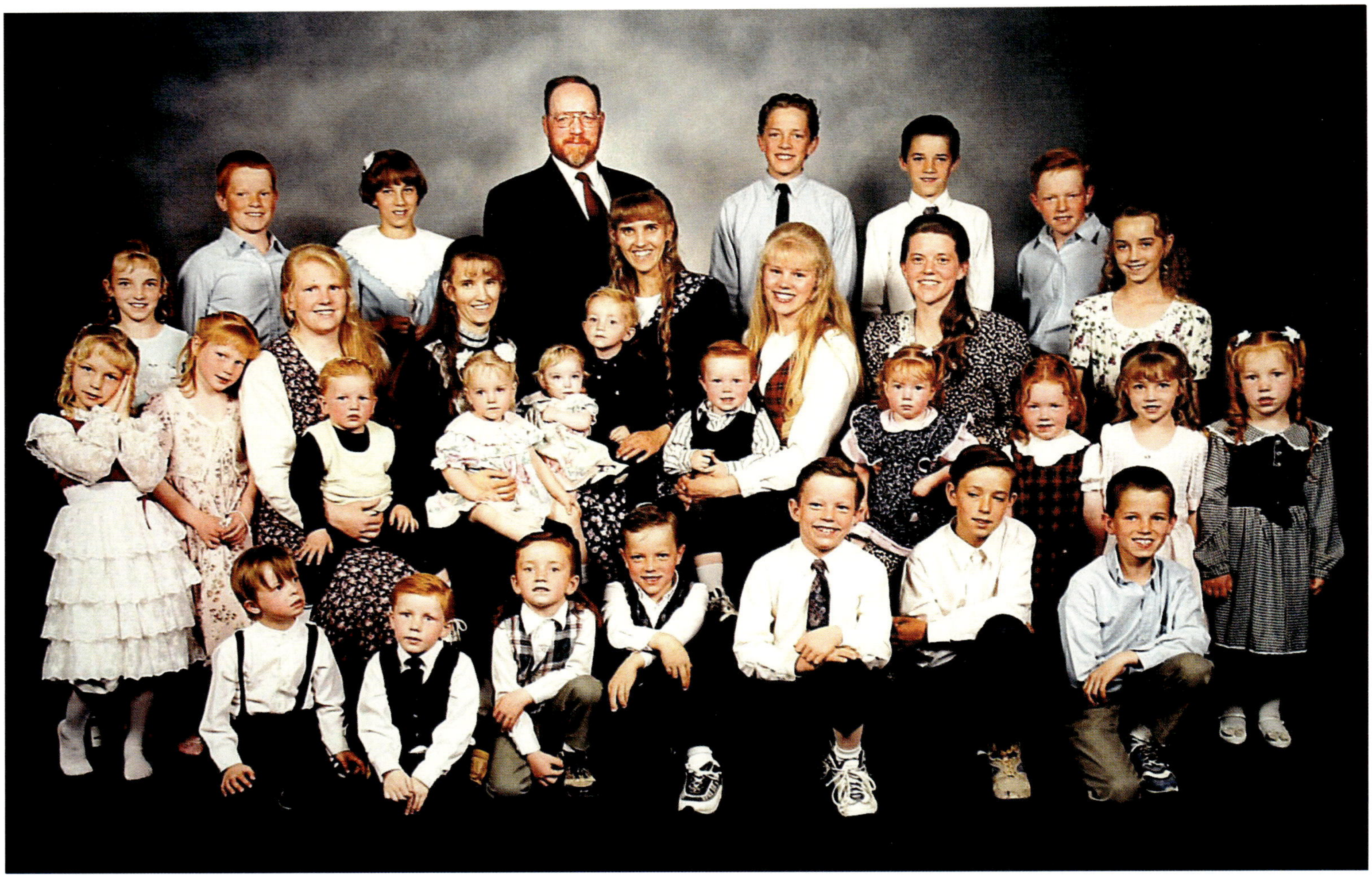

15TH MAY 2001 – PROVO, USA – THE FAMILY PHOTOGRAPH OF TOM GREEN (TOP, CENTER) SHOWING HIS FIVE WIVES AND SOME OF HIS TWENTY NINE CHILDREN, WHICH WAS PRESENTED AS EVIDENCE FOR THE DEFENCE AT HIS TRIAL FOR POLYGAMY IN UTAH. (DEFENSE EVIDENCE)

16TH MAY 2001 – PROVO, USA – SHIRLEY GREEN, ONE OF THE FIVE WIVES OF TOM GREEN, GIVING TESTIMONY DURING HIS TRIAL FOR POLYGAMY IN UTAH. (DAN LUND/THE DAILY HERALD)

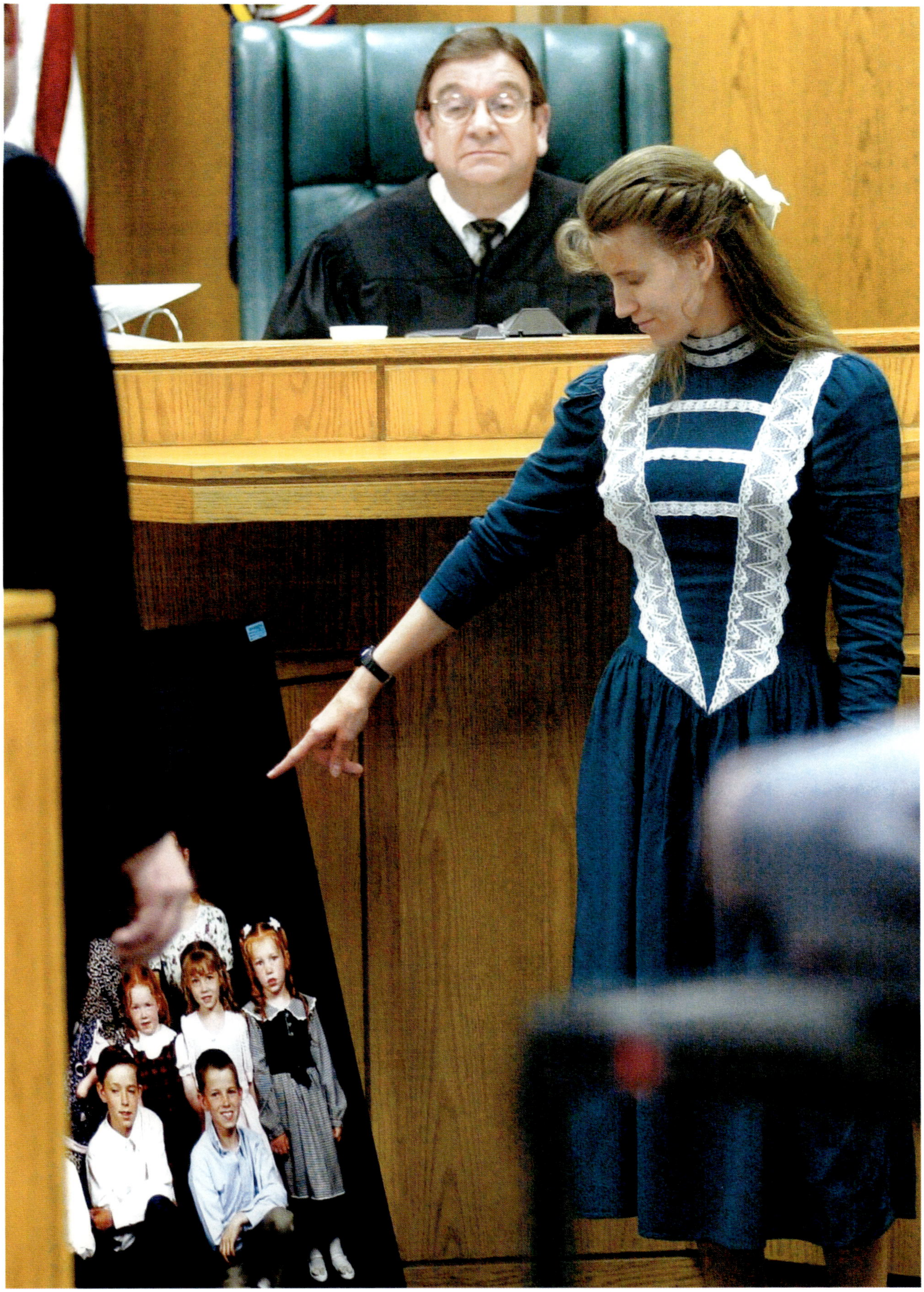

PASSION FOR SPORTS

AUTO-PRIX, ROUNDUP
SCHUMACHER WINS JAPAN GRAND PRIX FOR PERFECT END TO PERFECT SEASON
SUZUKA, JAPAN, OCT 14 (AFP) – WORLD CHAMPION MICHAEL SCHUMACHER ROMPED AWAY TO WIN THE JAPANESE GRAND PRIX SUNDAY, CAPPING A PERFECT END TO HIS PERFECT SEASON WITH YET ANOTHER RECORD IN THE HISTORY OF FORMULA ONE RACING.
THE FERRARI ACE, WHO SEALED HIS FOURTH WORLD TITLE IN AUGUST, FOUGHT OFF A DOGGED CHALLENGE FROM COLOMBIAN F1 ROOKIE JUAN PABLO MONTOYA IN A WILLIAMS TO STRETCH HIS RECORD OF CAREER WINS TO 53.
SCHUMACHER BROKE ALAIN PROST'S MARK OF 51 WHEN HE TRIUMPHED AT THE BELGIAN GRAND PRIX IN EARLY SEPTEMBER AFTER SEALING HIS SECOND STRAIGHT WORLD TITLE ONE ROUND EARLIER AT BUDAPEST.
SPS/BEN/CW01

CYCLING-WORLD-MEN-WIN
FREIRE OF SPAIN WINS THE MEN'S WORLD CHAMPIONSHIP ROAD RACE
LISBON, OCT 14 (AFP) – OSCAR FREIRE OF SPAIN WON THE MEN'S WORLD CHAMPIONSHIP ROAD RACE HERE SUNDAY AFTER 21 LAPS OF LISBON'S DEMANDING MONSANTO PARK CIRCUIT.
FREIRE, WHO CAME THIRD LAST YEAR AND LAST WON THE TITLE IN 1999, CAME THROUGH THE INSIDE IN A BUNCH SPRINT TO BEAT PAOLO BETTINI OF ITALY INTO SECOND PLACE.
ANDREJ HAUPTMAN OF SLOVENIA CAME THIRD.
JD/CW01

ATHLETICS-WORLD-100M-WIN
URGENT¥¥¥ GREENE RETAINS 100M WORLD TITLE
EDMONTON, CANADA, AUG 5 (AFP) – MAURICE GREENE OF THE UNITED STATES RETAINED HIS 100M WORLD TITLE HERE ON SUNDAY.
EM/GJ

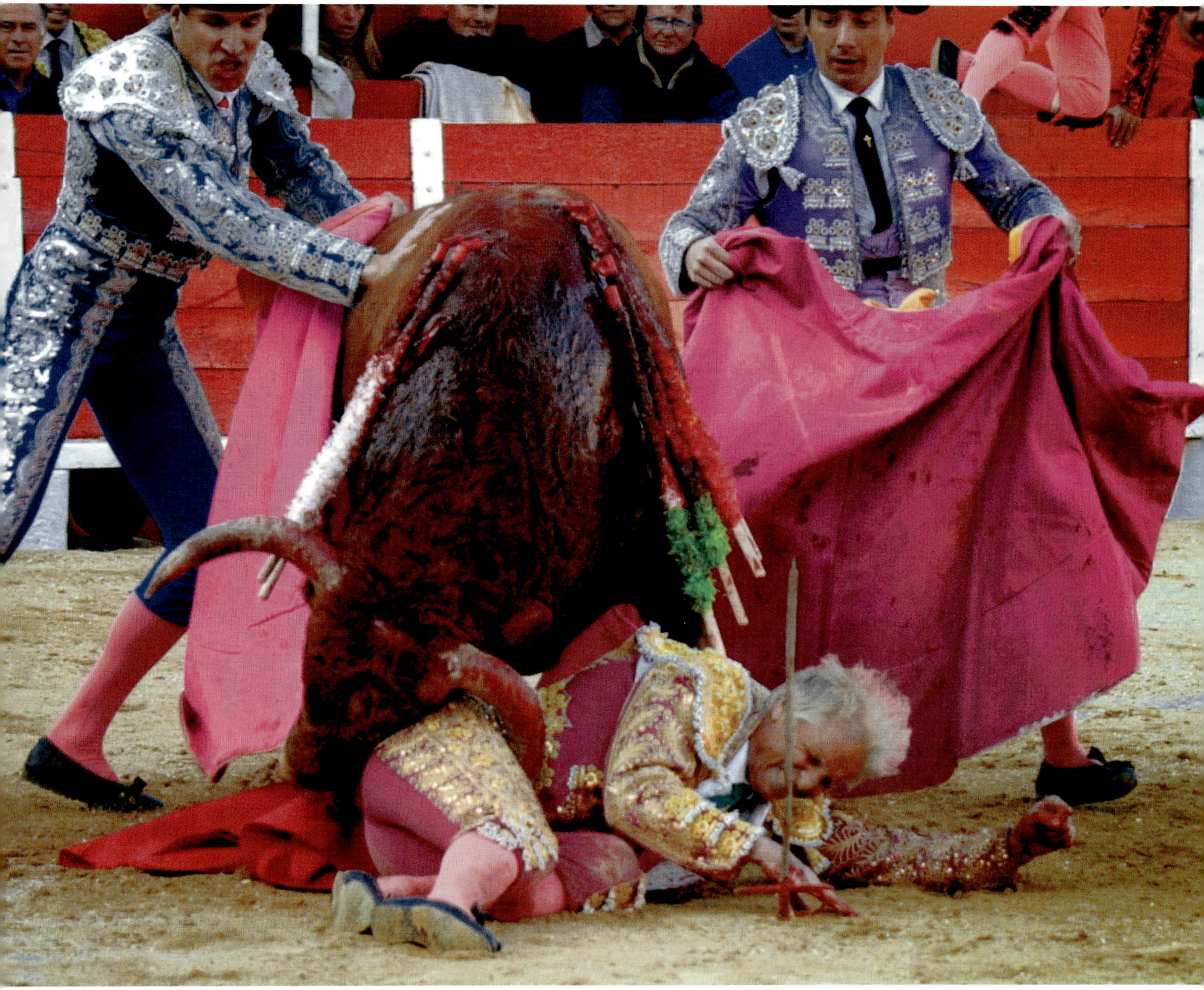

5TH MAY 2001 – PALAVAS-LES-FLOTS, FRANCE – SPANISH MATADOR EL CORDOBES IS KNOCKED TO THE GROUND BY A BULL. (DOMINIQUE FAGET)

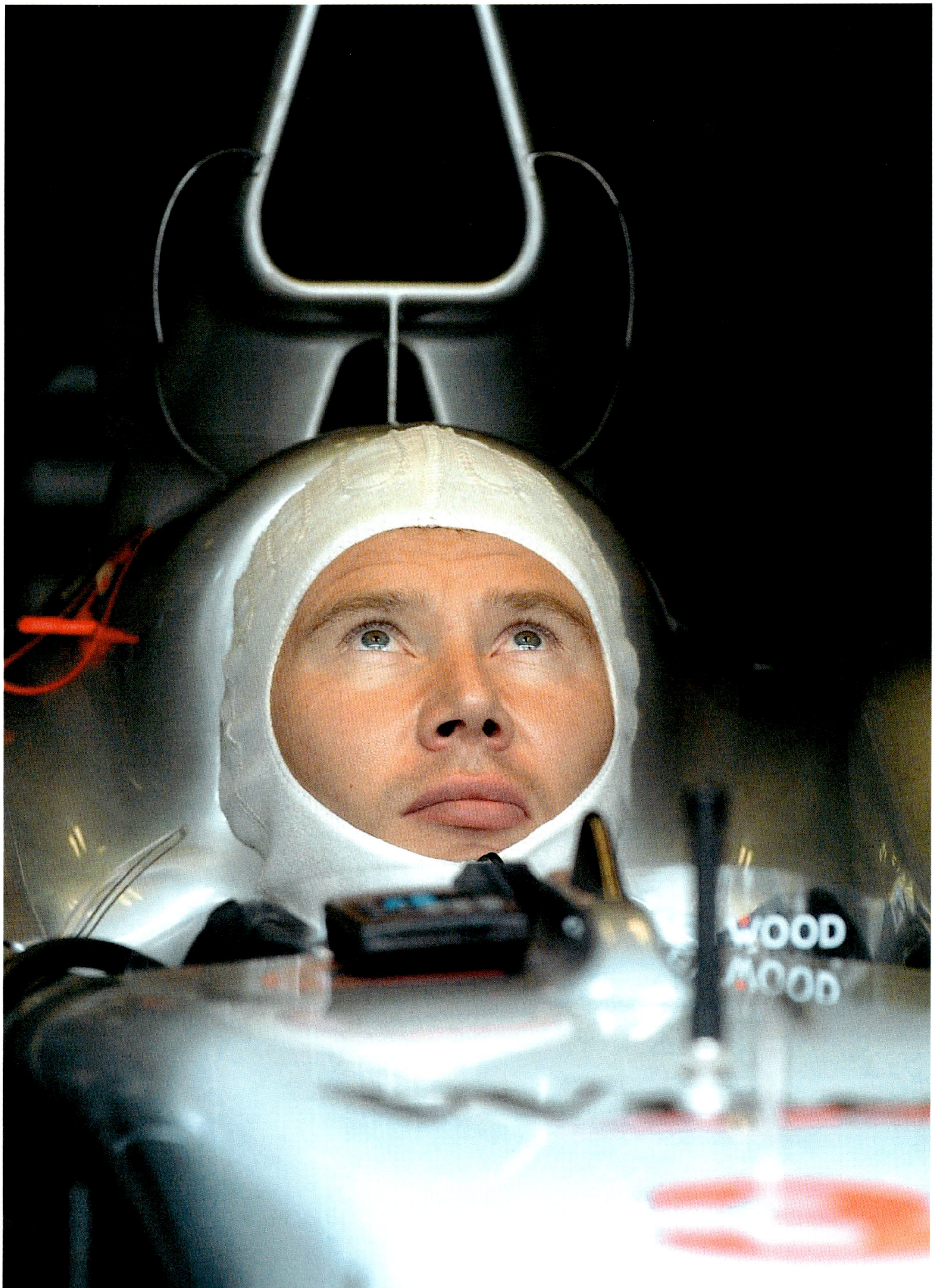
WOOD

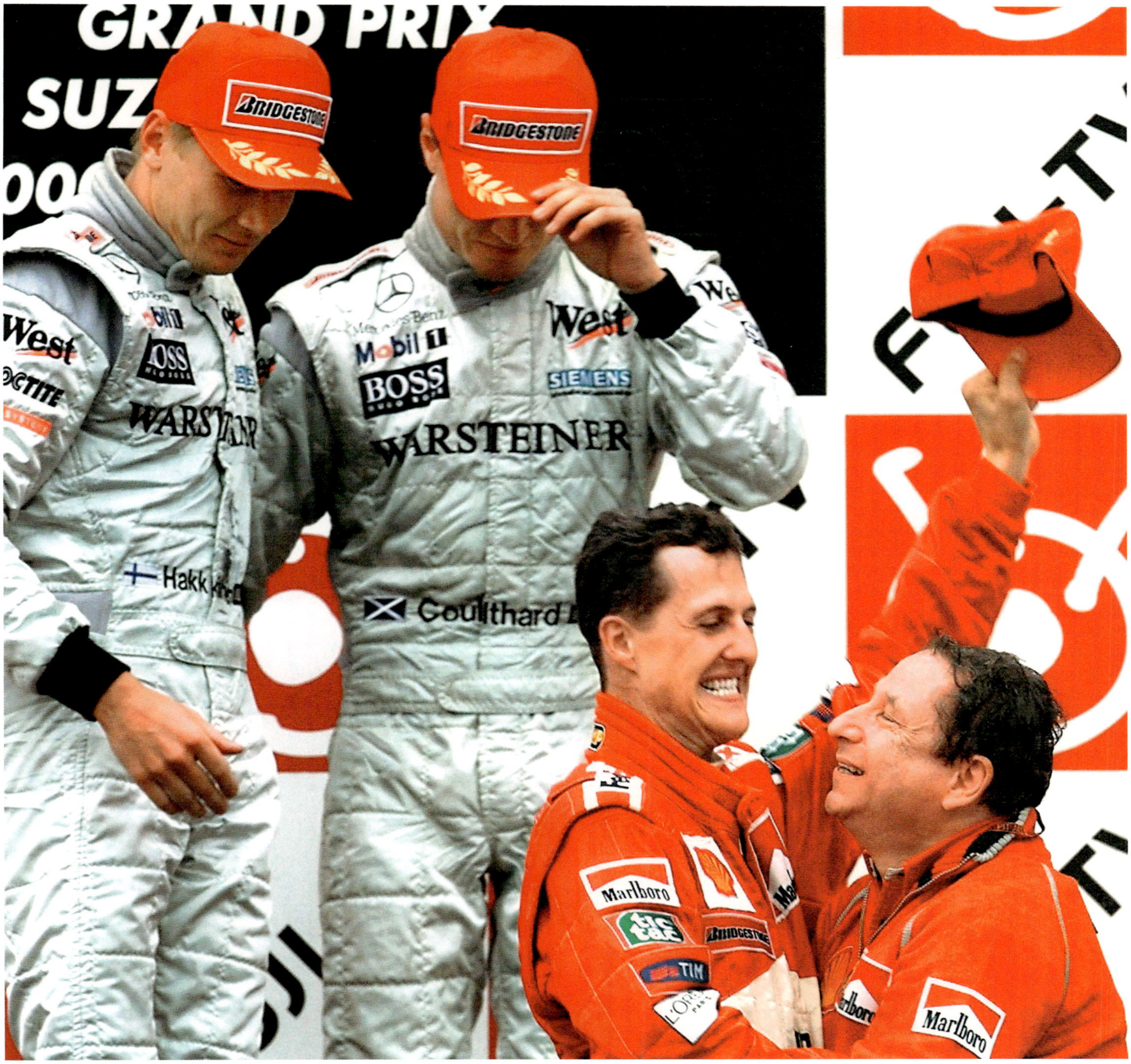

16TH MARCH 2001 – SEPANG, MALAYSIA – FINNISH FORMULA ONE ACE MIKA HAKKINEN WATCHES A TV MONITOR DURING PRACTICE FOR THE MALAYSIAN GRAND PRIX. (EMMANUEL DUNAND)

8TH OCTOBER 2000 – SUSUZA, JAPAN – MICHAEL SCHUMACHER CELEBRATES WITH TEAM MANAGER JEAN TODT ON THE PODIUM RACETRACK FOLLOWING SCHUMACHER'S WIN AT THE FORMULA ONE JAPAN GRAND PRIX. (PATRICK HERTZOG)

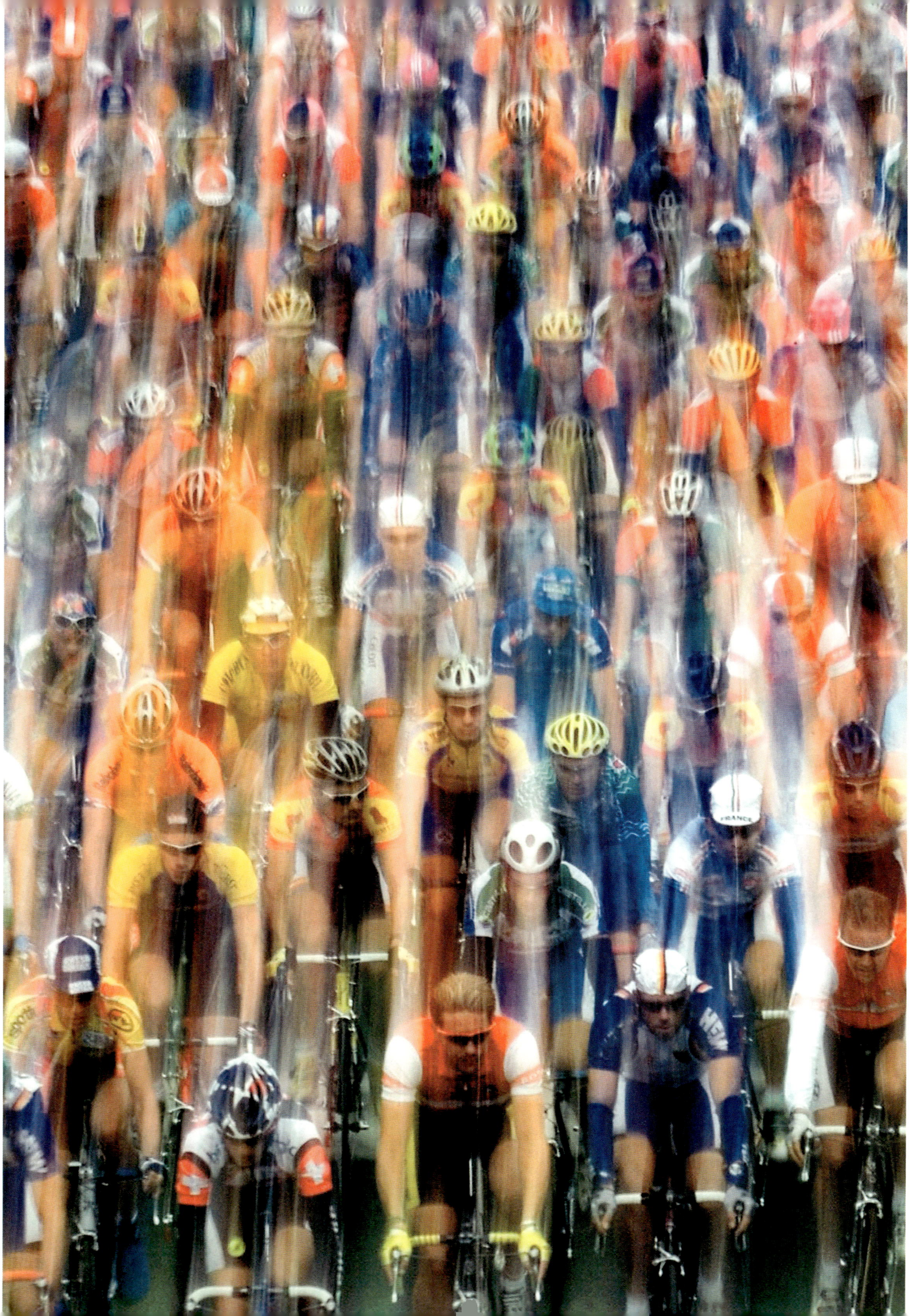

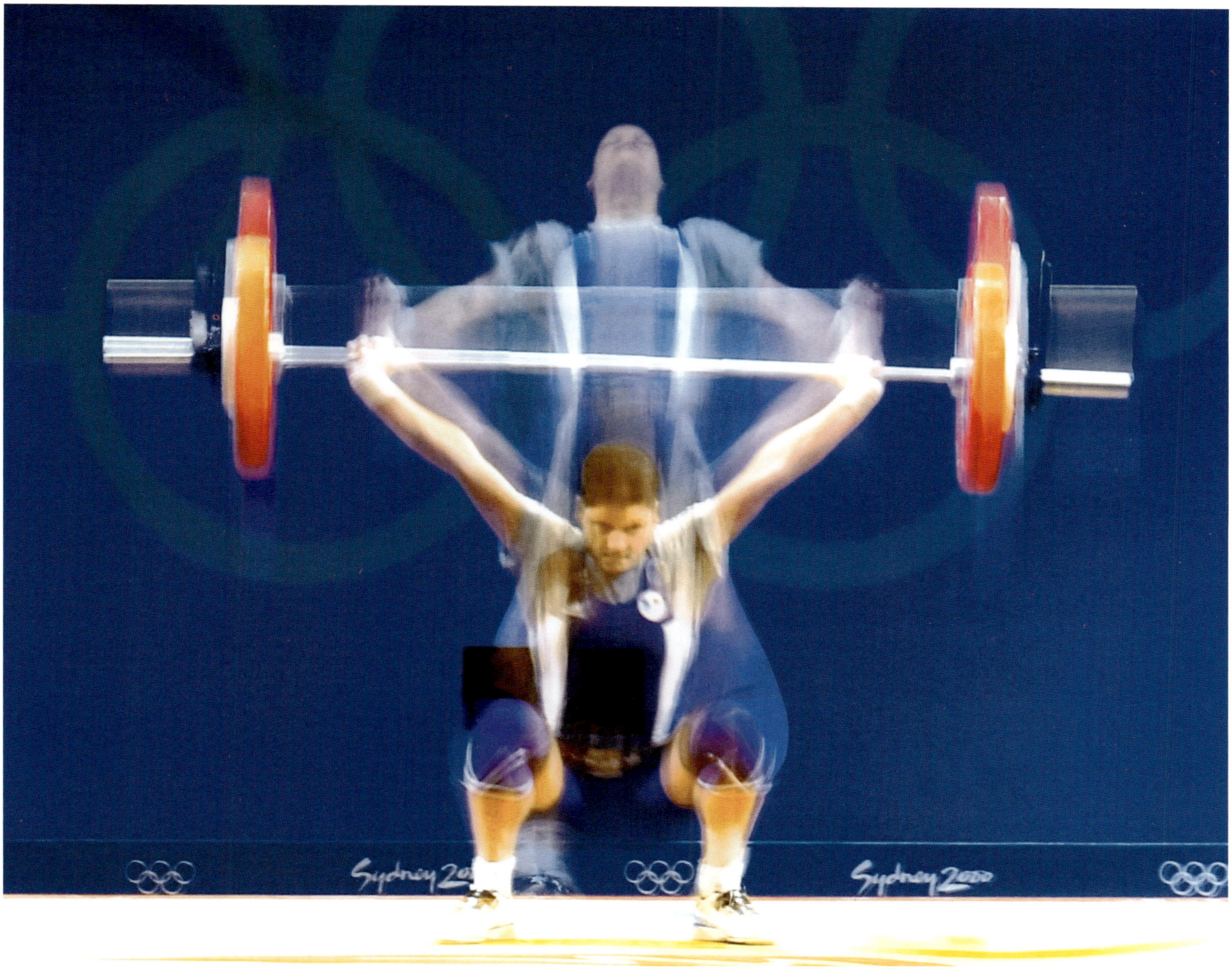

18TH SEPTEMBER 2000 – SYDNEY, AUSTRALIA – A DELAYED EXPOSURE SHOT OF TARANA ABBASOVA OF AZERBAIJAN DURING THE WOMEN'S 53 KG WEIGHTLIFTING COMPETITION AT THE OLYMPIC GAMES. ABBASOVA FINISHED 10TH. (PATRICK HERTZOG)

14TH OCTOBER 2001 – LISBON, PORTUGAL – RIDERS OF THE MEN'S WORLD ROAD CHAMPIONSHIP'S RACE START THE RACE. (JOËL SAGET)

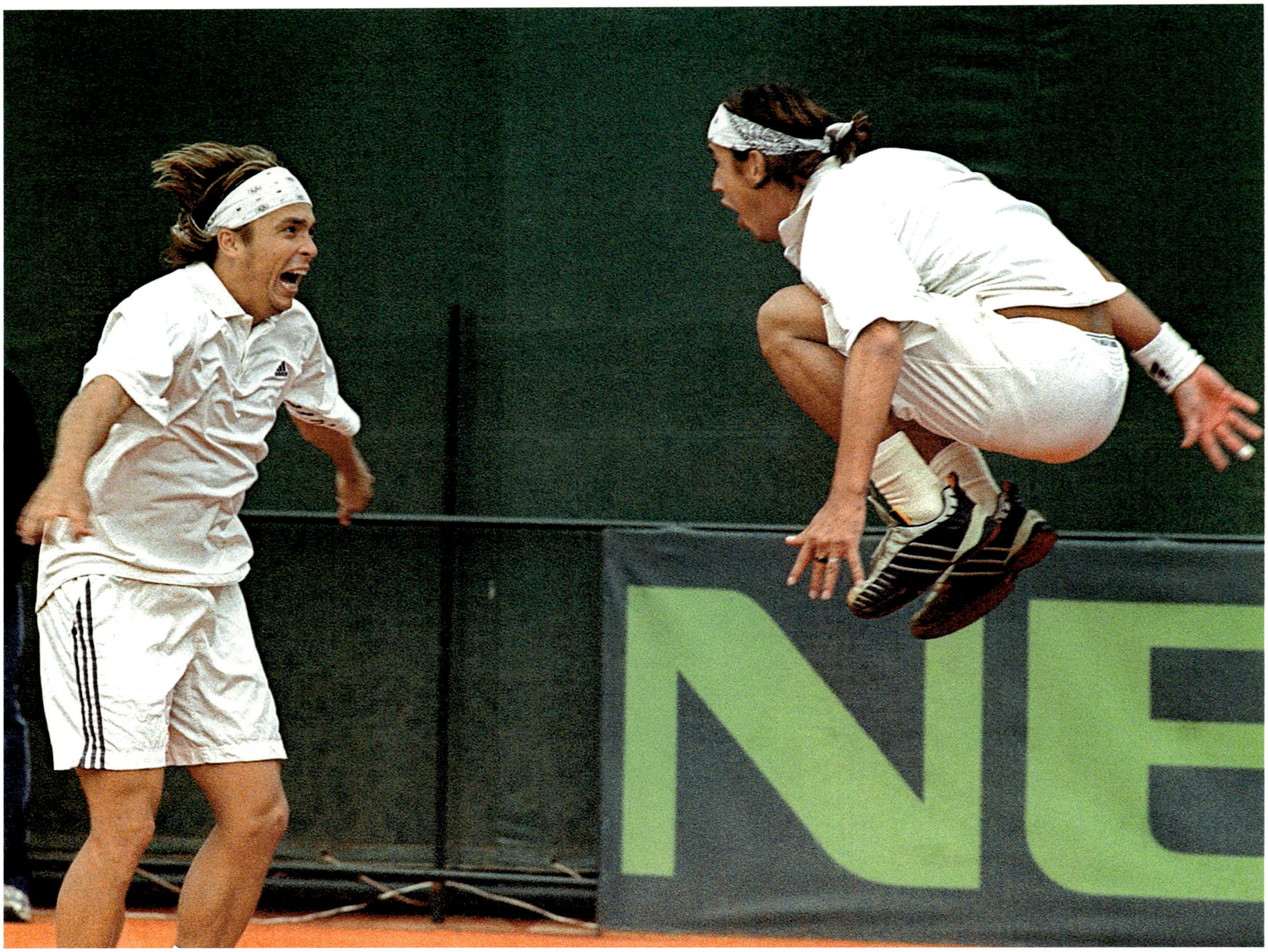

21ST JULY 2001 – MONTEVIDEO, URUGUAY – VENEZUELAN DOUBLES PARTNERS JIMY SZYMANSKI (LEFT) AND ANTONIO DE ARMAS CELEBRATE THEIR DAVIS CUP VICTORY OVER URUGUAY. (MIGUEL ROJO)

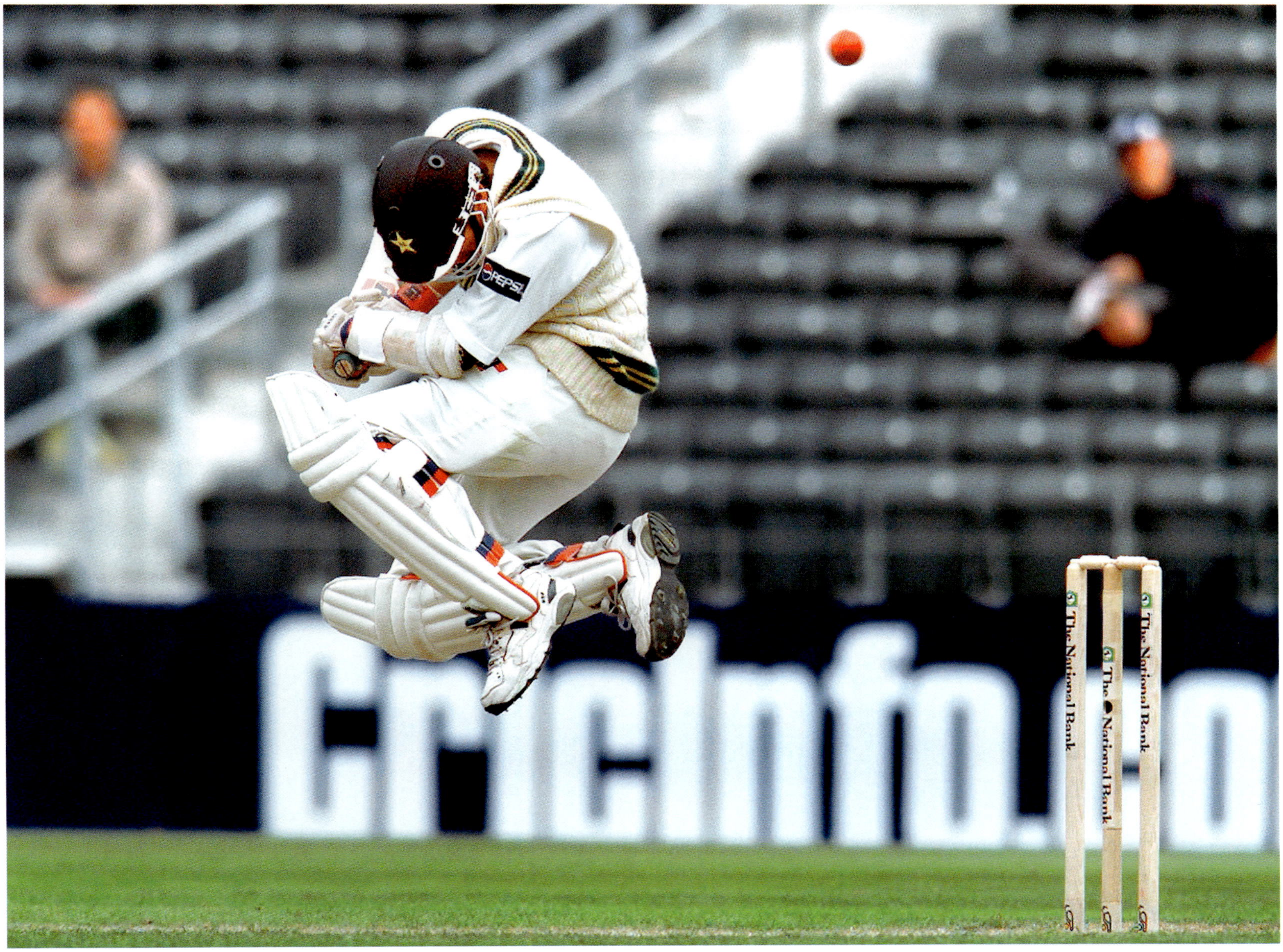

17TH MARCH 2001
– CHRISTCHURCH, NEW ZEALAND –
PAKISTAN BATSMAN YOUSUF YOUHANA DUCKS TO AVOID A BOUNCER BOWLED BY NEW ZEALAND FAST BOWLER DARYL TUFFEWY DURING THE SECOND TEST MATCH. (WILLIAM WEST)

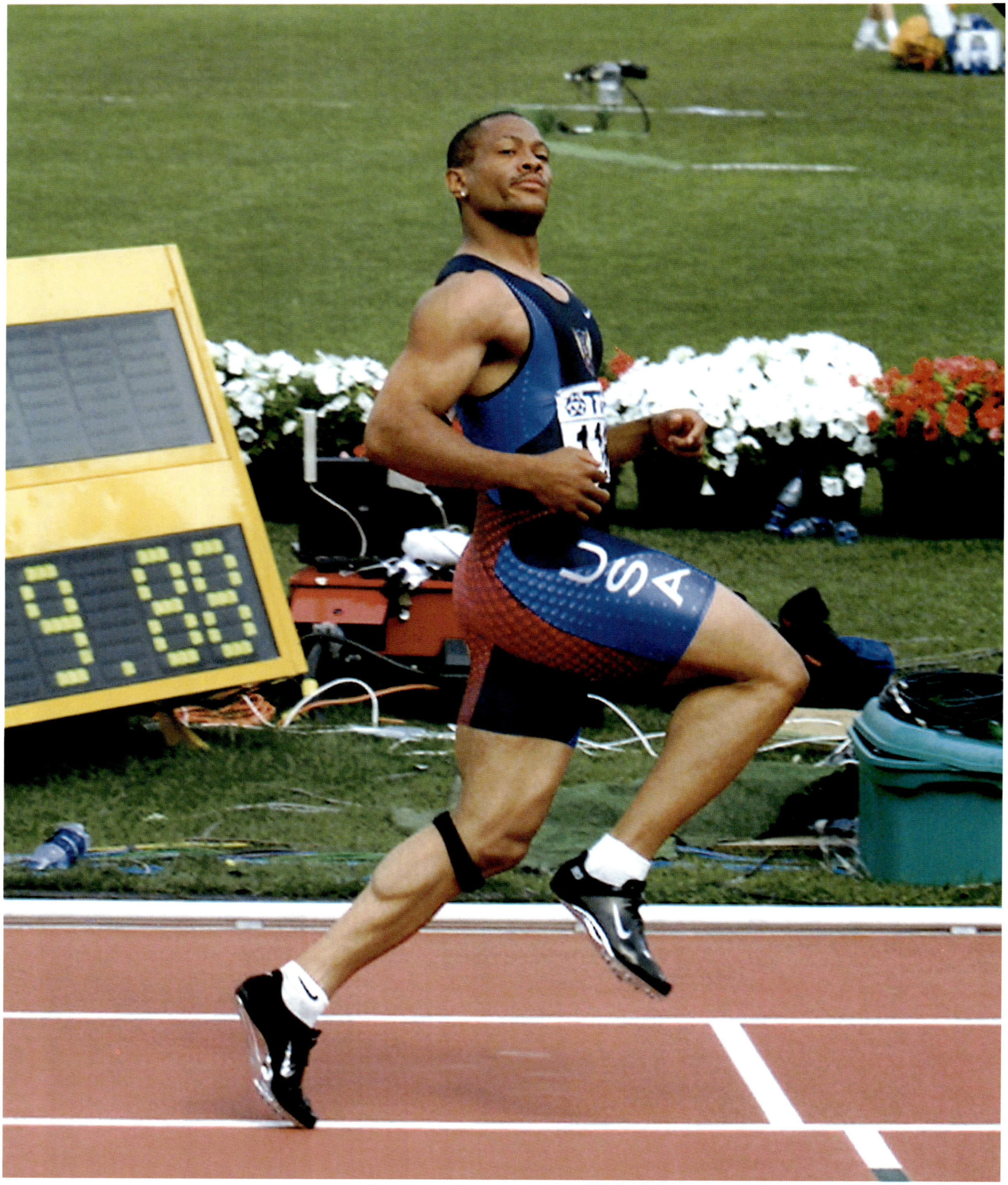
9.88
USA

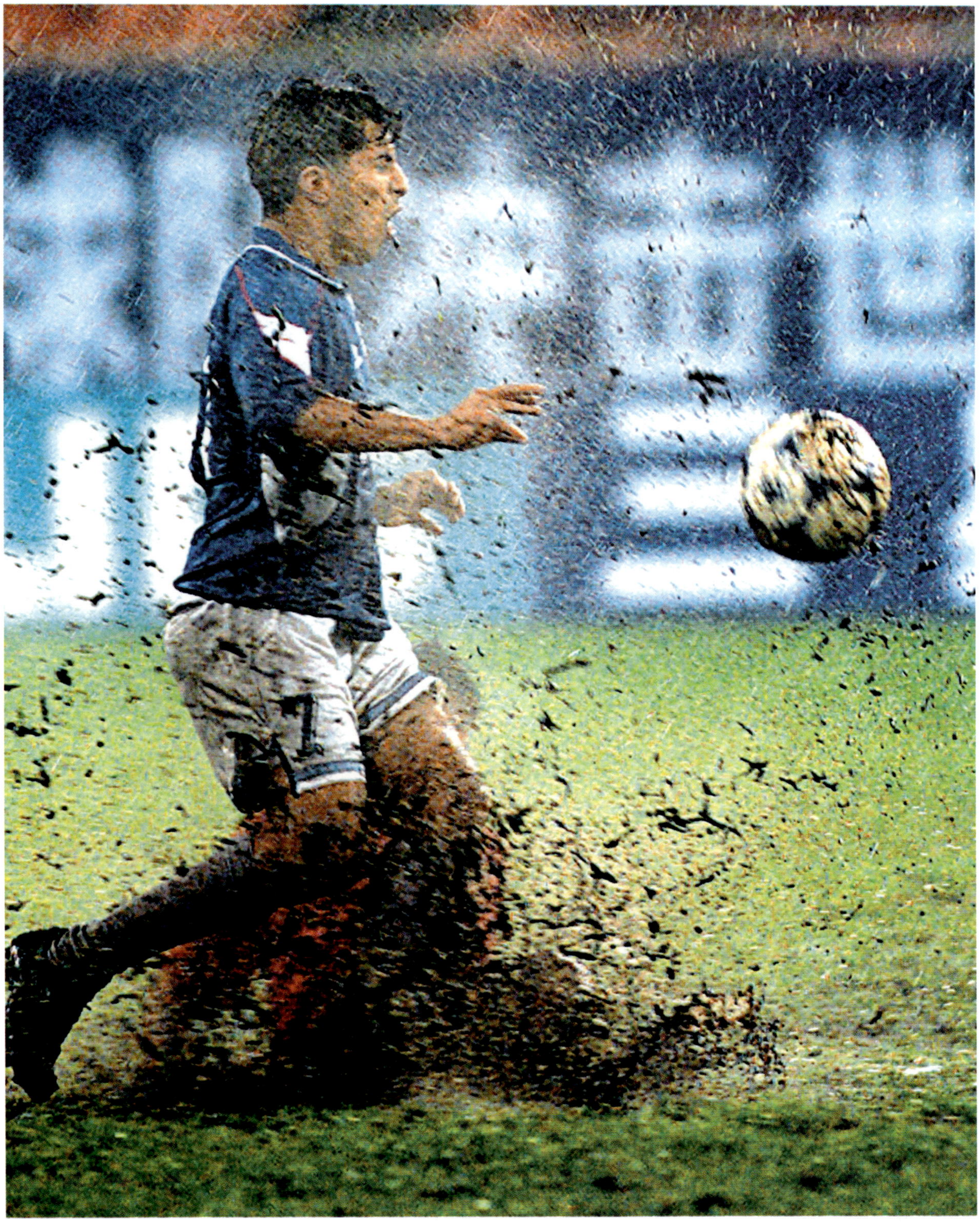

4TH AUGUST 2001 – EDMONTON, CANADA – MAURICE GREENE OF THE UNITED STATES STRUTS HIS WAY TO VICTORY IN THE MEN'S 100 M QUARTER-FINAL AT THE WORLD ATHLETICS CHAMPIONSHIPS. (TIMOTHY A. CLARY)

5TH AUGUST 2001 – SHANGHAI, CHINA – KHALEF M M S ALMUTAIRI OF KUWAIT FIGHTS FOR THE BALL WITH A NORTH KOREAN DEFENDER IN HIS COUNTRY'S DEFEAT ON PENALTIES BY THE KOREANS IN THE FOUR NATIONS CHAMPIONSHIP. (LIU JIN)

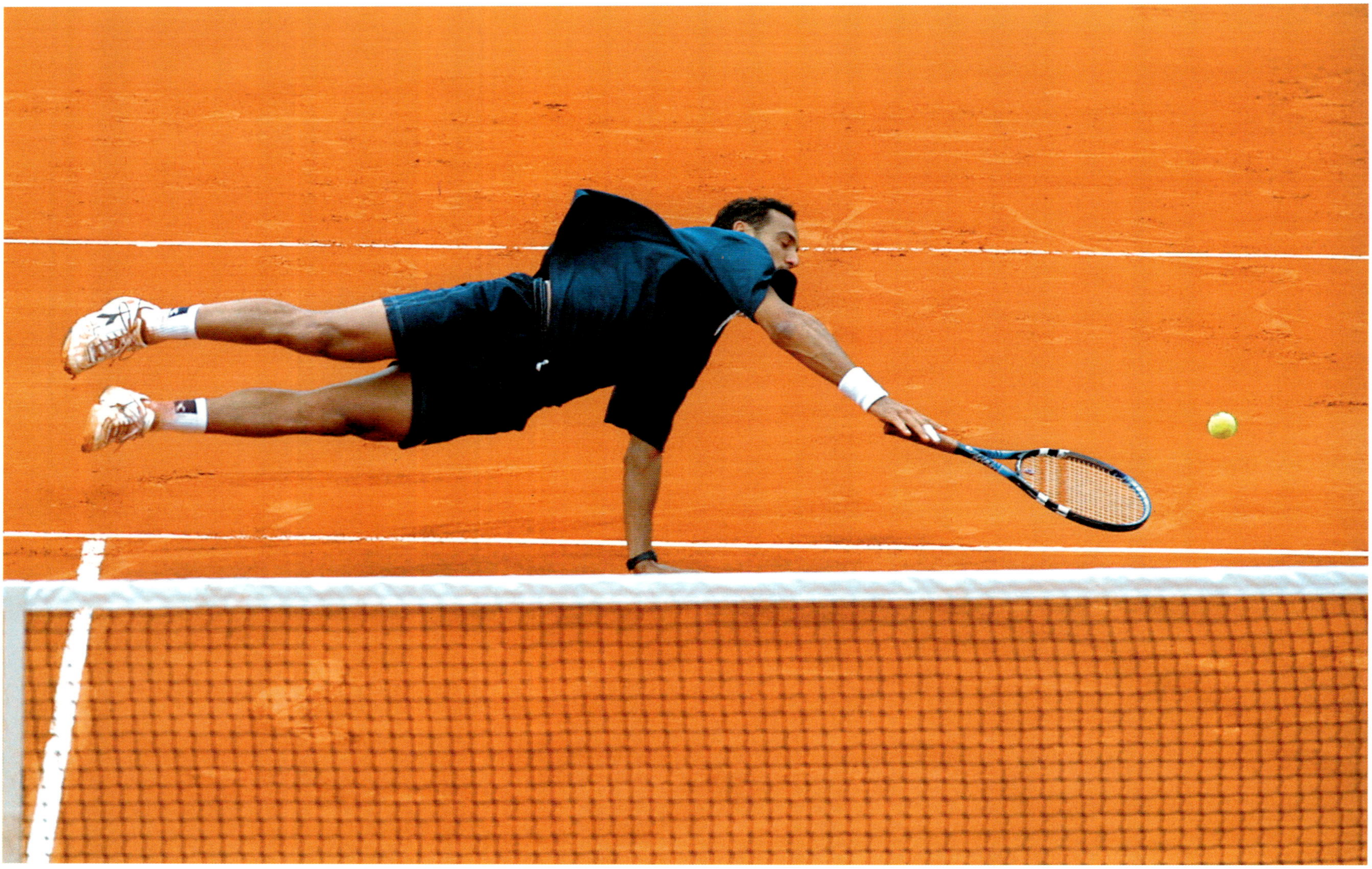

1ST JUNE 2001 – PARIS, FRANCE – KARIM ALAMI DIVES FOR THE BALL DURING HIS THIRD ROUND DEFEAT AT THE FRENCH OPEN BY EVENTUAL CHAMPION GUSTAVO KUERTEN OF BRAZIL. (JACQUES DEMARTHON)

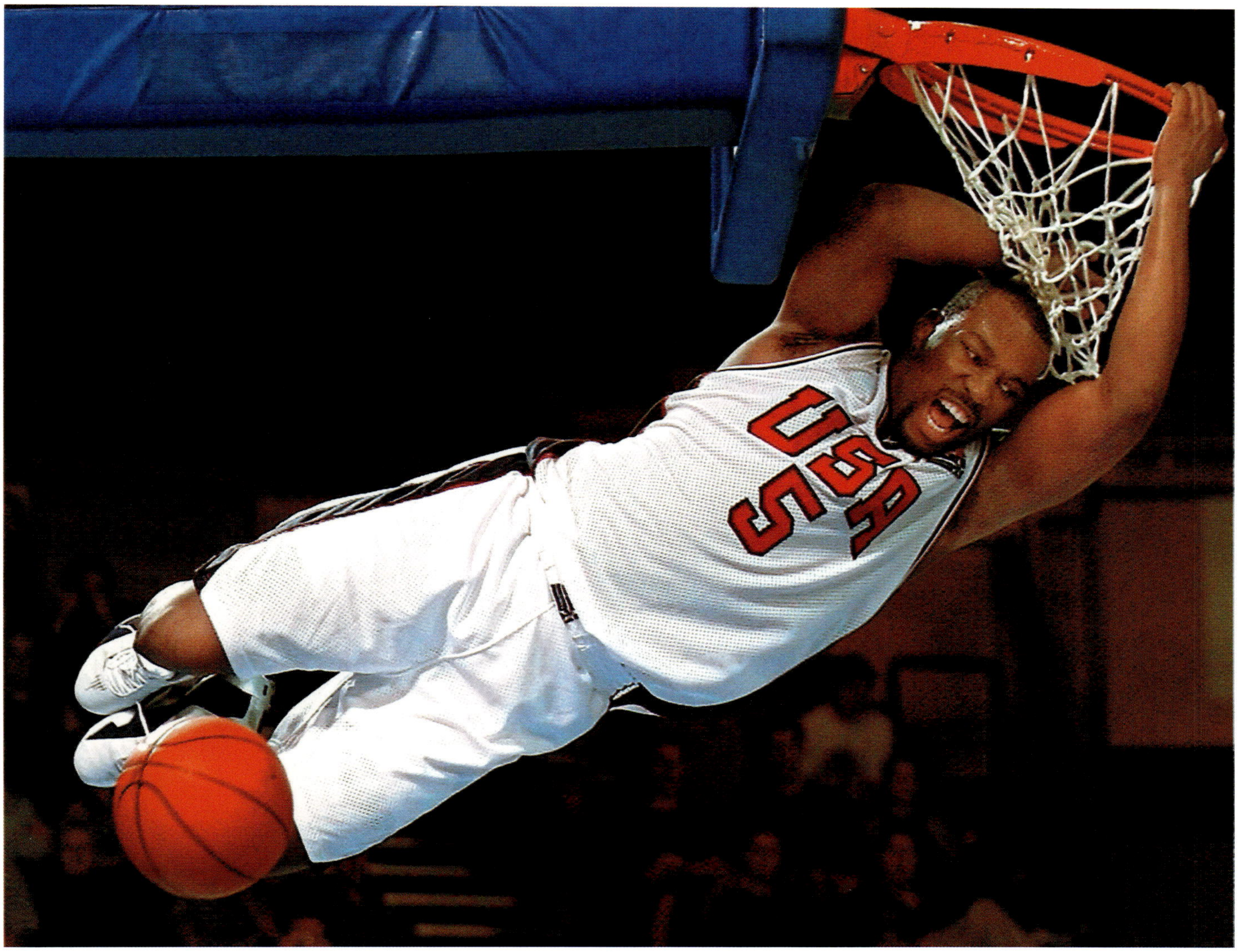

8TH SEPTEMBER 2001 – BRISBANE, AUSTRALIA – BARON DAVIS OF THE UNITED STATES SCORES A SLAM-DUNK AS THE AMERICANS BEAT BRAZIL 106-98 IN OVERTIME IN THEIR GOODWILL GAMES SEMI-FINAL. (WILLIAM WEST)

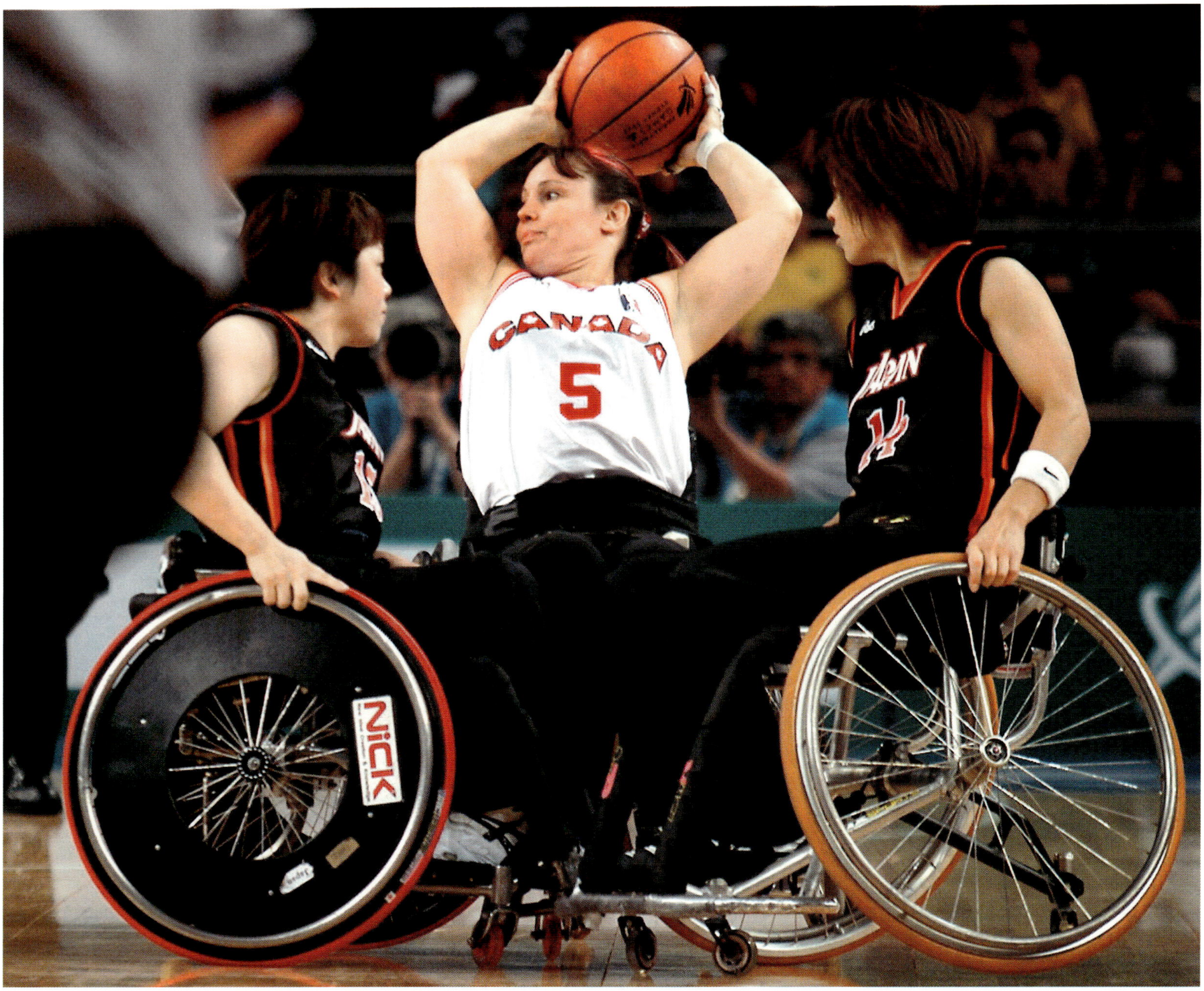

23RD OCTOBER 2000 – SYDNEY, AUSTRALIA – MARNI ABBOTT OF CANADA SURROUNDED BY TWO JAPANESE DEFENDERS IN THE 11TH PARALYMPICS. (WILLIAM WEST)

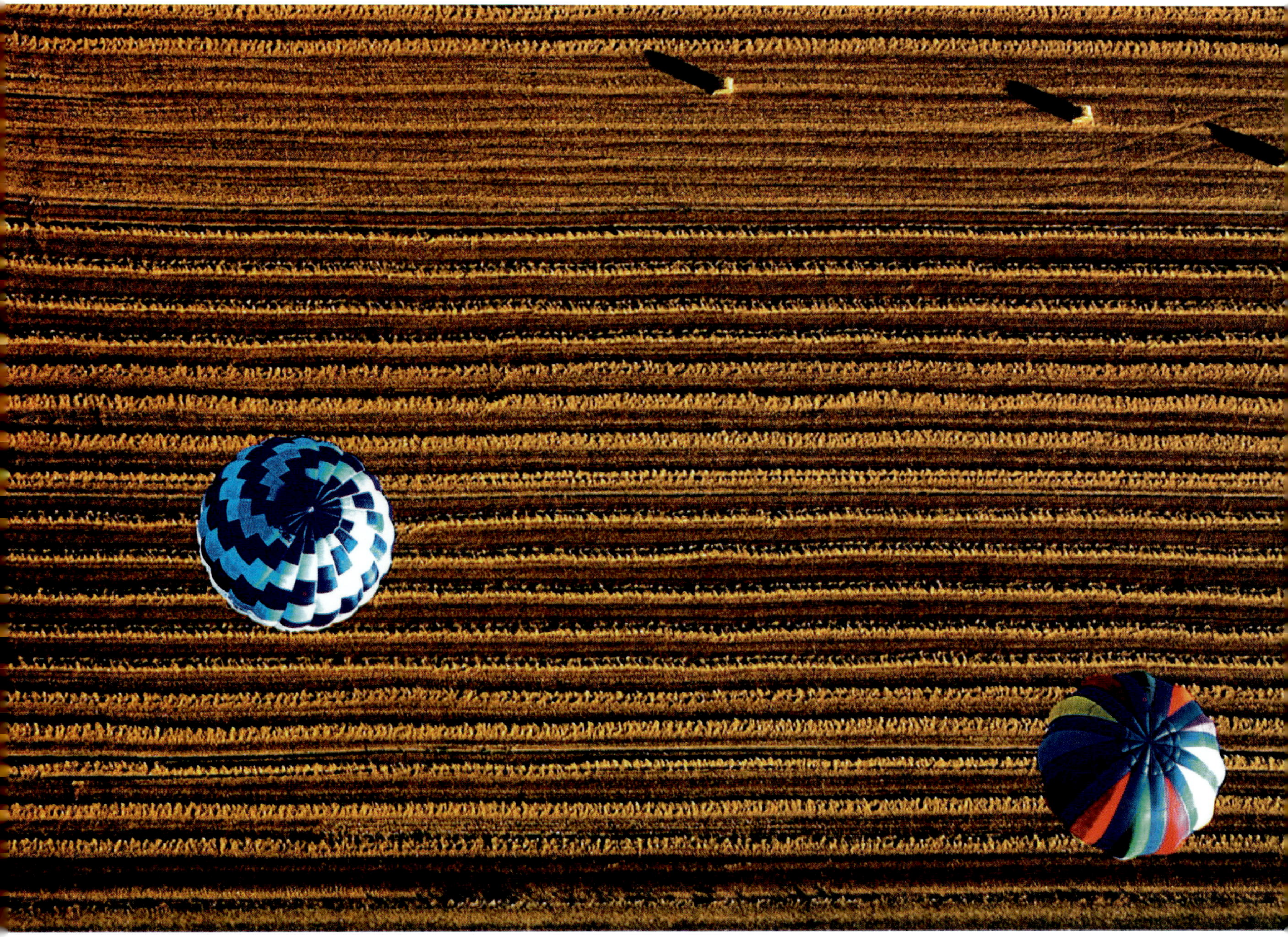

30TH JULY 2001 – CHAMBLEY, FRANCE – AN AERIAL VIEW OF HOT-AIR BALLOONS ABOVE A NEWLY-PLOUGHED FIELD. (DAMIEN MAYER)

FROM NEW YORK TO KABUL

14.55
BULLETIN¥¥¥
NEW YORK – PLANE CRASHES INTO NEW YORK WORLD TRADE CENTER.
MM/CW

15.09
BULLETIN¥¥¥
NEW YORK – SECOND PLANE HITS WORLD TRADE CENTER TOWERS – MEDIA
BUR/CW

15.47
BULLETIN¥¥¥
WASHINGTON, SEPT 11 (AFP) – TWO EXPLOSIONS ROCKED THE SIDE OF THE PENTAGON TUESDAY, A WITNESS SAID
"I HEARD TWO LOUD BOOMS - ONE LARGE, ONE SMALL" SAID LISA BURGESS, A REPORTER FOR STARS AND STRIPES NEWSPAPER. SHE SAID SHE SAW SMOKE BILLOWING FROM ONE SIDE OF THE BUILDING.
JM/MDLUS-PLANE-COLLAPSE

16.01
URGENT¥¥¥
ONE OF THE WORLD TRADE CENTER'S TWIN TOWERS COLLAPSES
NEW YORK, SEPT 11 (AFP) – THE SOUTHERN OF THE WORLD TRADE CENTER'S TWIN TOWERS, HIT BY AN AIRPLANE, COMPLETELY COLLAPSED AFTER EXPLODING IN A MASSIVE CLOUD OF SMOKE AND DEBRIS.
MM/LG/MDL

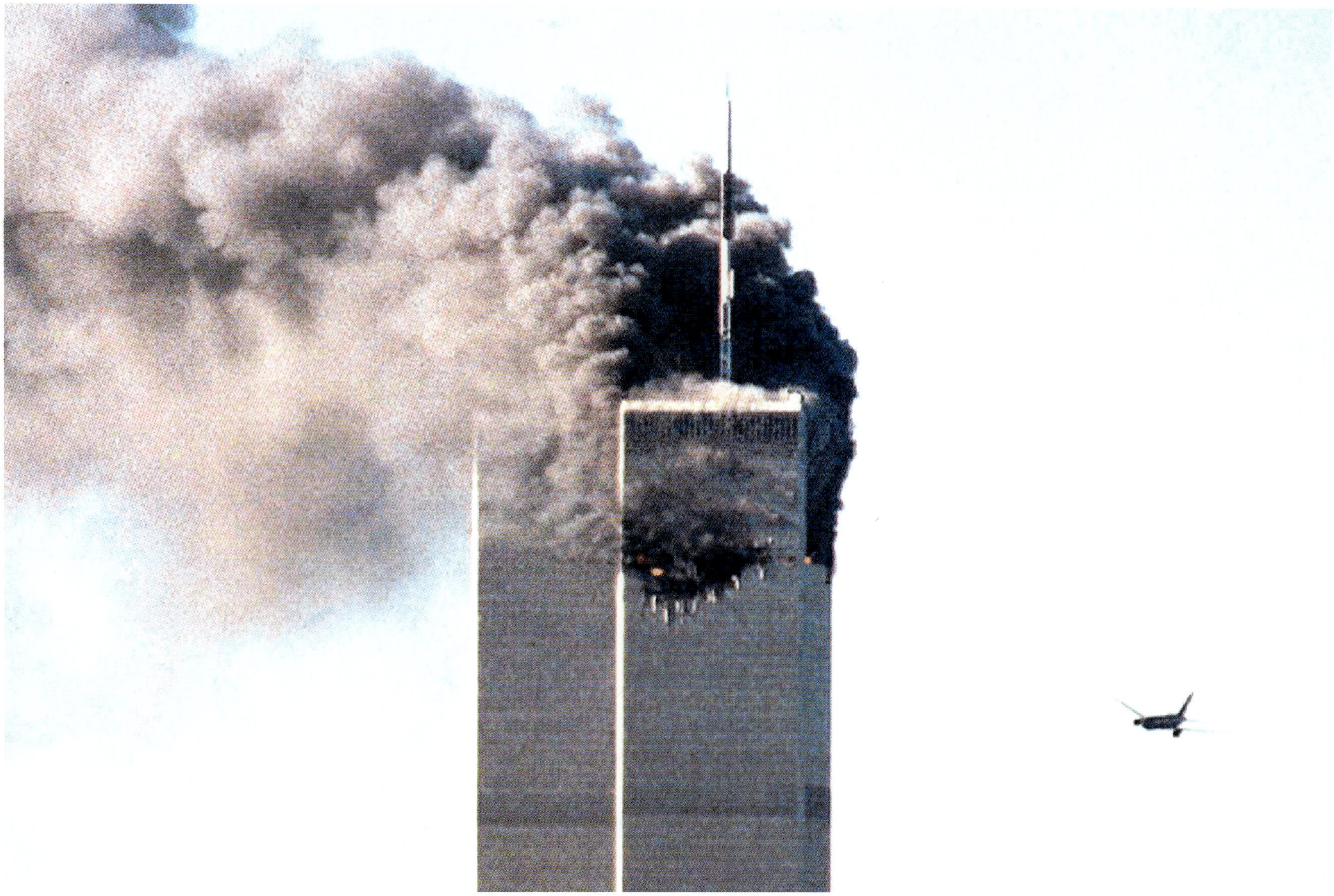

11TH SEPTEMBER 2001 – NEW YORK, USA – A HIJACKED COMMERCIAL AIRLINER APPROACHES THE NORTH TOWER OF THE WORLD TRADE CENTER BEFORE PLOUGHING INTO THE BUILDING. (SETH McCALLISTER)

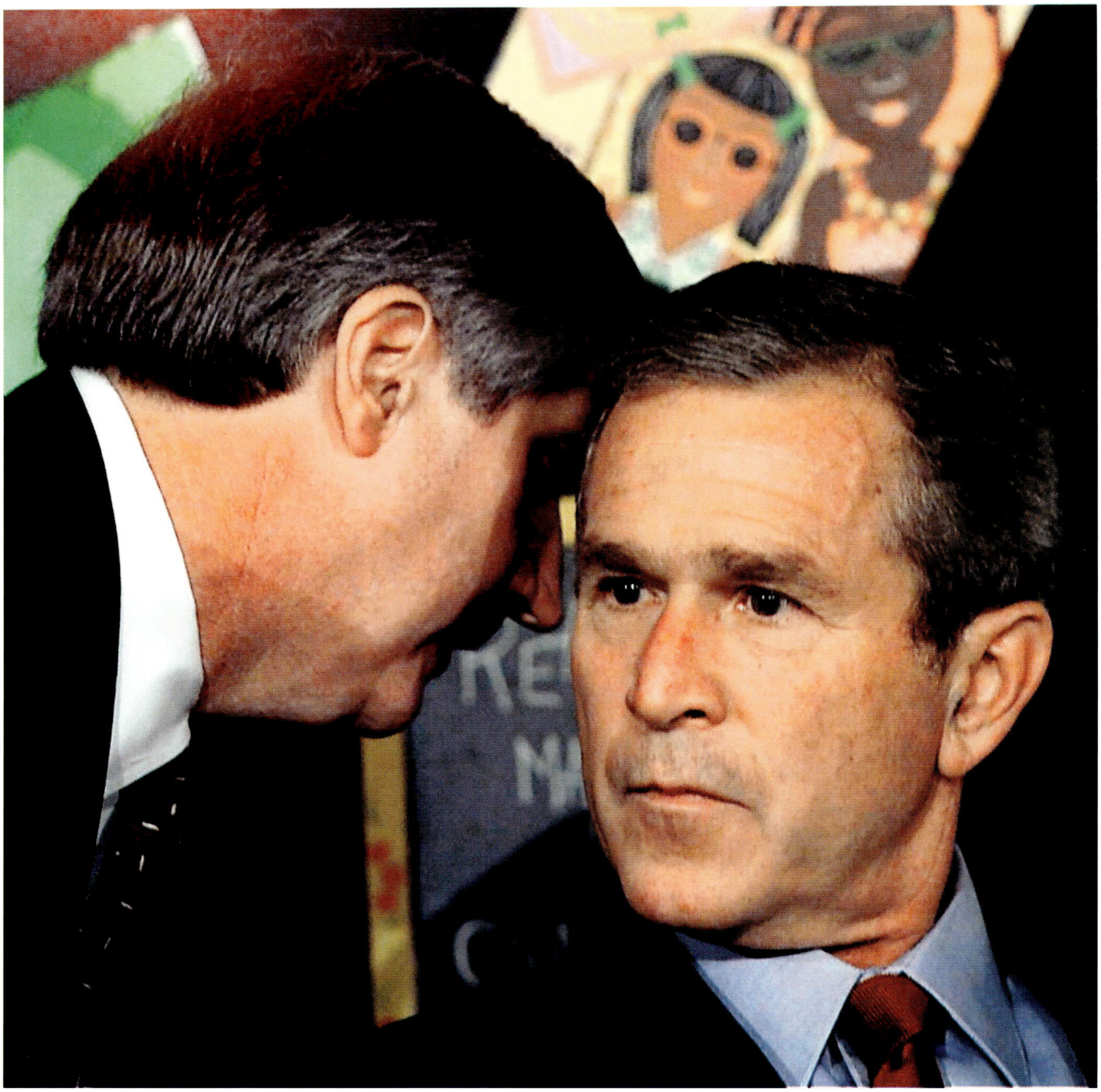

11TH SEPTEMBER 2001 – SARASOTA, USA – PRESIDENT GEORGE W. BUSH IS INFORMED OF THE TERRORIST ATTACKS ON THE WORLD TRADE CENTER BY CHIEF OF STAFF ANDREW CARD AS HE ATTENDS A MORNING SCHOOL READING. (PAUL J. RICHARDS)

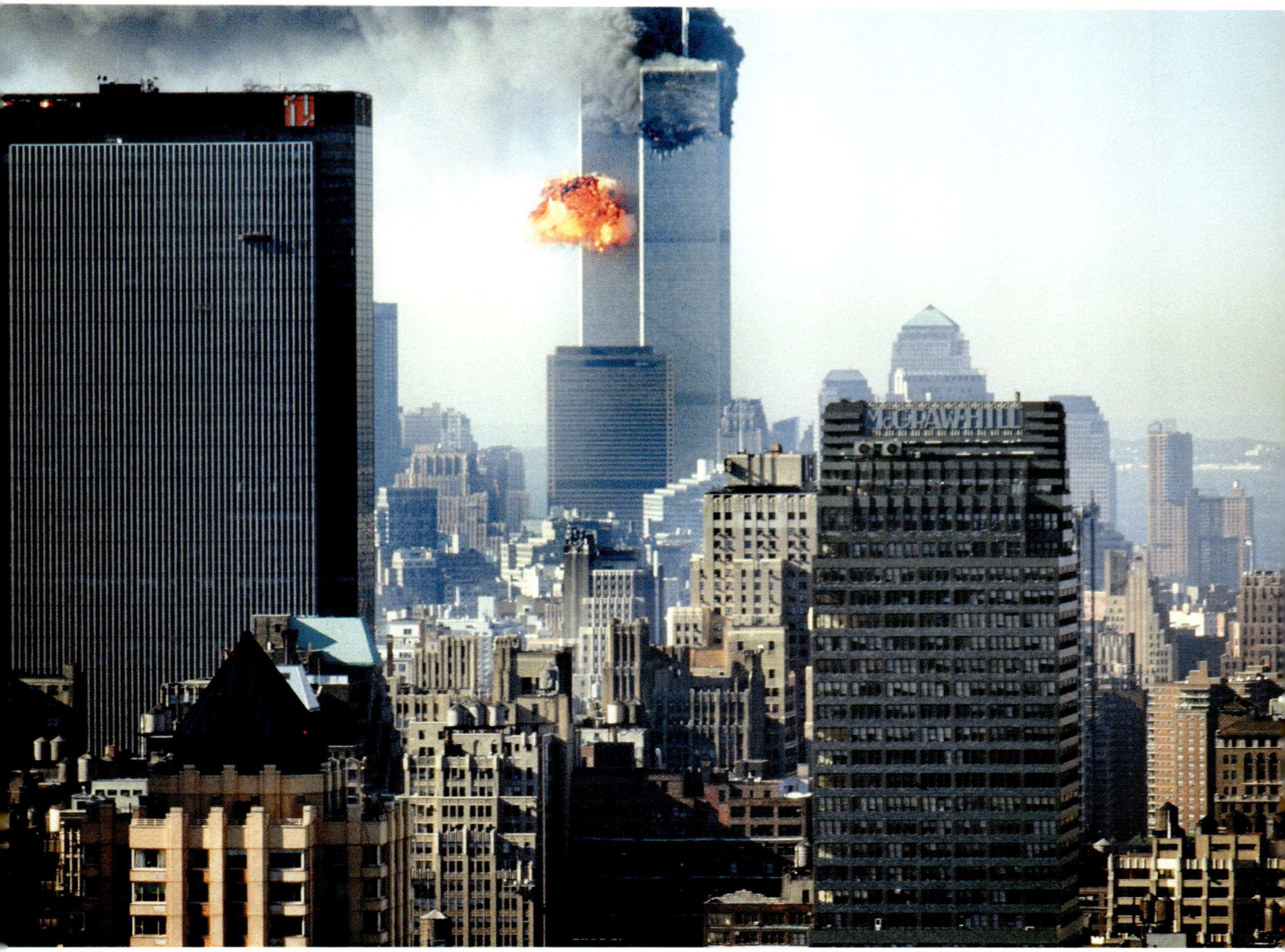

11TH SEPTEMBER 2001 – NEW YORK, USA – A SECOND HIJACKED AIRLINER CRASHES INTO THE WORLD TRADE CENTER. (SETH McCALLISTER)

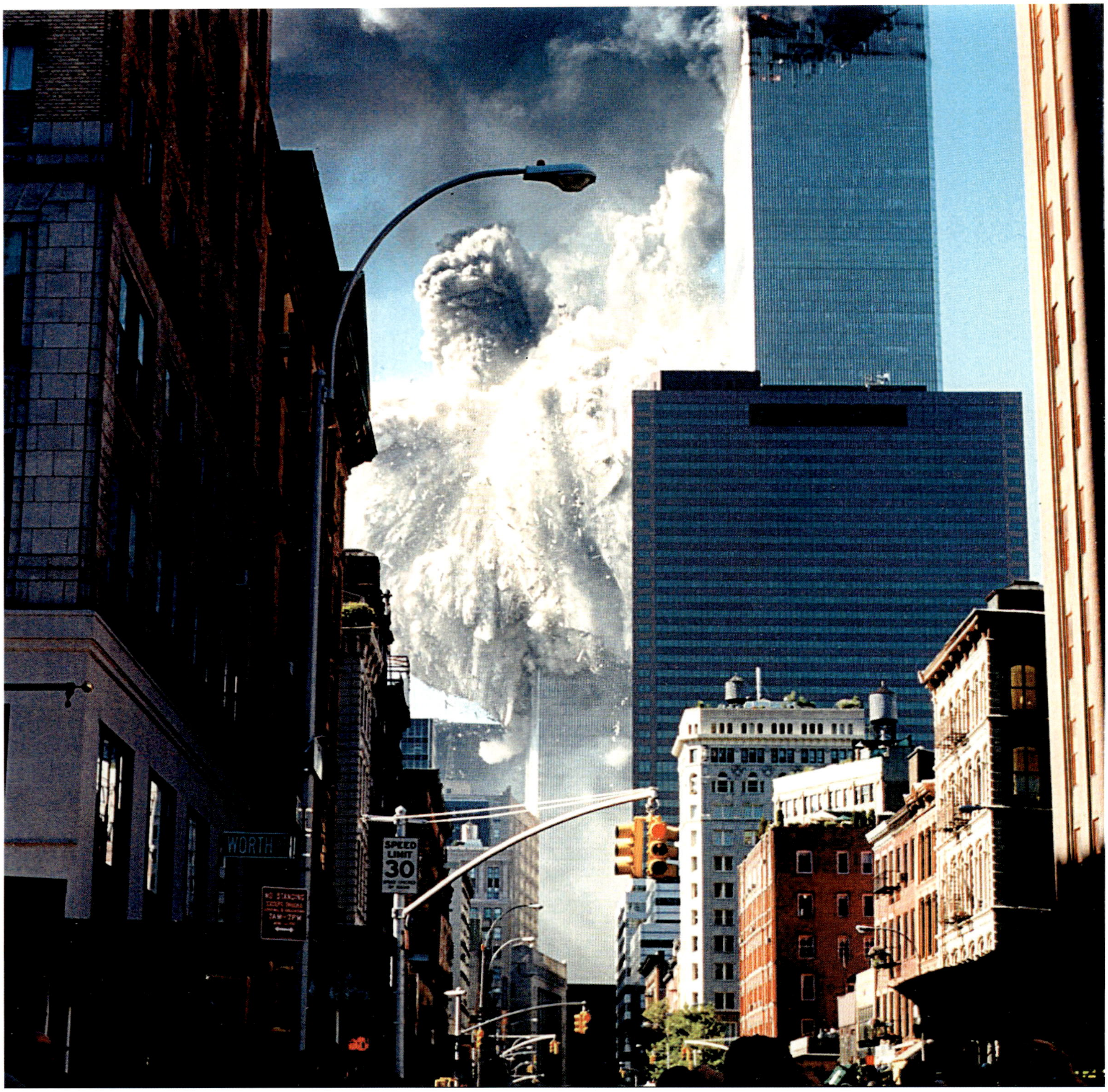

11TH SEPTEMBER 2001 – NEW YORK, USA – THE SOUTH TOWER OF THE WORLD TRADE CENTER CASCADES INTO THE STREETS BELOW. (AARON MILESTON)

11TH SEPTEMBER 2001 – NEW YORK, USA – PEDESTRIANS FLEE AS ONE OF THE WORLD TRADE CENTER TOWERS COLLAPSES. (DOUG KANTER)

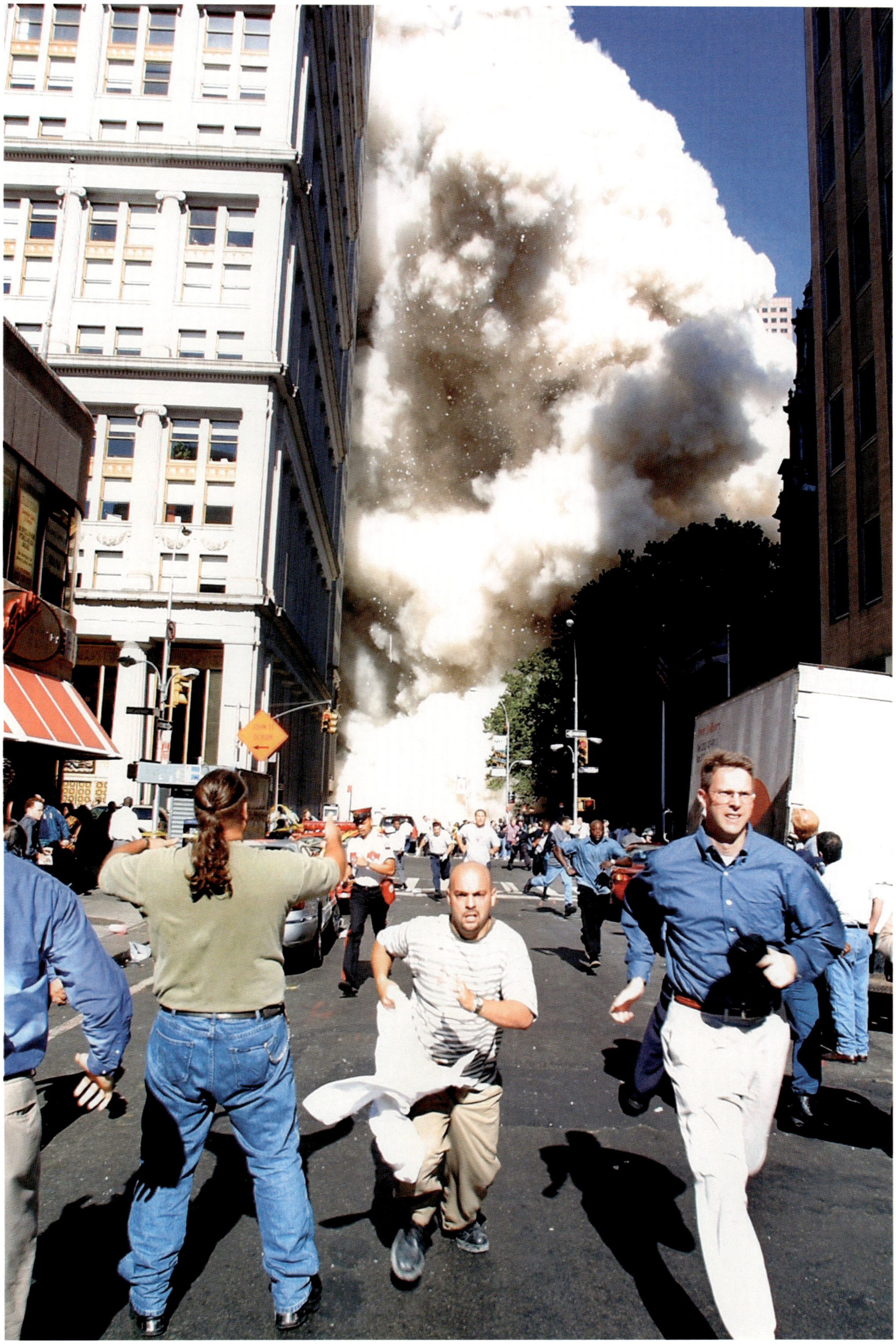

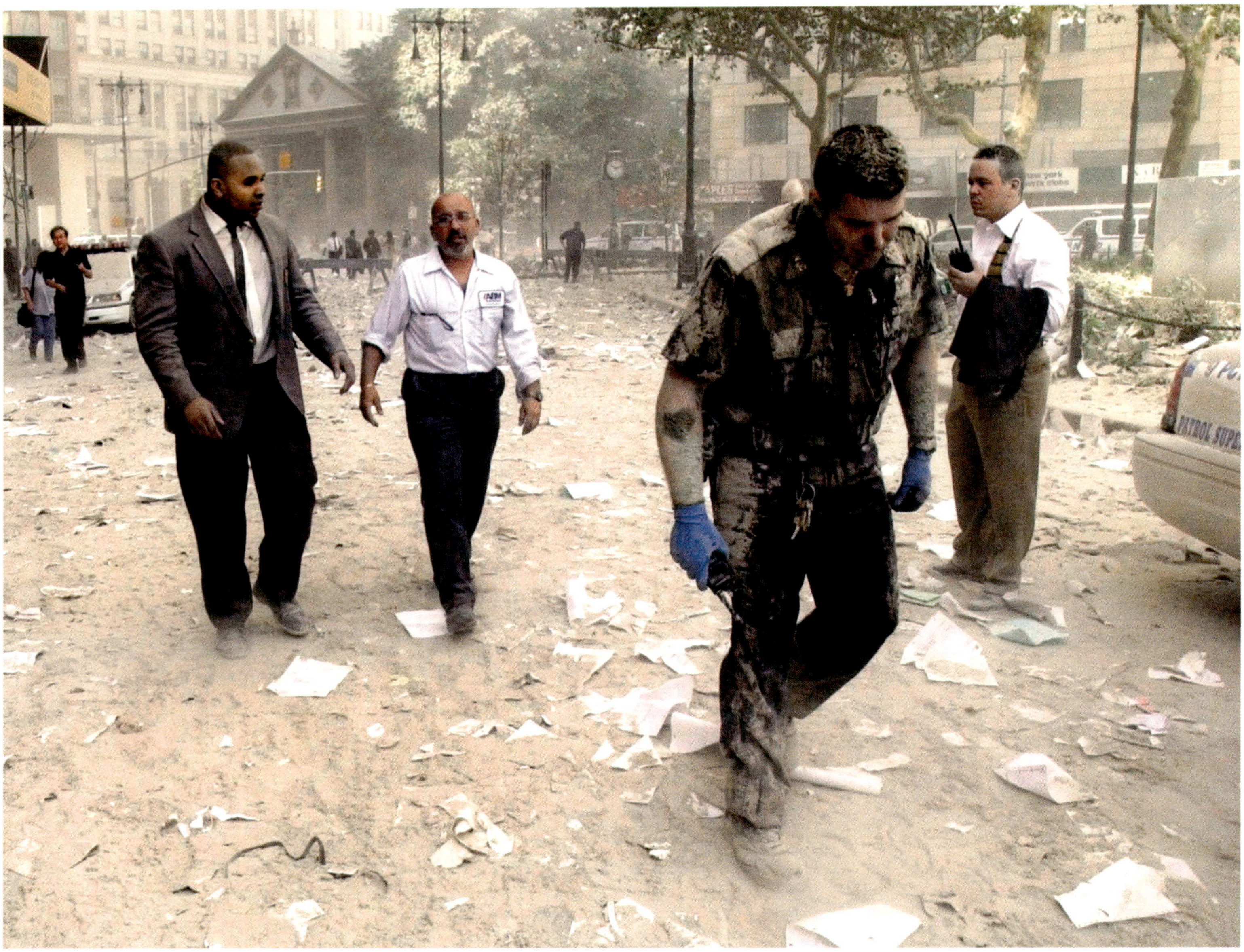

11TH SEPTEMBER 2001 – NEW YORK, USA – STUNNED POLICE AND BYSTANDERS WADE THROUGH DEBRIS WHICH HAD FALLEN INTO THE STREET AFTER THE COLLAPSE OF THE WORLD TRADE CENTER. (STAN HONDA)

11TH SEPTEMBER 2001 – NEW YORK, USA – GEORGE SLEIGH, WHO MIRACULOUSLY SURVIVED THE TERRORIST ATTACK ON THE WORLD TRADE CENTER WHERE HE WORKED ON THE 91ST FLOOR, STAGGERS HIS WAY THROUGH THE DEBRIS ON HIS WAY HOME. (STAN HONDA)

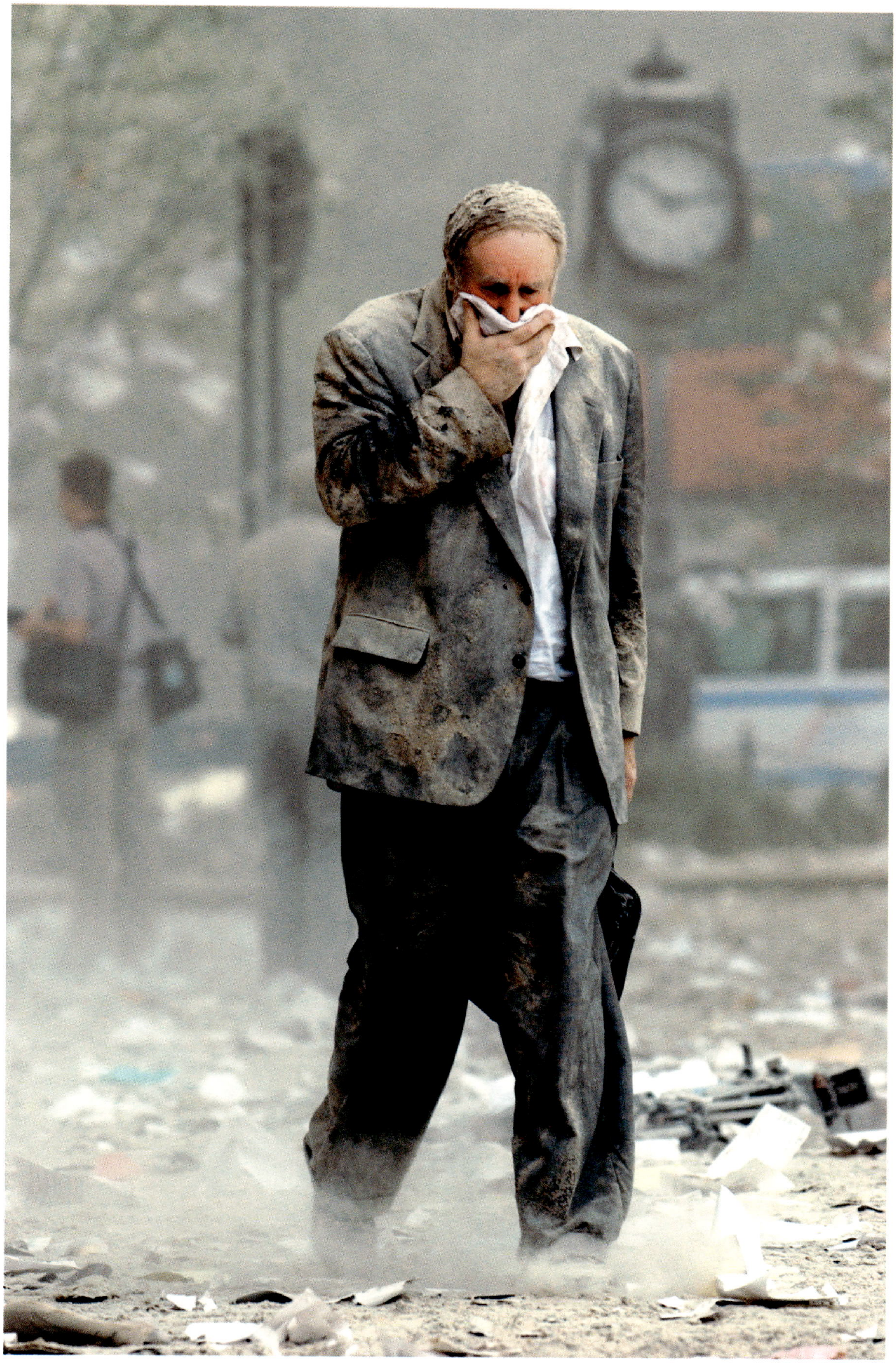

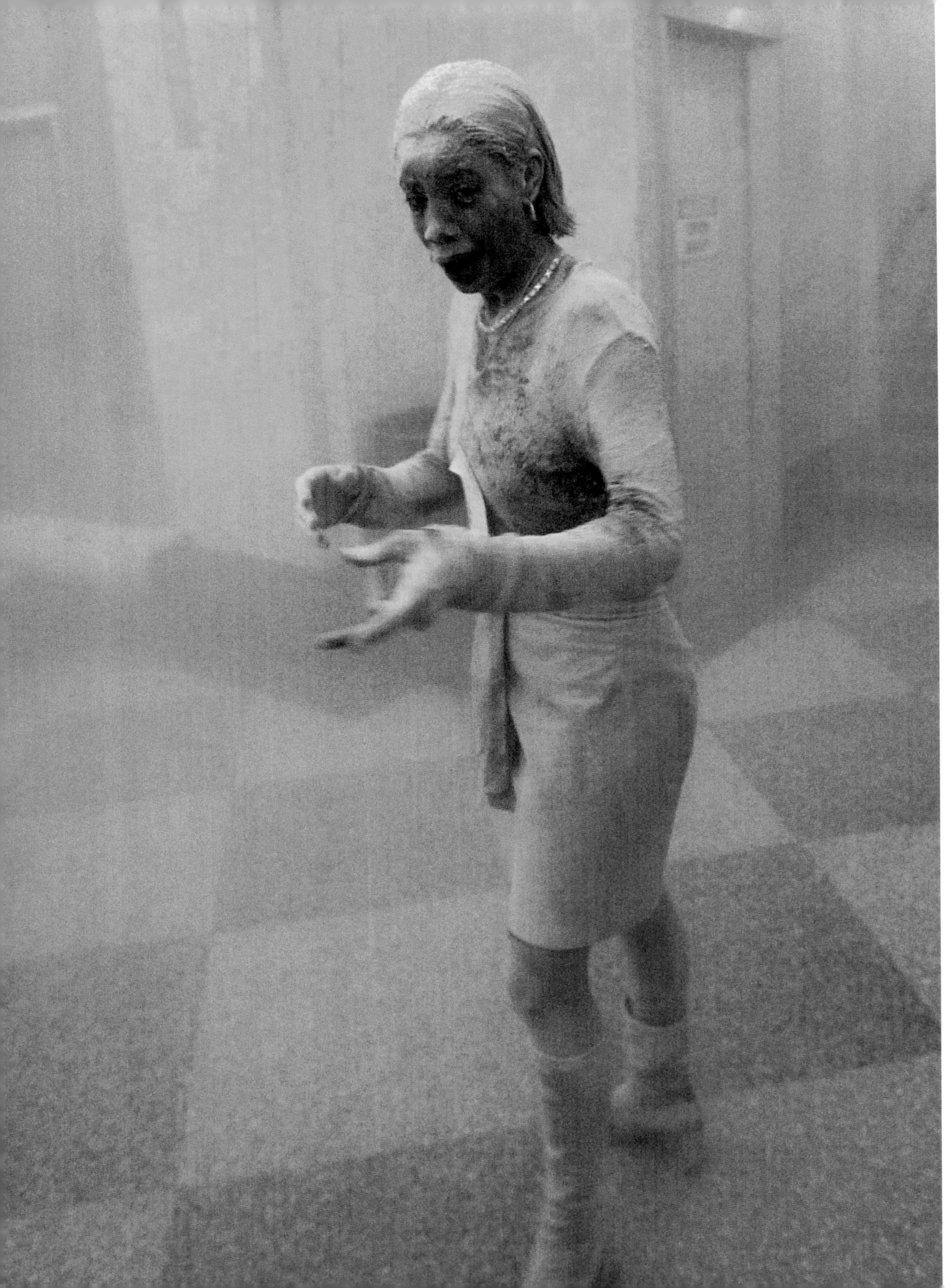

11TH SEPTEMBER 2001
– NEW YORK, USA –
A WOMAN COVERED IN DUST AFTER THE COLLAPSE OF THE TWIN TOWERS OF THE WORLD TRADE CENTER FOLLOWING THE TERRORIST ATTACK ON THE BUILDINGS. (STAN HONDA)

12TH SEPTEMBER 2001
– WASHINGTON, USA –
A SCENE FROM A CANDLELIGHT VIGIL IN FRONT OF THE US CAPITOL IN MEMORY OF THE VICTIMS OF THE 11TH SEPTEMBER ATTACKS. (ROBYN BECK)

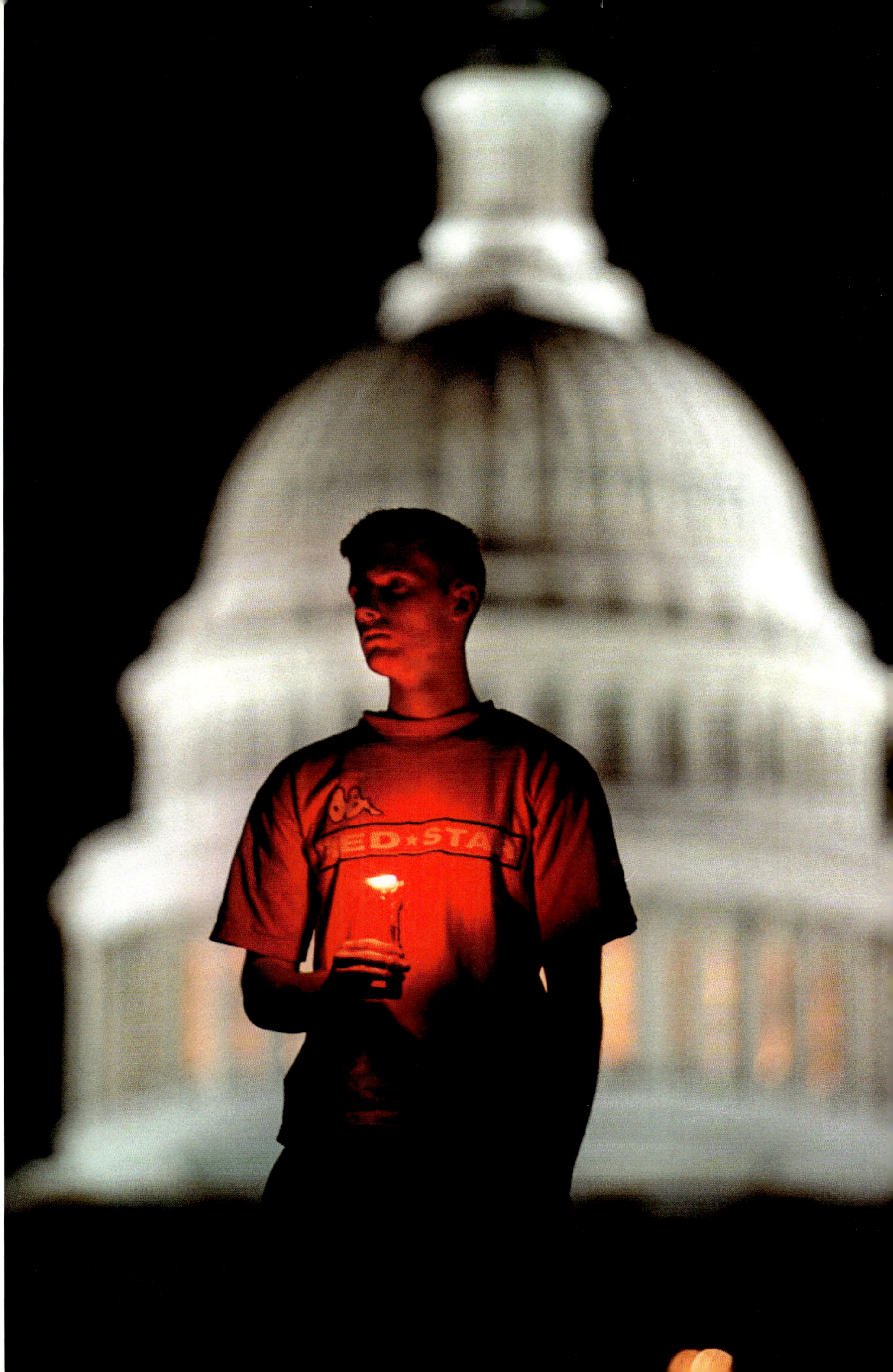

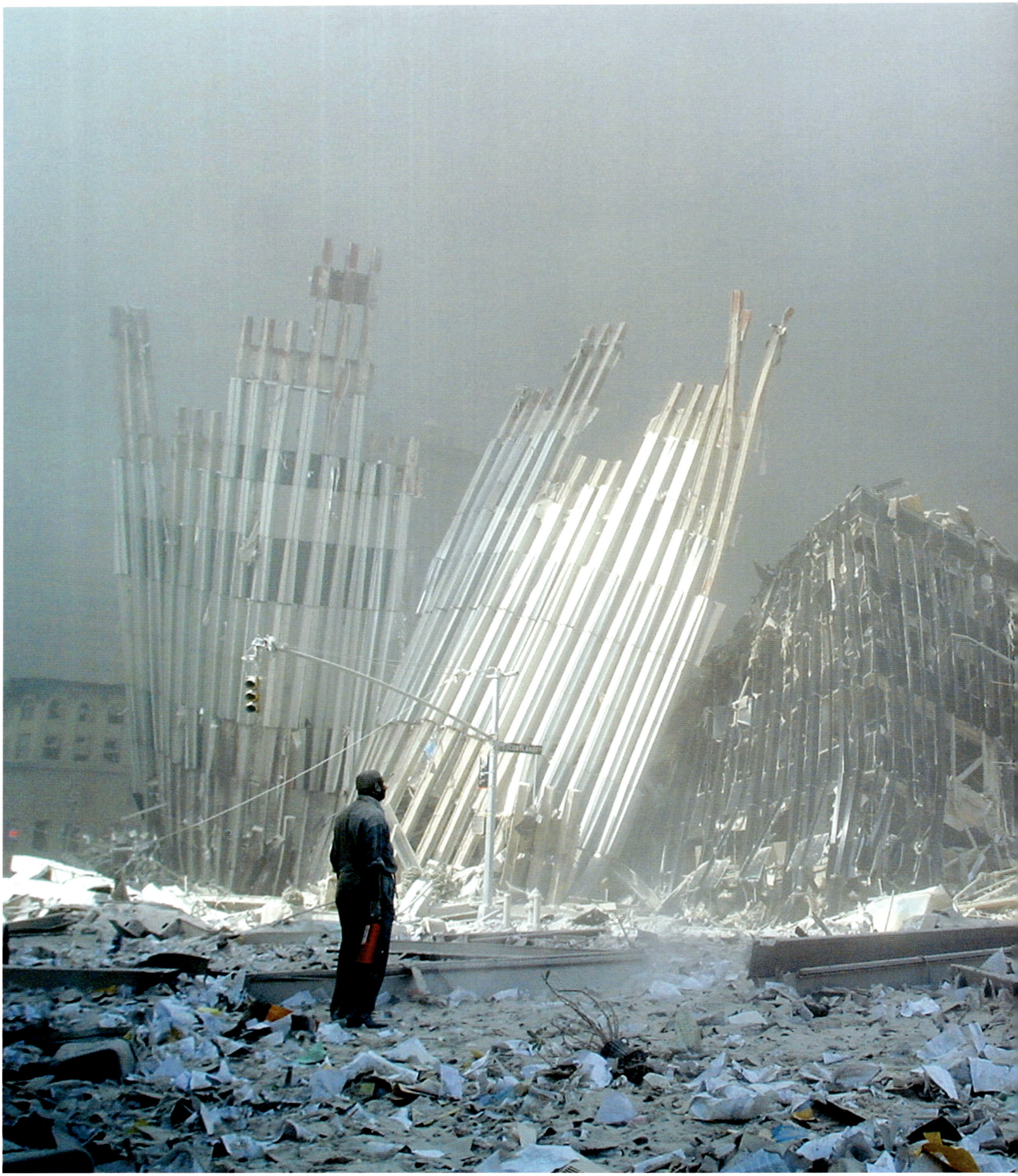

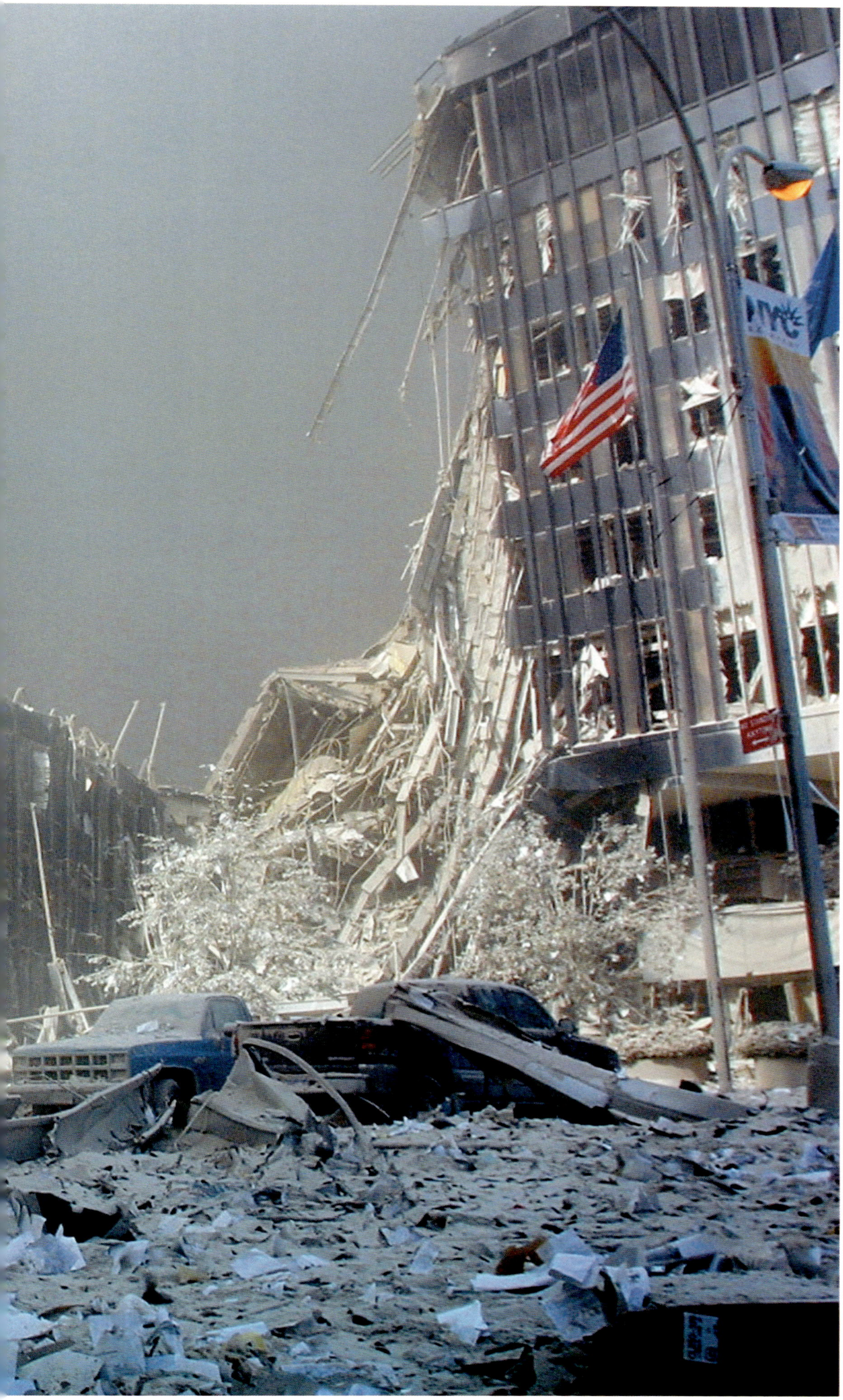

11TH SEPTEMBER 2001 – NEW YORK, USA – A LONE FIGURE STANDS AMONG THE WRECKAGE OF THE WORLD TRADE CENTER. (DOUG KANTER)

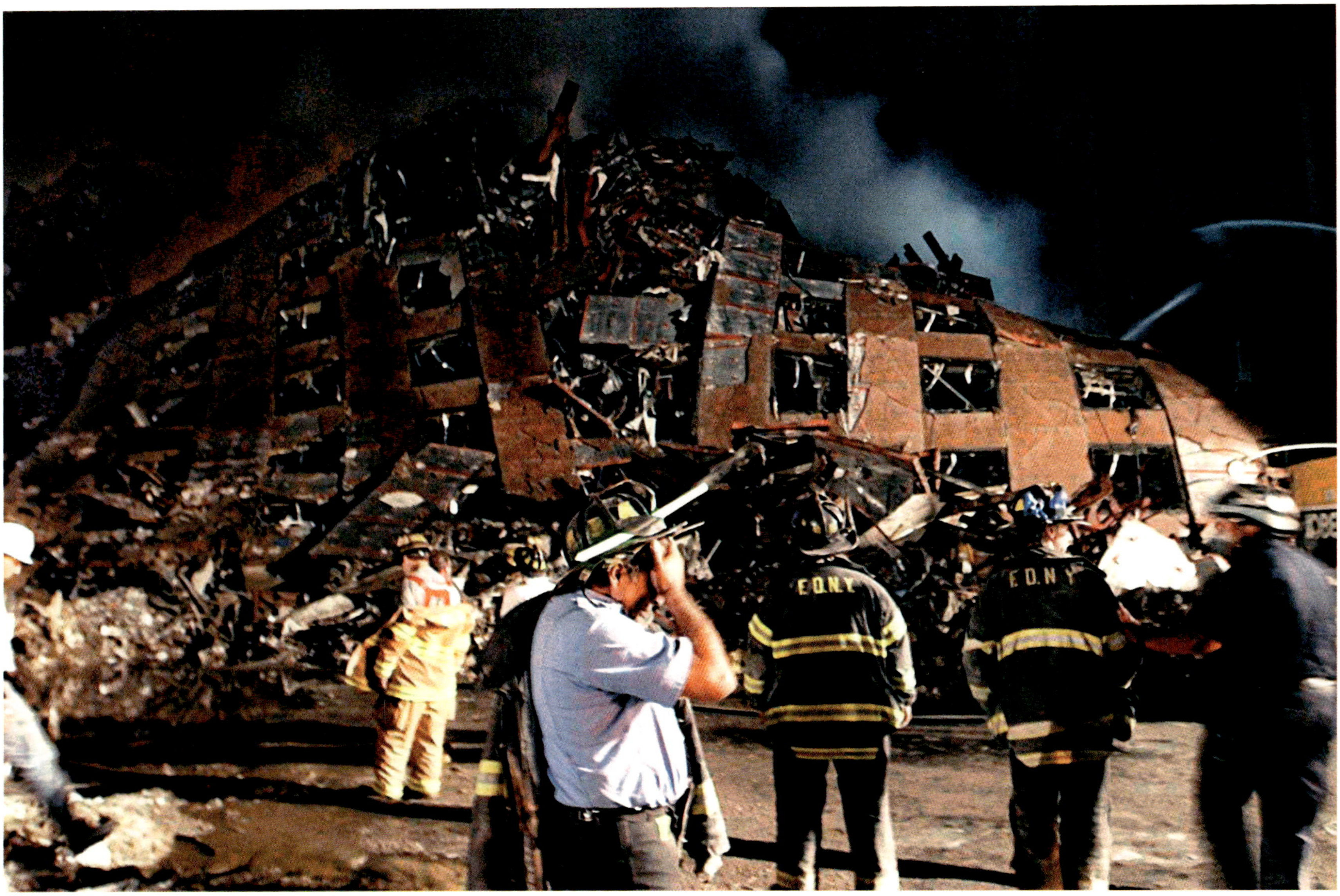

12TH SEPTEMBER 2001 – NEW YORK, USA – FIREFIGHTERS AT THE END OF A SHIFT SIFTING THROUGH THE WRECKAGE OF THE WORLD TRADE CENTER. (MARCOS TOWNSEND)

18TH SEPTEMBER 2001 – NEW YORK, USA – AN AERIAL VIEW OF THE STILL-SMOULDERING WRECKAGE OF THE WORLD TRADE CENTER. (NEW YORK MAYOR'S OFFICE)

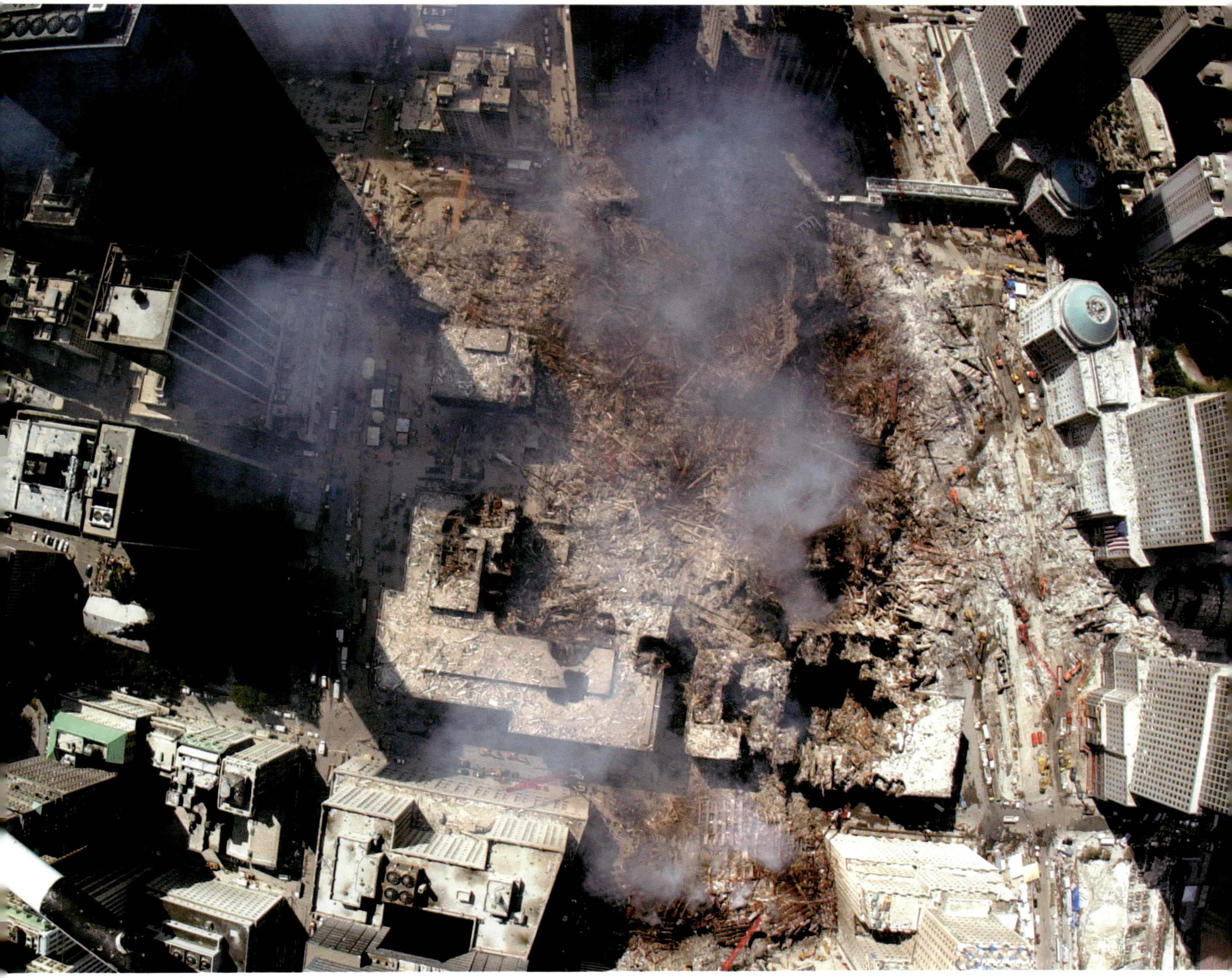

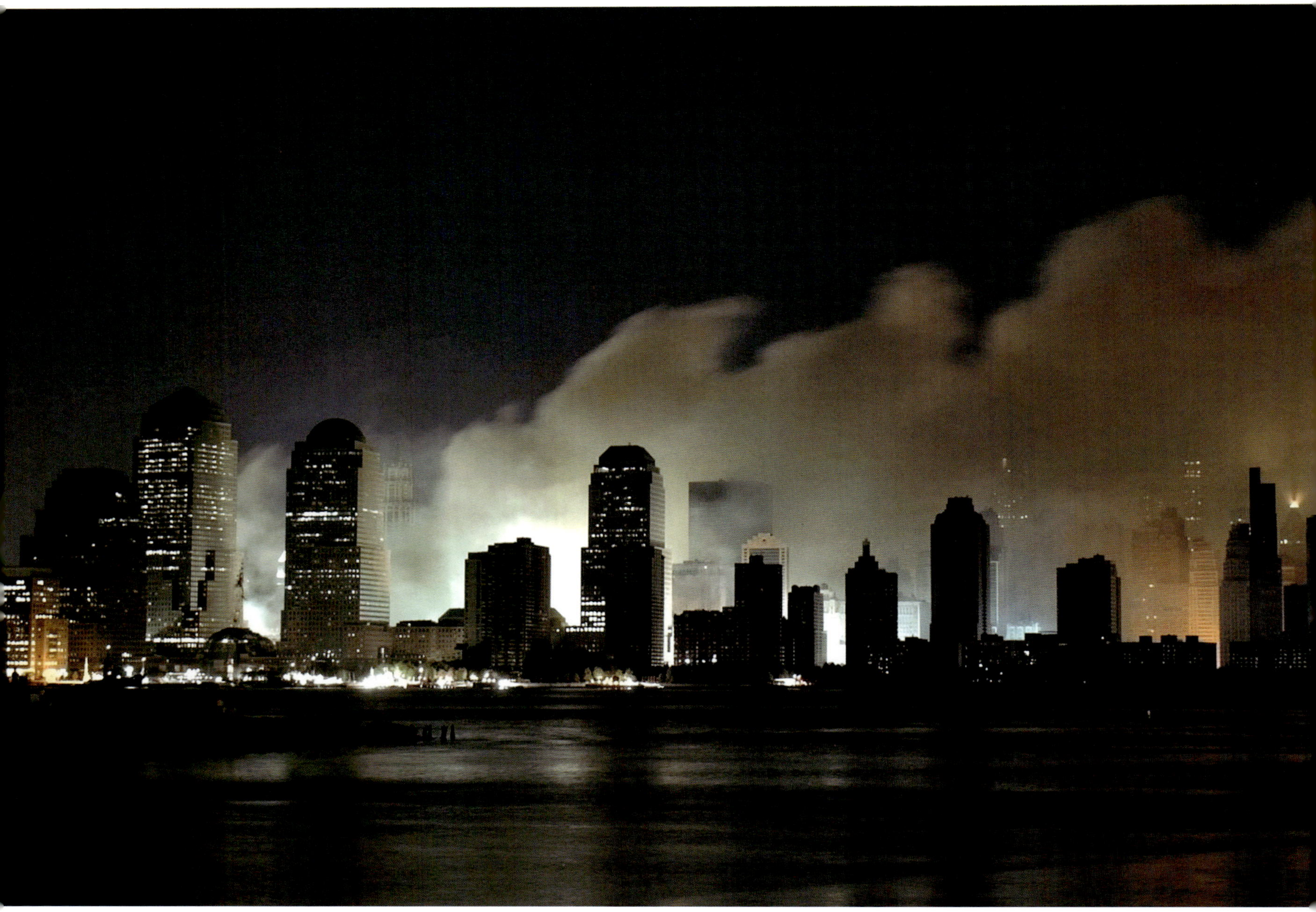

12TH SEPTEMBER 2001
– JERSEY CITY, USA –
A VIEW FROM ACROSS THE RIVER SHOWS SMOKE AND ASH BILLOWING ACROSS THE MANHATTAN SKYLINE AFTER THE DEMOLITION OF THE WORLD TRADE CENTER IN THE 11TH SEPTEMBER ATTACK. (TANNEN MAURY)

11TH SEPTEMBER 2001 – WASHINGTON, USA – THE STARS AND STRIPES FLIES AT HALF-MAST OVER THE WHITE HOUSE AS A MARK OF RESPECT FOR THE VICTIMS IN THE TERRORIST ATTACKS ON NEW YORK AND WASHINGTON. (TIM SLOAN)

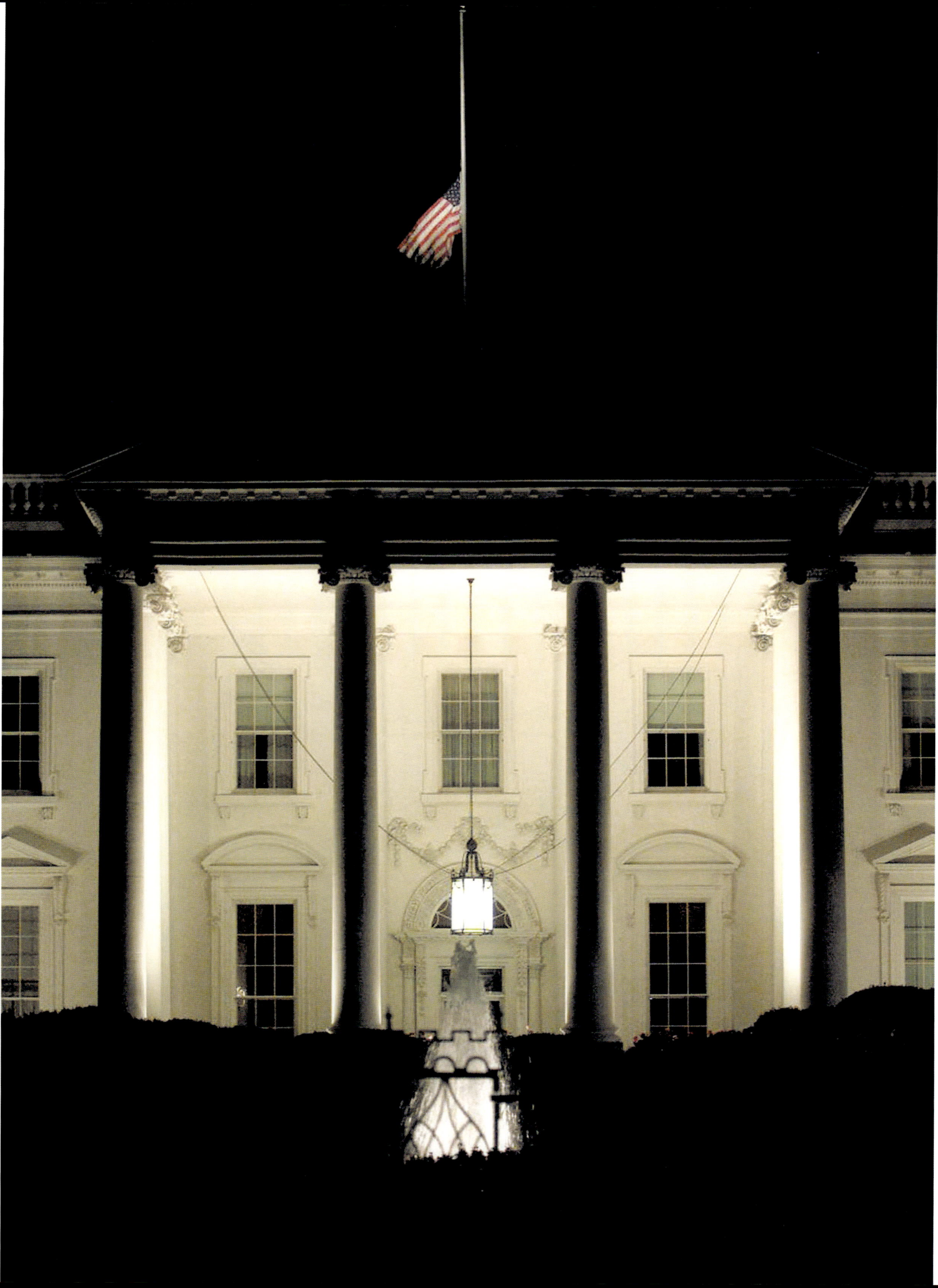

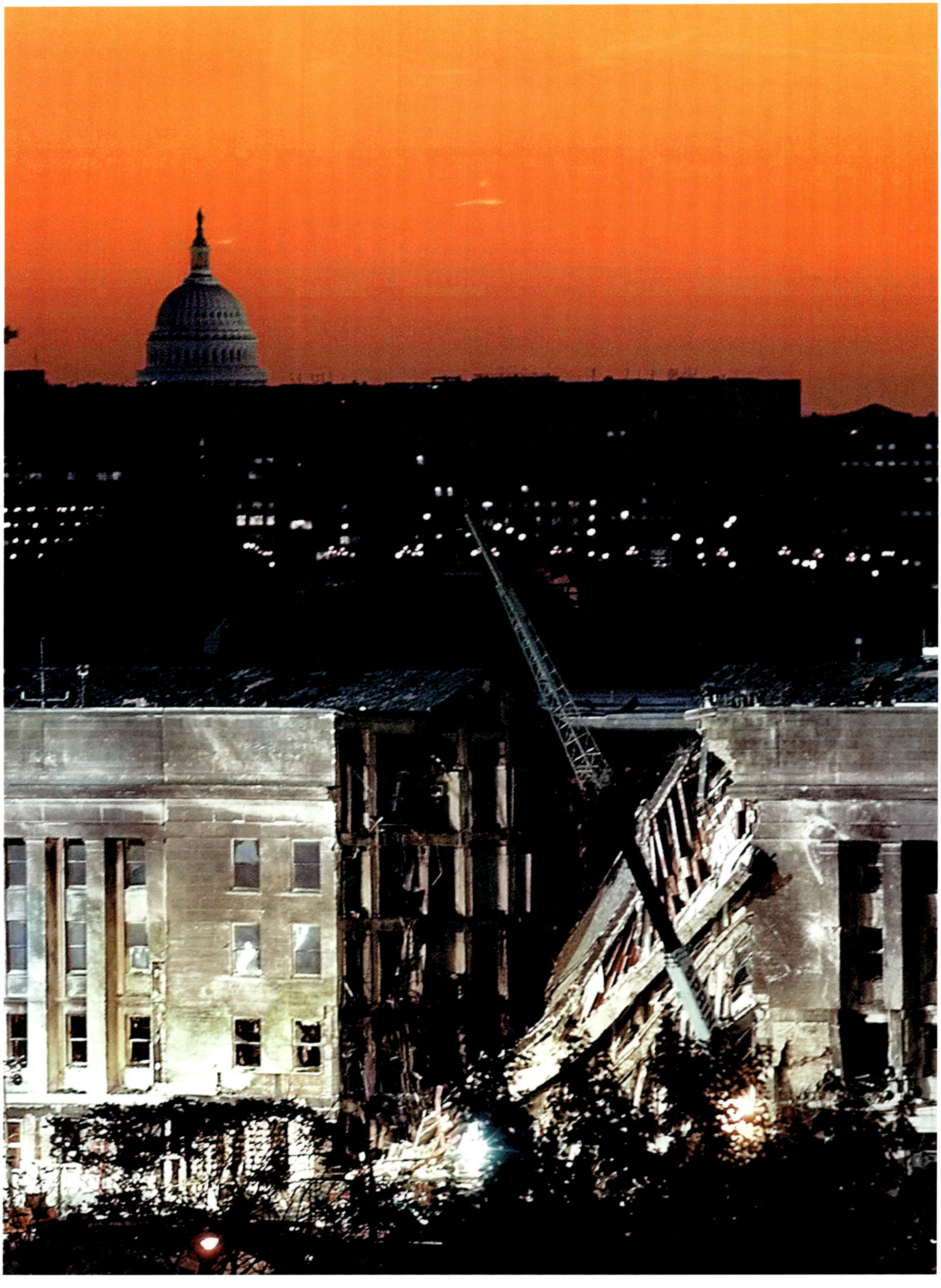

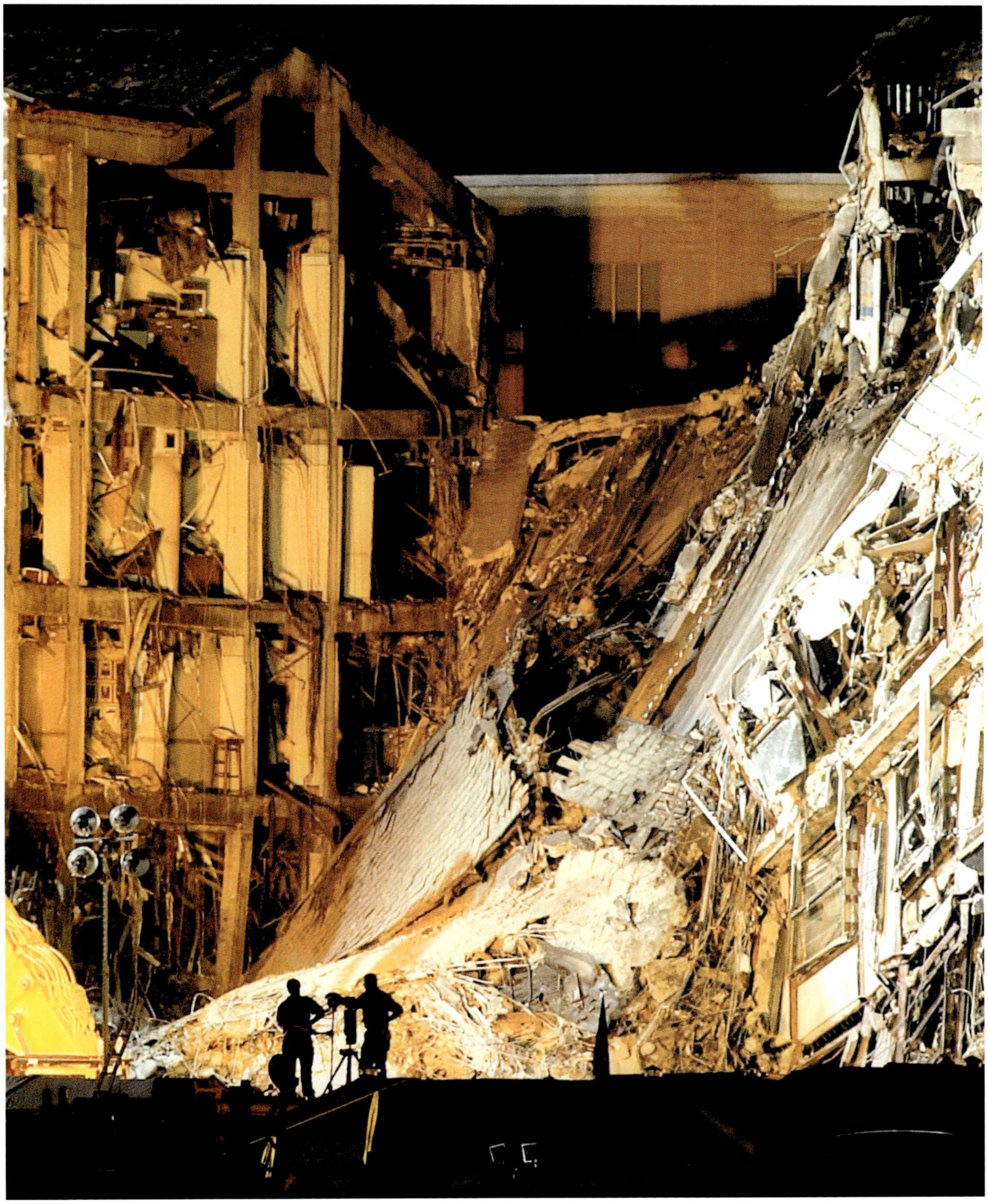

15TH SEPTEMBER 2001 – WASHINGTON, USA – A VIEW OF THE DAMAGE AT THE PENTAGON IN THE WAKE OF THE 11TH SEPTEMBER TERRORIST ATTACK. (SHAWN THEW)

13TH SEPTEMBER 2001 – WASHINGTON, USA – THE SUN RISES OVER WASHINGTON AND THE DAMAGED AREA OF THE PENTAGON AFTER THE 11TH SEPTEMBER TERRORIST ATTACK. (LUKE FRAZZA)

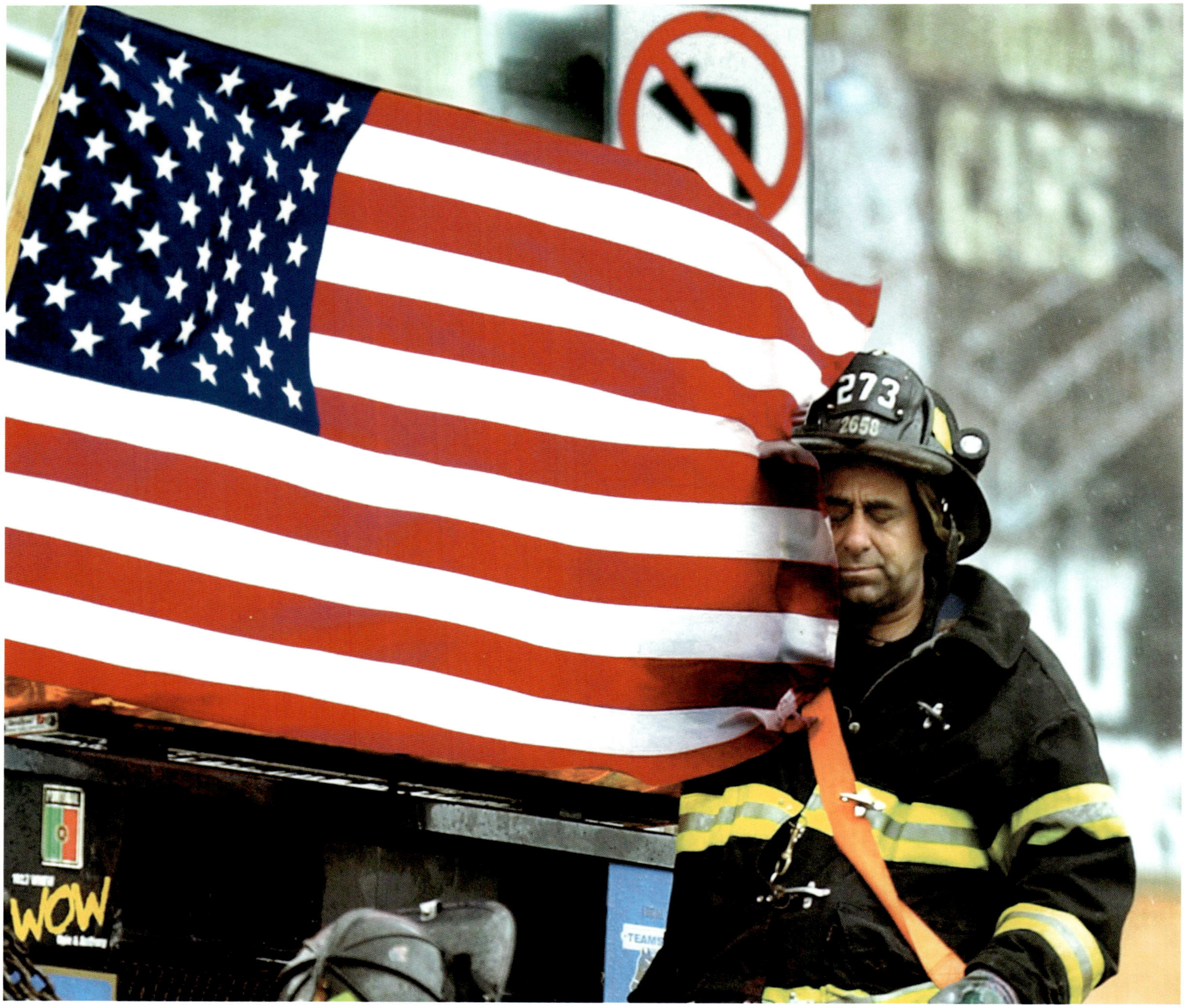

14TH SEPTEMBER 2001 – NEW YORK, USA – A FIREMAN LEANS AGAINST THE STARS AND STRIPES WHILE TAKING A BREAK FROM SEARCHING THE WRECKAGE OF THE WORLD TRADE CENTER FOR SURVIVORS. (TANNEN MAURY)

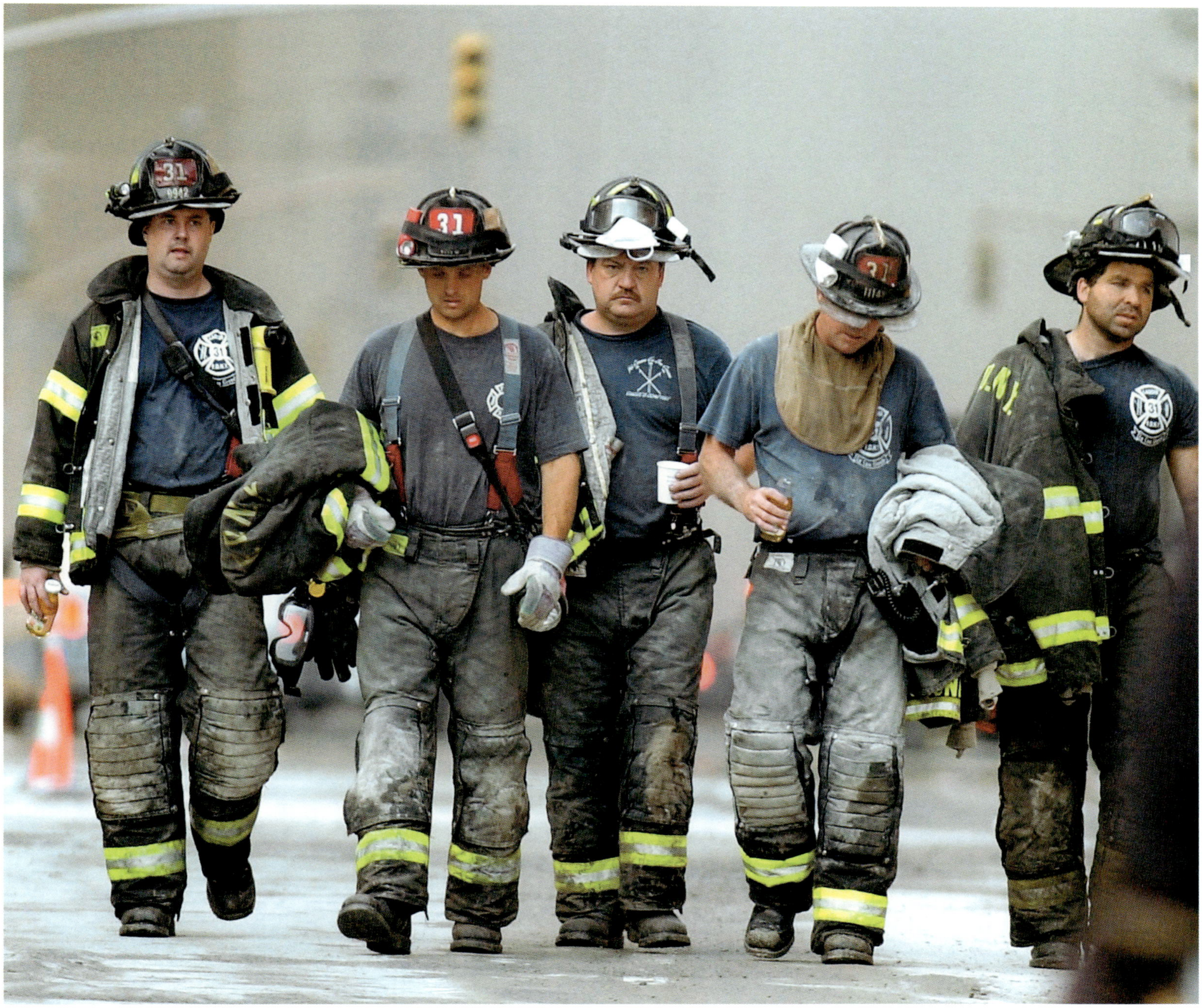

13TH SEPTEMBER 2001 – NEW YORK, USA – WEARY FIREMEN LEAVE THE SITE OF THE WORLD TRADE CENTER AT THE END OF THEIR SHIFT TWO DAYS AFTER THE TWIN TOWERS WERE DESTROYED. (ROBERTO SCHMIDT)

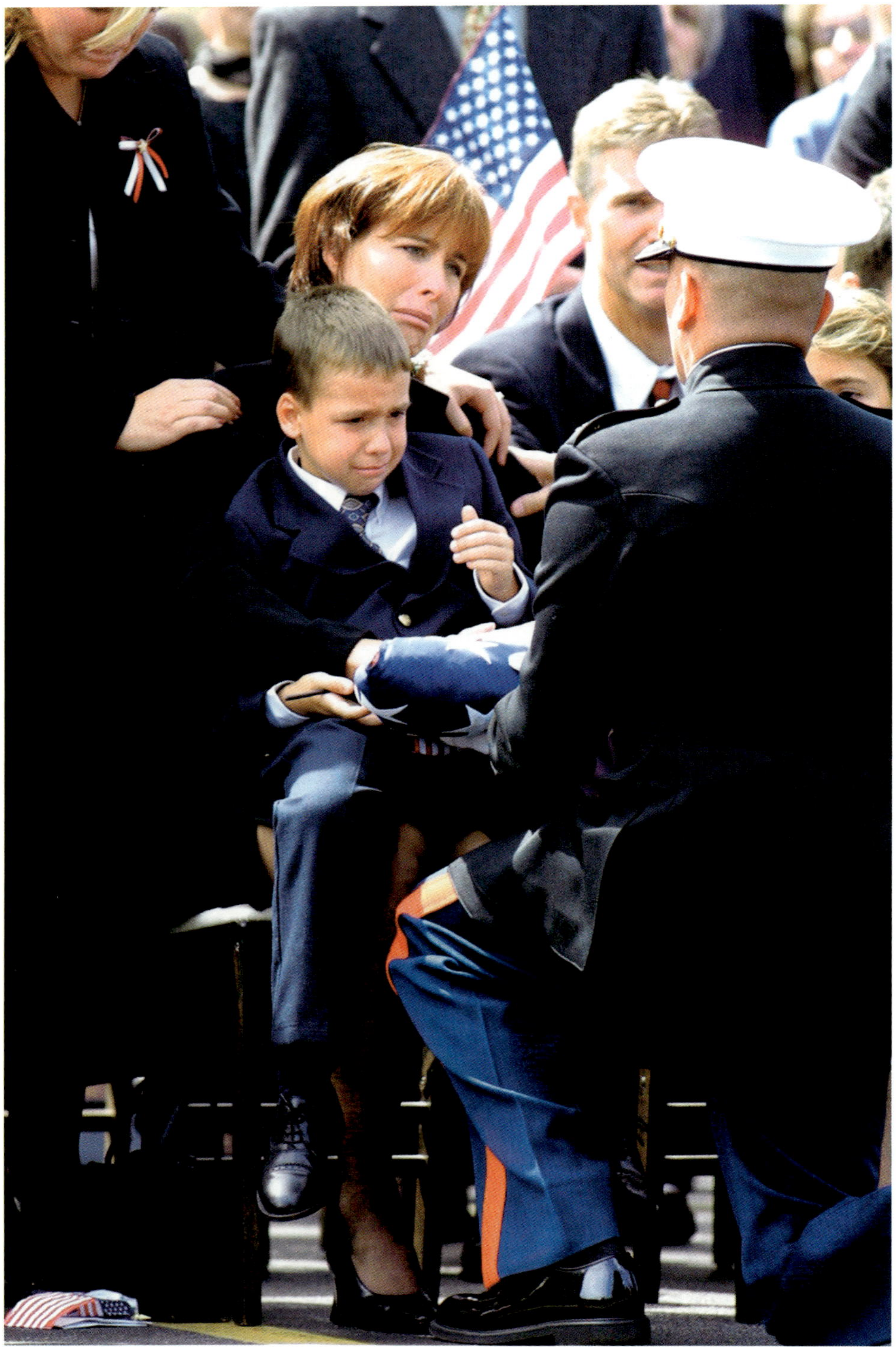

17TH SEPTEMBER 2001 – MEDIA, USA – MIRIAM HORROCKS, THE WIDOW OF UNITED AIRLINES CO-PILOT MICHAEL HORROCKS, WITH THEIR SIX-YEAR-OLD SON MICHAEL, RECEIVE A US FLAG FROM A MARINE IN COMMEMORATION OF HER LATE HUSBAND'S DEATH WHEN THE PLANE HE WAS FLYING PLOUGHED INTO THE SOUTH TOWER OF THE WORLD TRADE CENTER. (TOM MIHALEK)

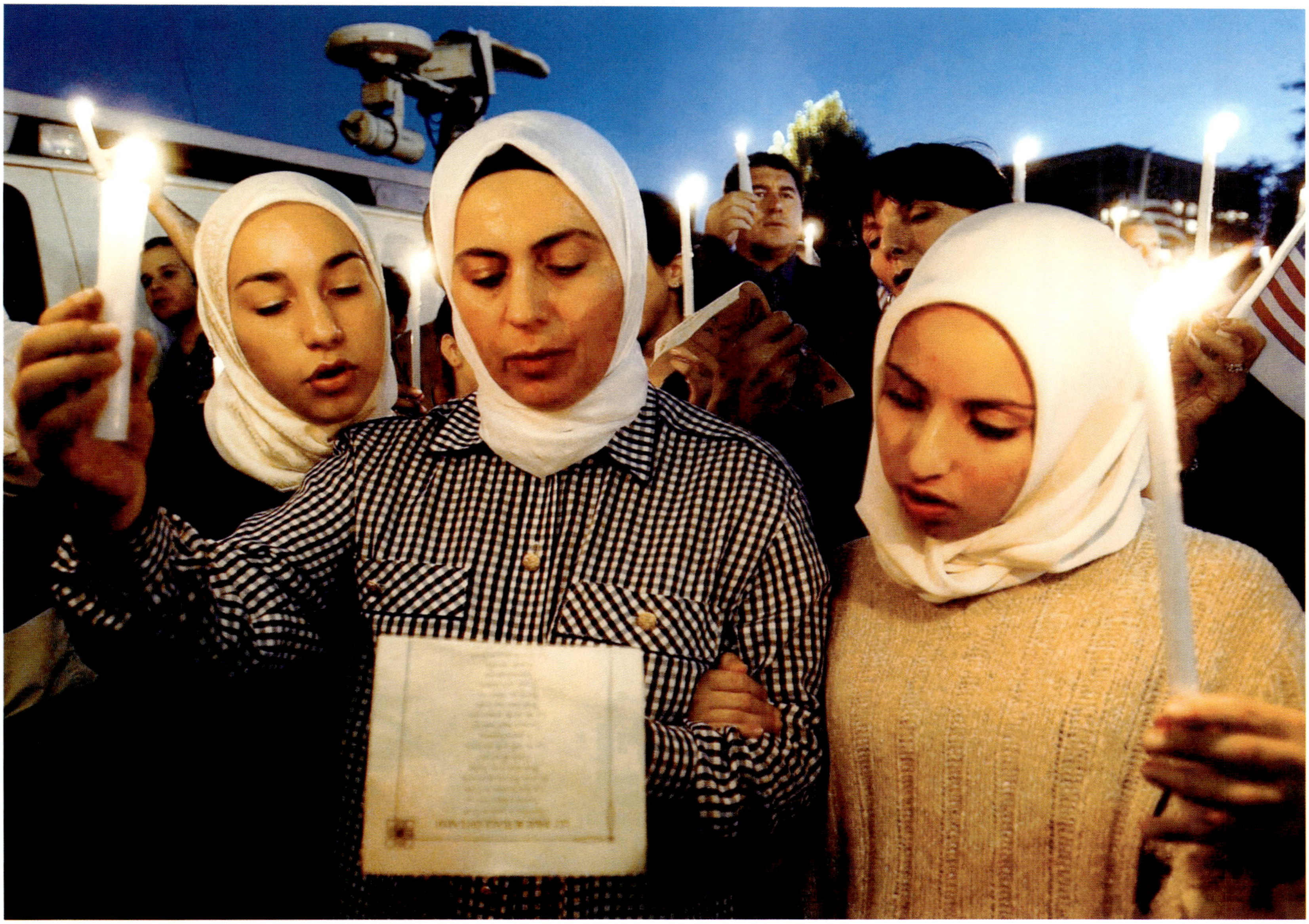

13TH SEPTEMBER 2001
– PASADENA, USA –
MUSLIM WOMEN SINGING
"GOD BLESS AMERICA" AT
AN INTER-DENOMINATIONAL
MEMORIAL SERVICE FOR
THE VICTIMS IN THE NEW YORK
AND WASHINGTON TERRORIST
ATTACKS. (LUCY NICHOLSON)

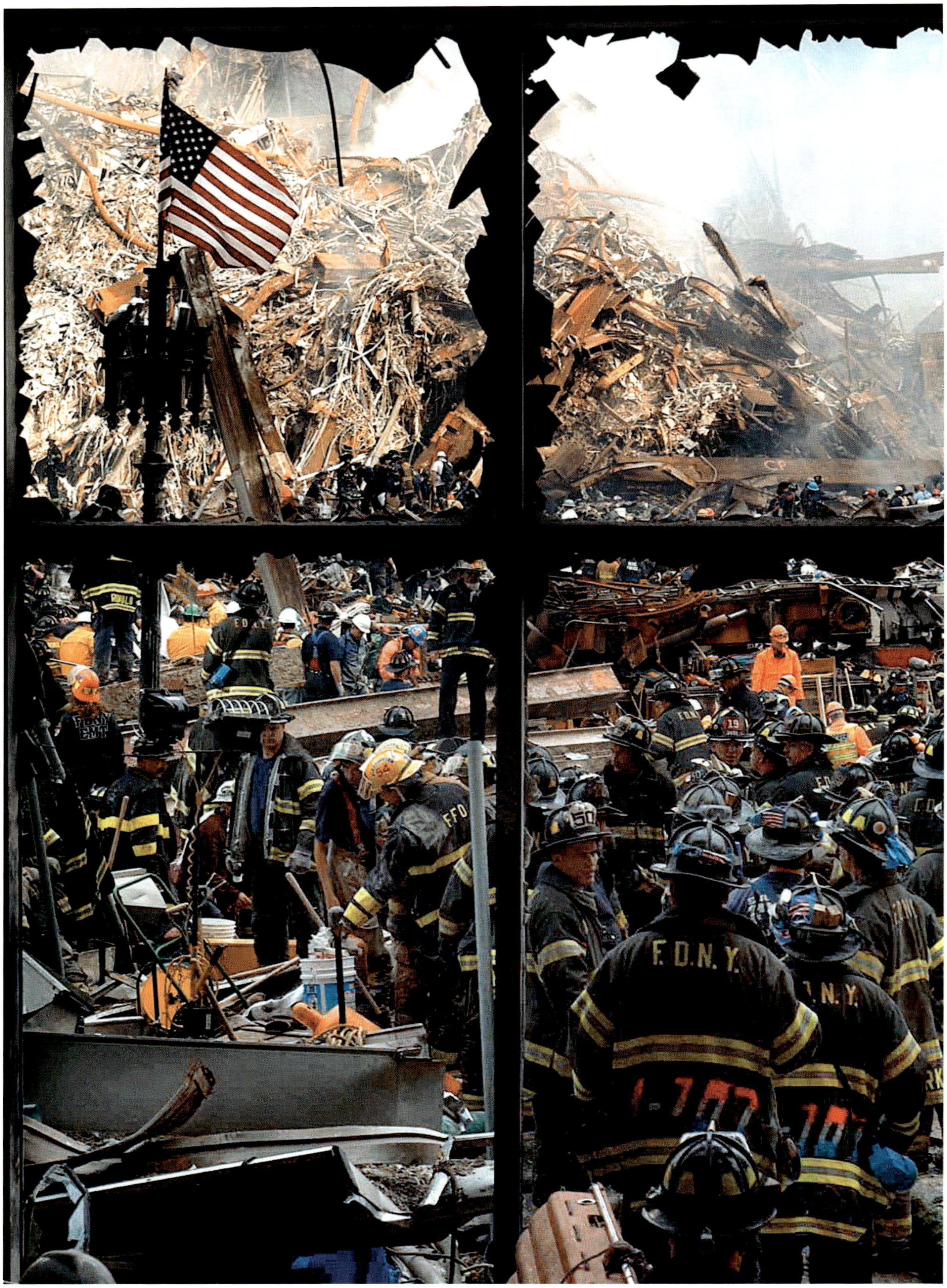
F.D.N.Y.

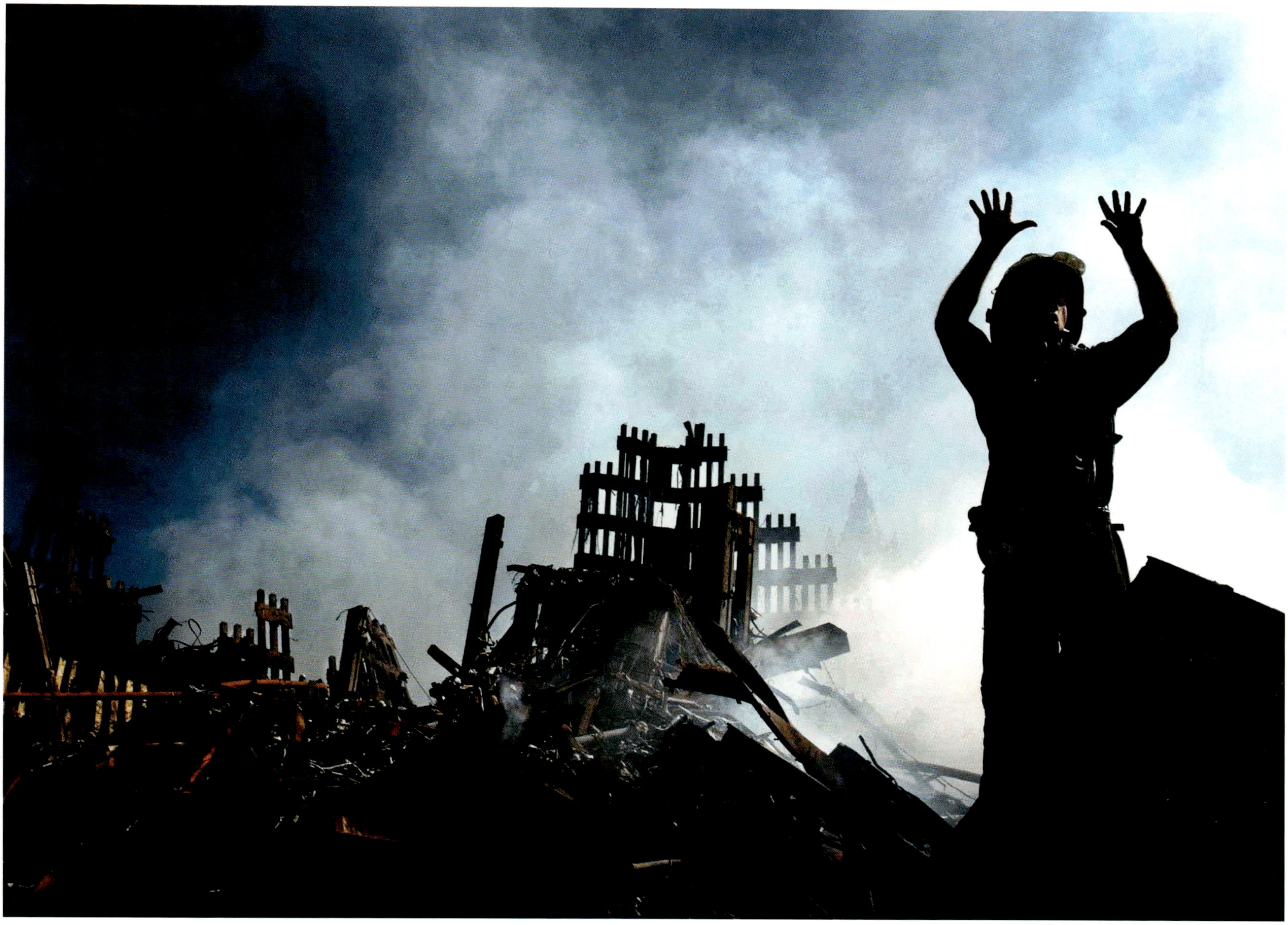

15TH SEPTEMBER 2001 – NEW YORK, USA – A NEW YORK FIREMAN CALLS FOR TEN REINFORCEMENTS TO JOIN HIM IN THE SEARCH TROUGH THE RUBBLE OF THE WORLD TRADE CENTER. (PRESTON KERES/US NAVY)

14TH SEPTEMBER 2001 – NEW YORK, USA – A VIEW OF THE WRECKAGE OF WHAT WAS ONCE THE WORLD TRADE CENTER. (PRESTON KERES/US NAVY)

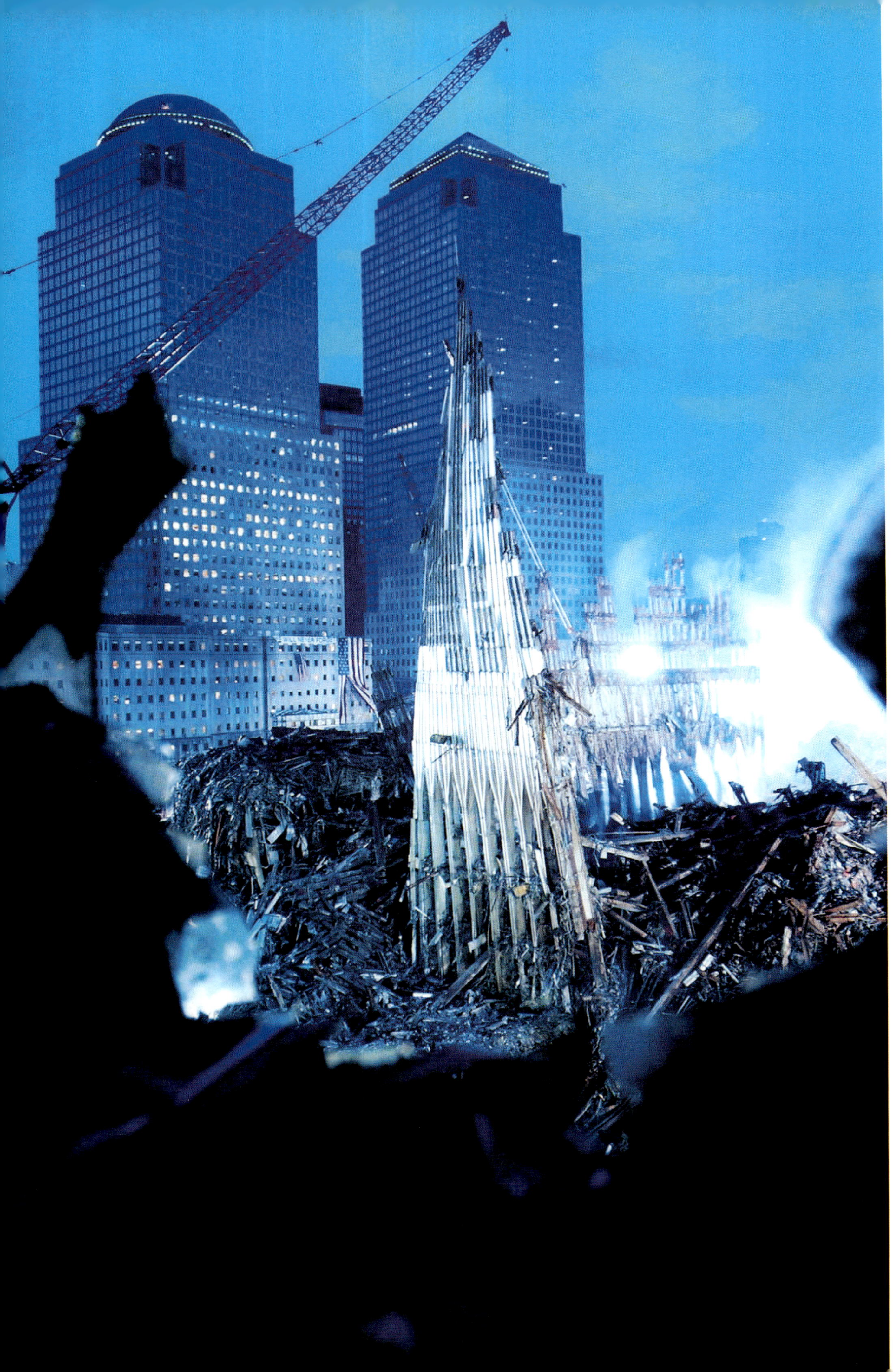

25TH SEPTEMBER 2001
– NEW YORK, USA –
AN EARLY MORNING VIEW OF THE REMAINS OF THE WORLD TRADE CENTER. (ÉRIC FEFERBERG)

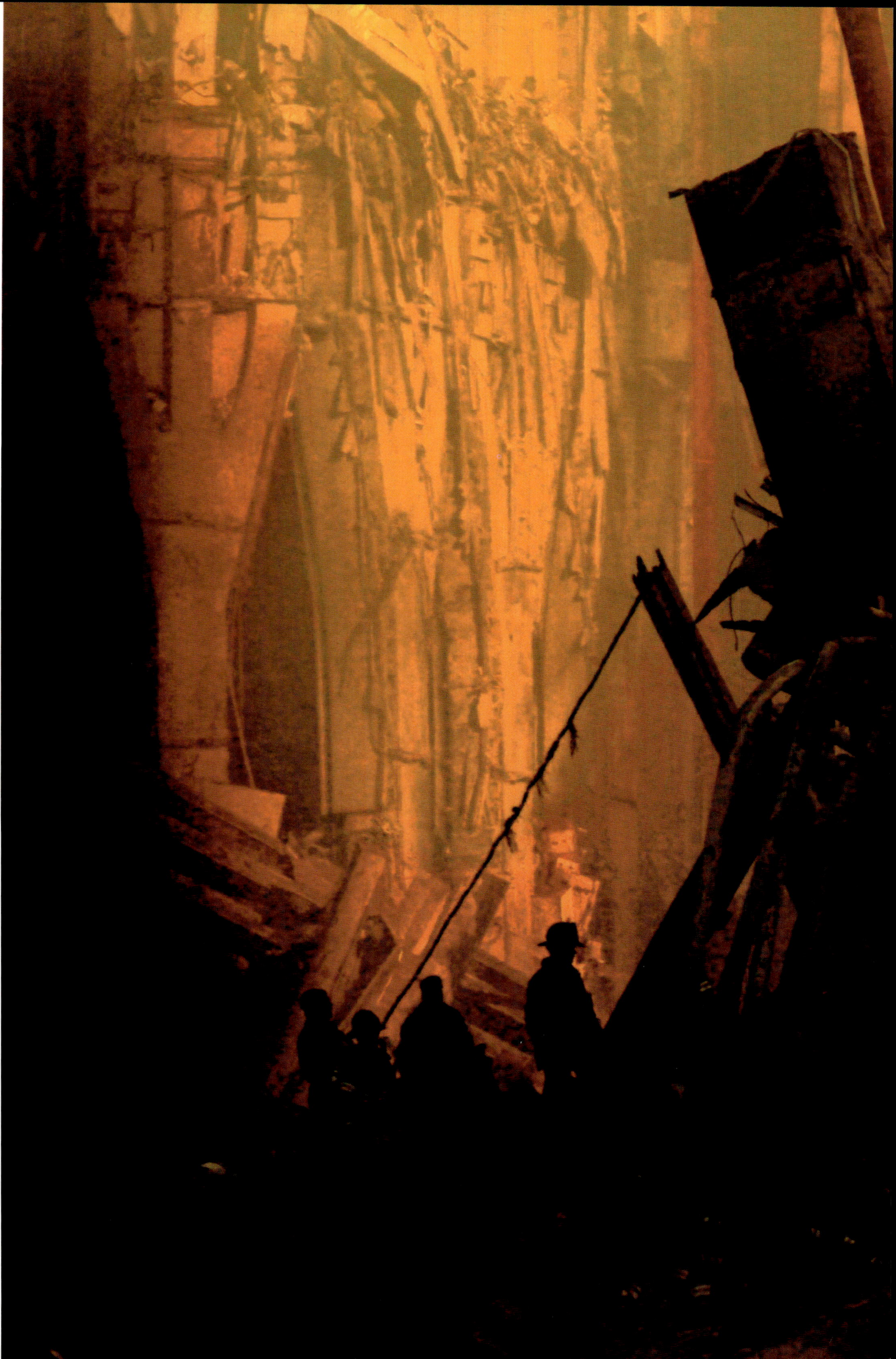

14TH SEPTEMBER 2001 – NEW YORK, USA – RESCUE WORKERS CONTINUE THEIR SEARCH THROUGH THE WRECKAGE OF THE WORLD TRADE CENTER. (JIM WATSON/US NAVY)

13TH SEPTEMBER 2001 – CHICAGO, USA – A SOLITARY TRADER SITS AT HIS DESK ON THE FLOOR OF THE DOW JONES INDUSTRIAL AVERAGE STOCK INDEX FUTURES WHILE OPPOSITE TRADERS RESUME BUSINESS ON THE CHICAGO FUTURES EXCHANGES AFTER THE SEPTEMBER 11TH TERRORIST ATTACKS ON NEW YORK AND WASHINGTON. (SCOTT OLSON)

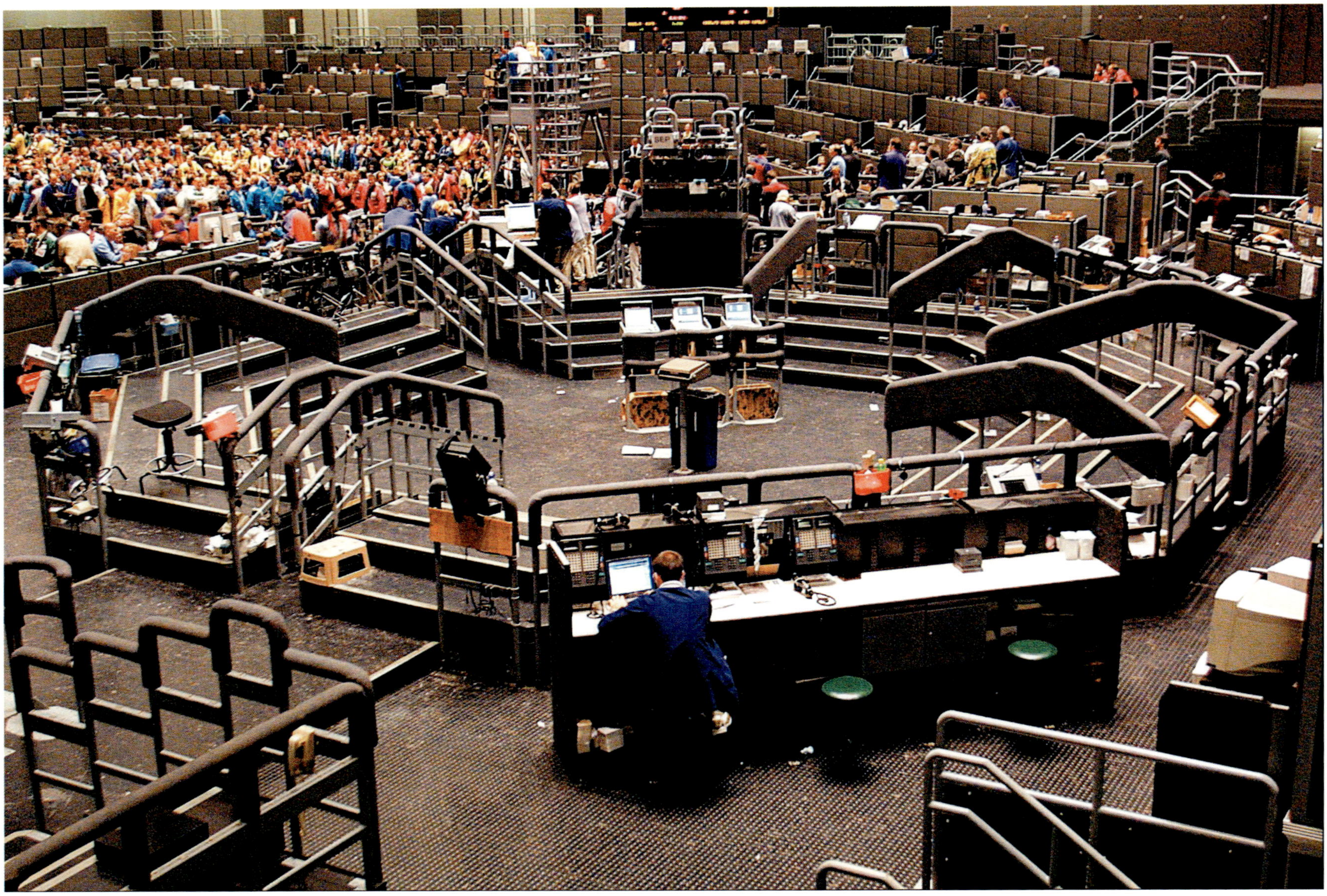

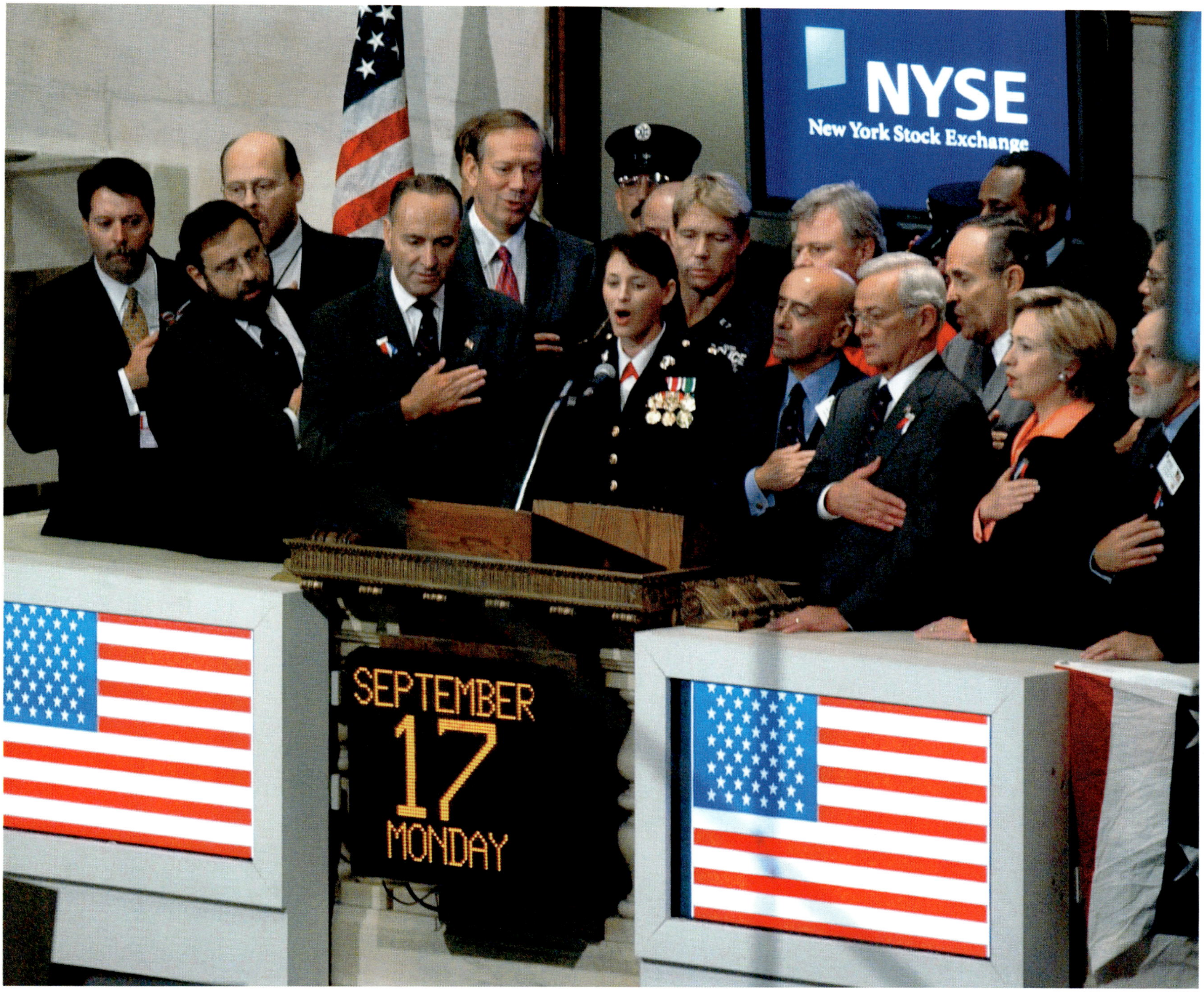

17TH SEPTEMBER 2001 – NEW YORK, USA – MAJOR ROSE-ANNE SGRIGNOLI LEADS A CHORUS OF GOD BLESS AMERICA BEFORE THE START OF TRADING AT THE NEW YORK STOCK EXCHANGE FOLLOWING ITS CLOSURE IN THE WAKE OF THE SEPTEMBER 11 TERRORIST ATTACKS. SHE IS ACCOMPANIED BY SENATOR HILLARY RODHAM CLINTON, TREASURY SECRETARY PAUL O'NEILL, NYSE CHAIRMAN RICHARD GRASSO AND SENATOR CHUCK SCHUMER. (STAN HONDA)

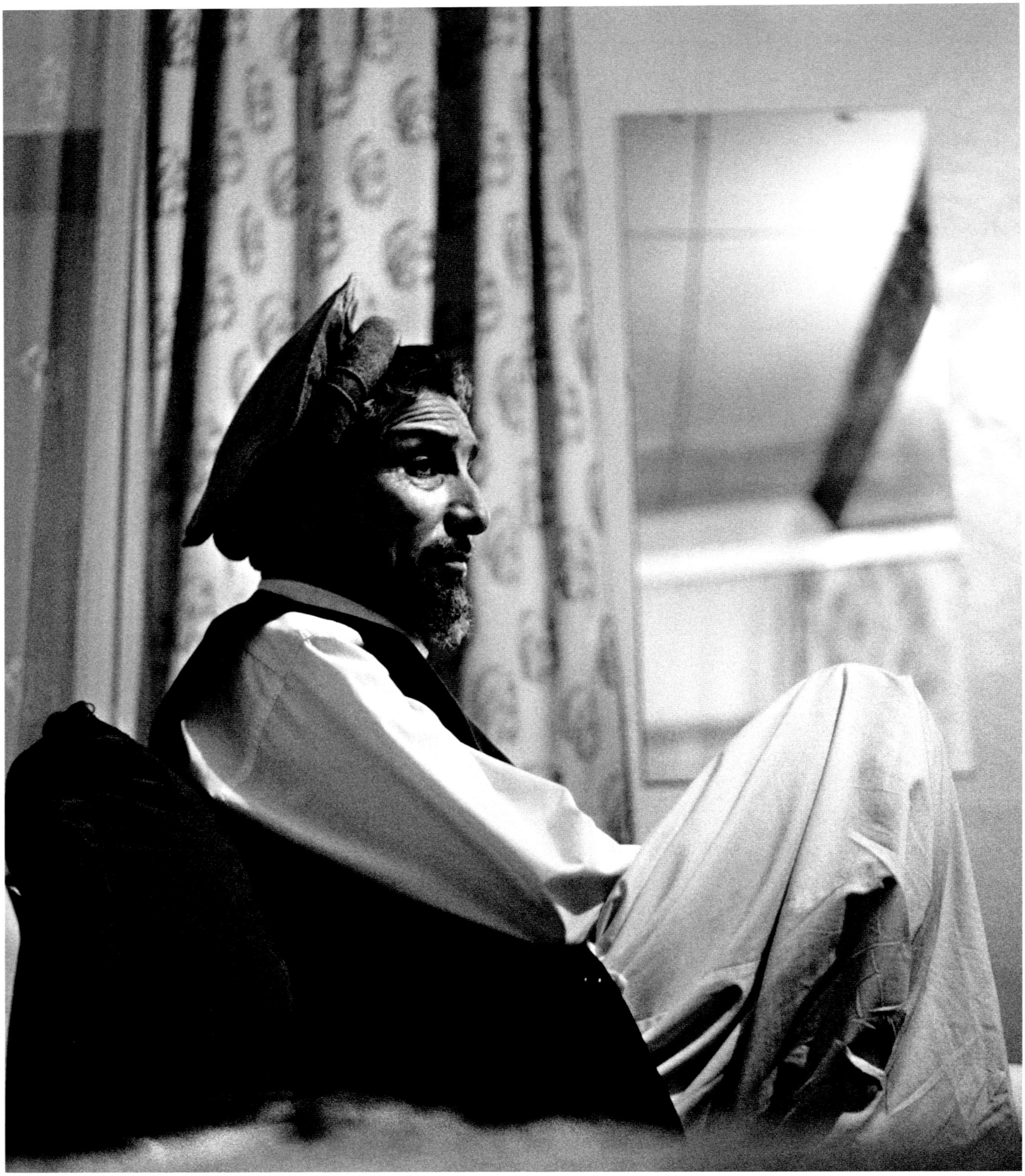

28TH JUNE 2001 – KHWAJA BAHAUDDIN, AFGHANISTAN – AFGHAN OPPOSITION MILITIA LEADER AHMAD SHAH MASOOD IN CONVERSATION WITH AN AFP JOURNALIST THREE MONTHS BEFORE HIS MURDER. (JOËL ROBINE)

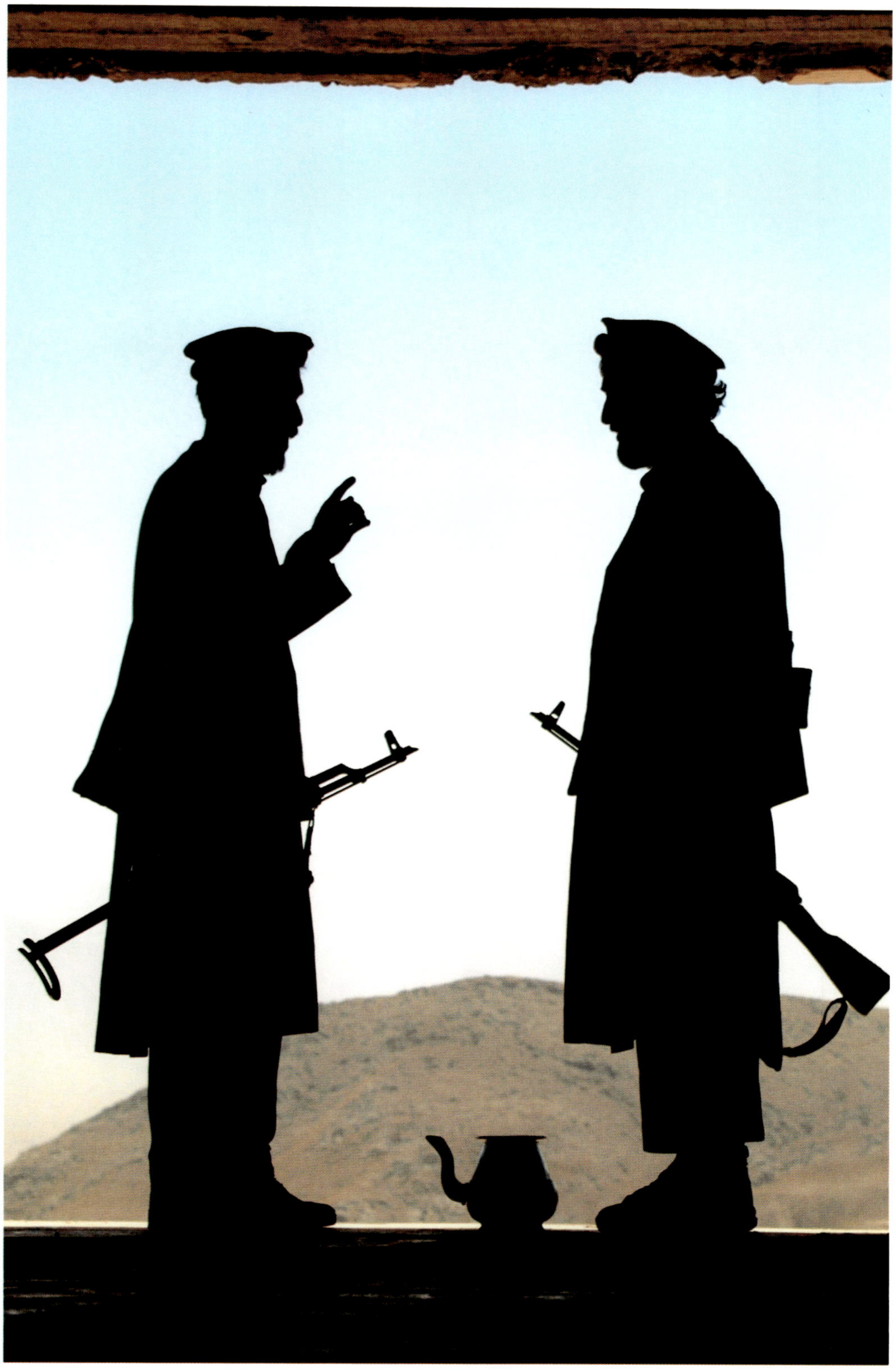

27TH SEPTEMBER 2001 – BAGRAM, PAKISTAN – NORTHERN ALLIANCE FIGHTERS ARE SILHOUETTED AGAINST THE HILLSIDE NORTH OF KABUL. (ALEXANDER NEMENOV)

1ST JANUARY 1989 – JALALABAD, AFGHANISTAN – AN ARCHIVE PHOTO OF OSAMA BIN LADEN, THE CHIEF SUSPECT IN THE SEPTEMBER 11TH ATTACKS IN NEW YORK AND WASHINGTON.

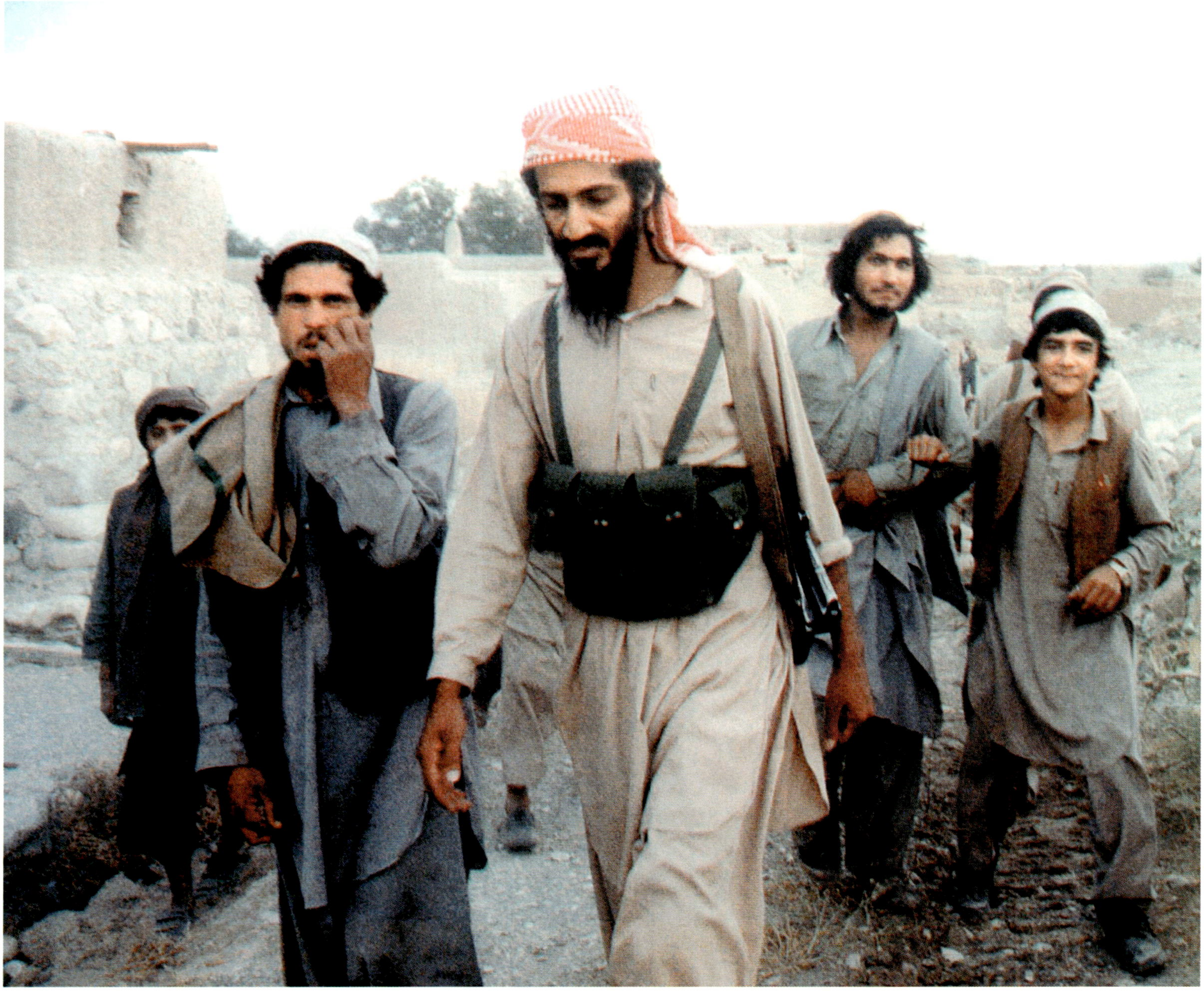

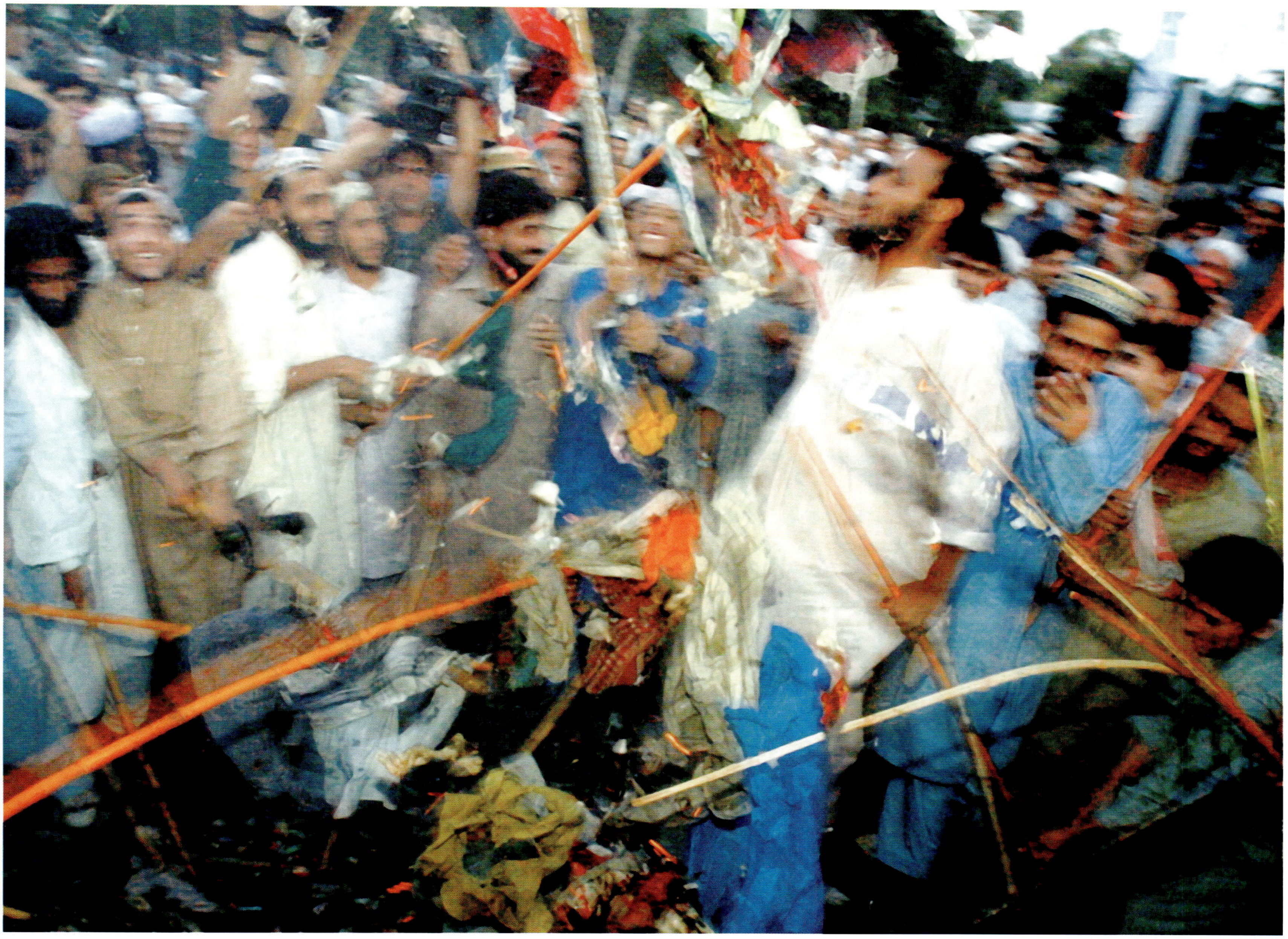

14TH OCTOBER 2001 – ISLAMABAD, PAKISTAN – PRO-TALIBAN PROTESTERS BEAT AND TEAR APART A BURNING EFFIGY OF US PRESIDENT GEORGE W. BUSH DURING AN ANTI-US RALLY. (STEPHEN SHAVER)

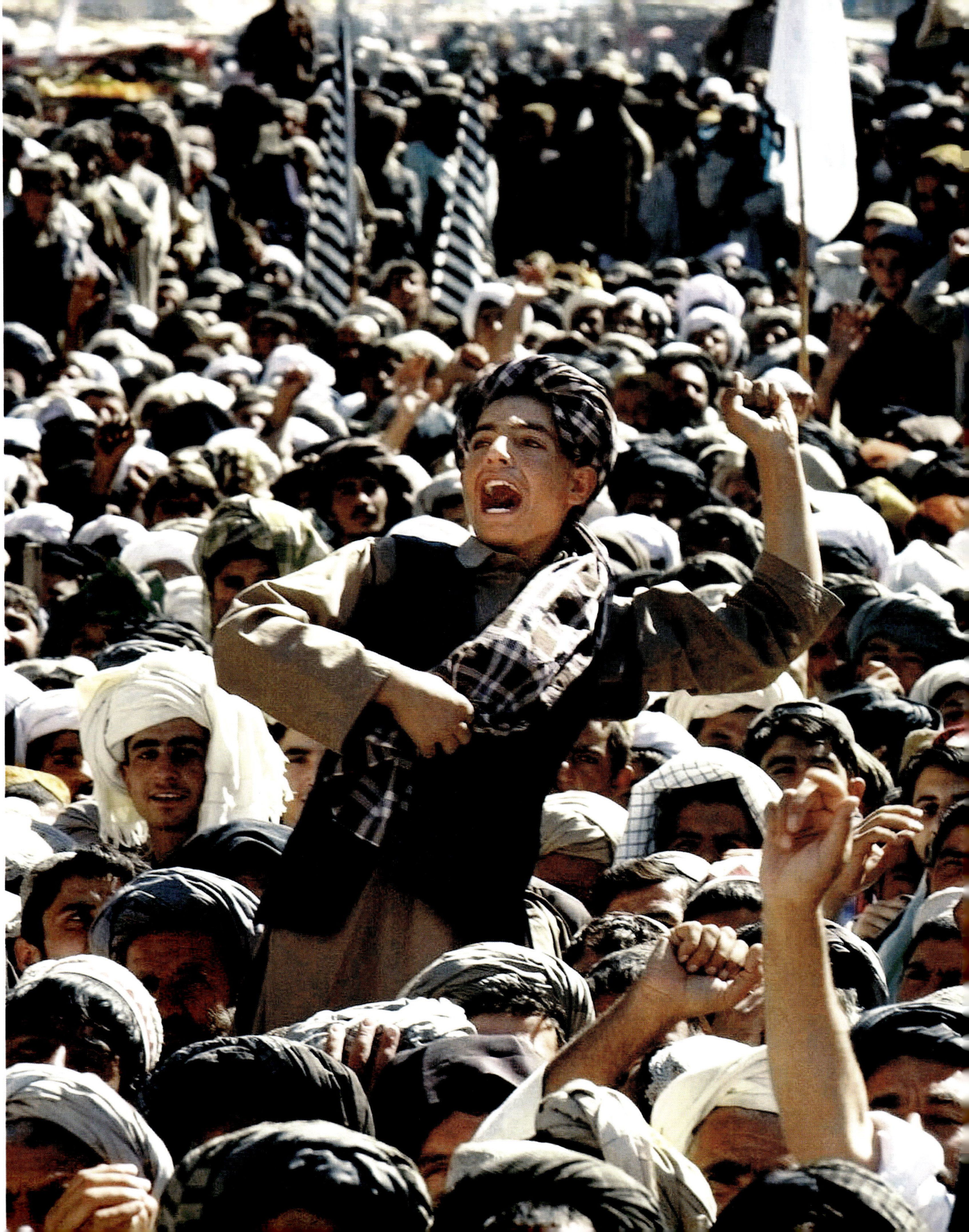

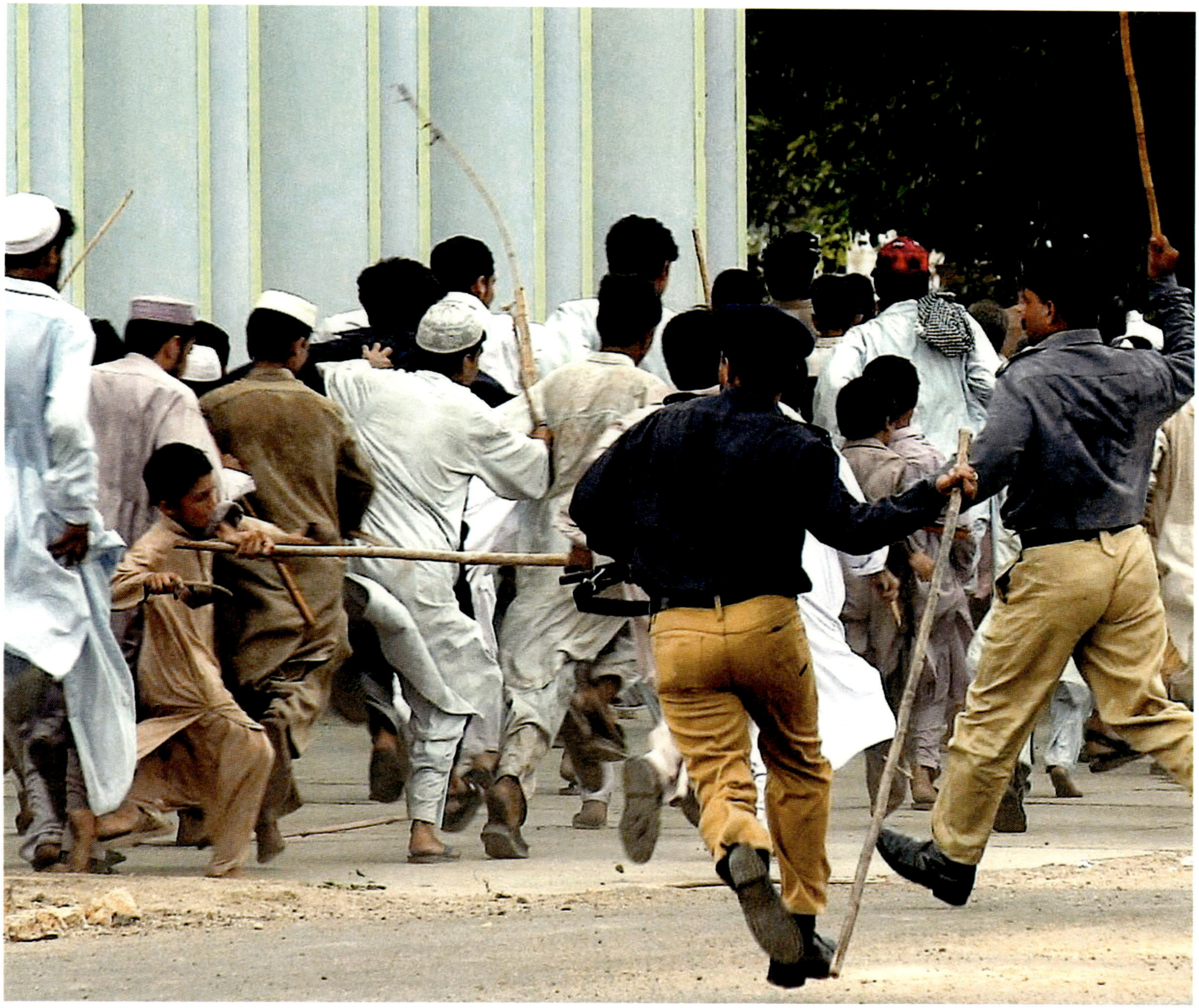

8TH OCTOBER 2001 – CHAMAN, PAKISTAN – PAKISTANI DEMONSTRATORS VENT THEIR ANGER AGAINST THE USA STRIKES ON AFGHANISTAN. (SAEED KHAN)

21ST SEPTEMBER 2001 – KARACHI, PAKISTAN – DEMONSTRATORS AND PAKISTANI POLICE CLASH AS MILITANTS STAGE A PROTEST AGAINST IMMINENT US STRIKES AGAINST AFGHANISTAN. (AAMIR QURESHI)

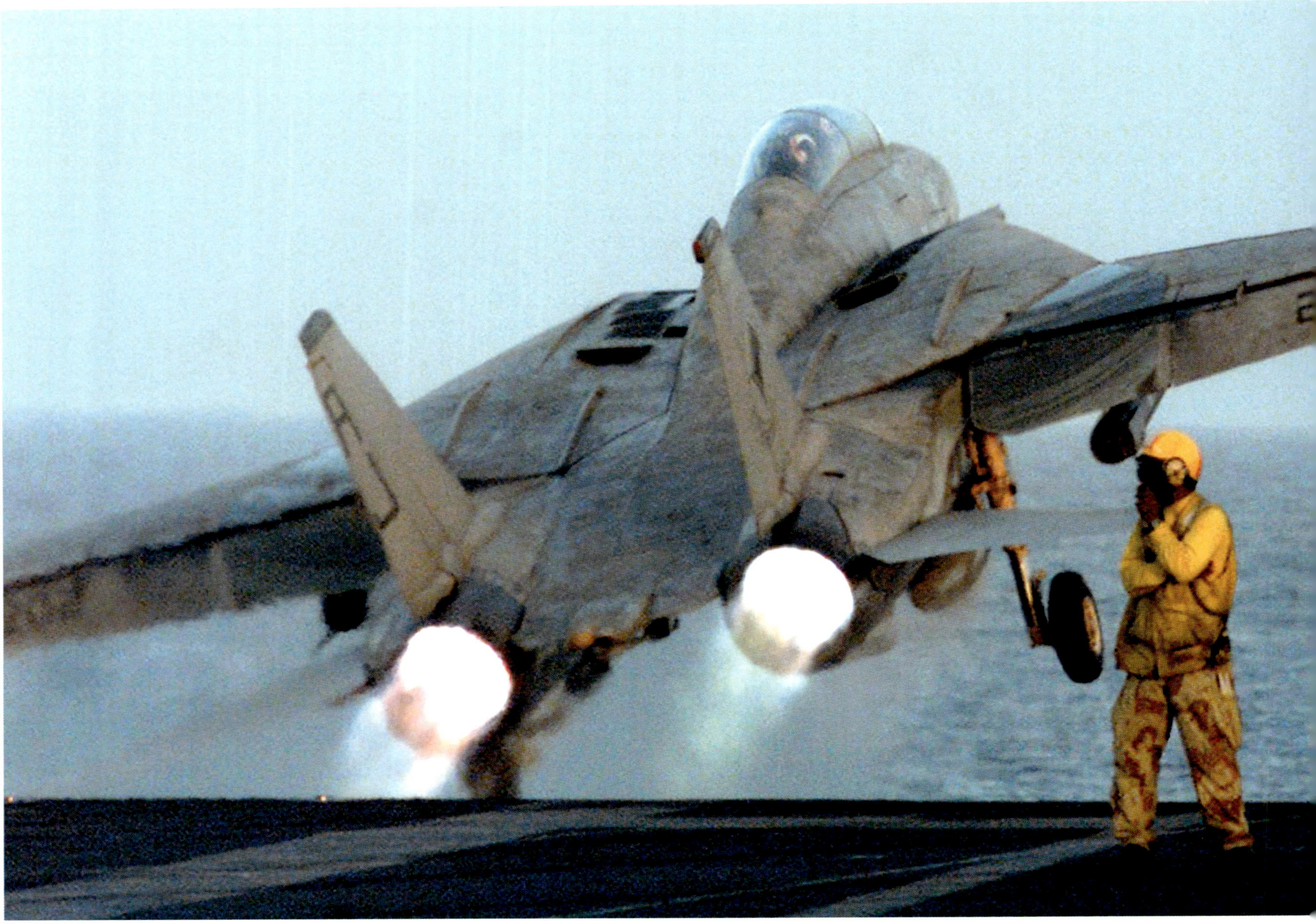

9TH OCTOBER 2001 – ABOARD USS ENTERPRISE – A US F-14 FIGHTER TAKES OFF ON A US-LED RAID AGAINST THE AFGHAN CAPITAL KABUL. (RABIH MOGHRABI)

7TH OCTOBER 2001 – ABOARD USS PHILIPPINE – A TOMAHAWK CRUISE MISSILE IS FIRED IN THE US-LED RETALIATORY ATTACKS AGAINST AFGHANISTAN IN THE WAKE OF THE SEPTEMBER 11TH TERRORIST ATTACKS AGAINST NEW YORK AND WASHINGTON. (BARRY IVERSON/TIME)

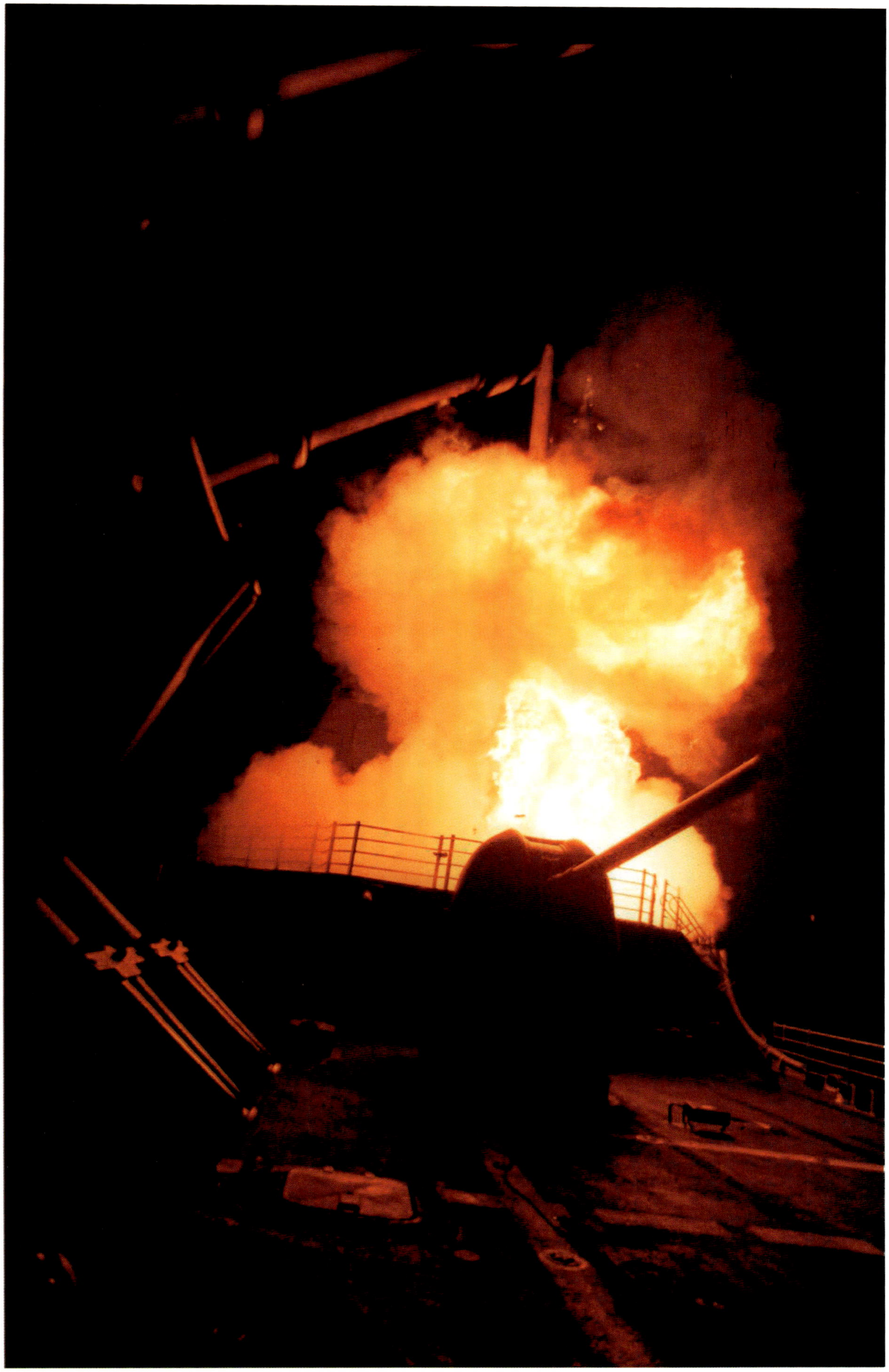

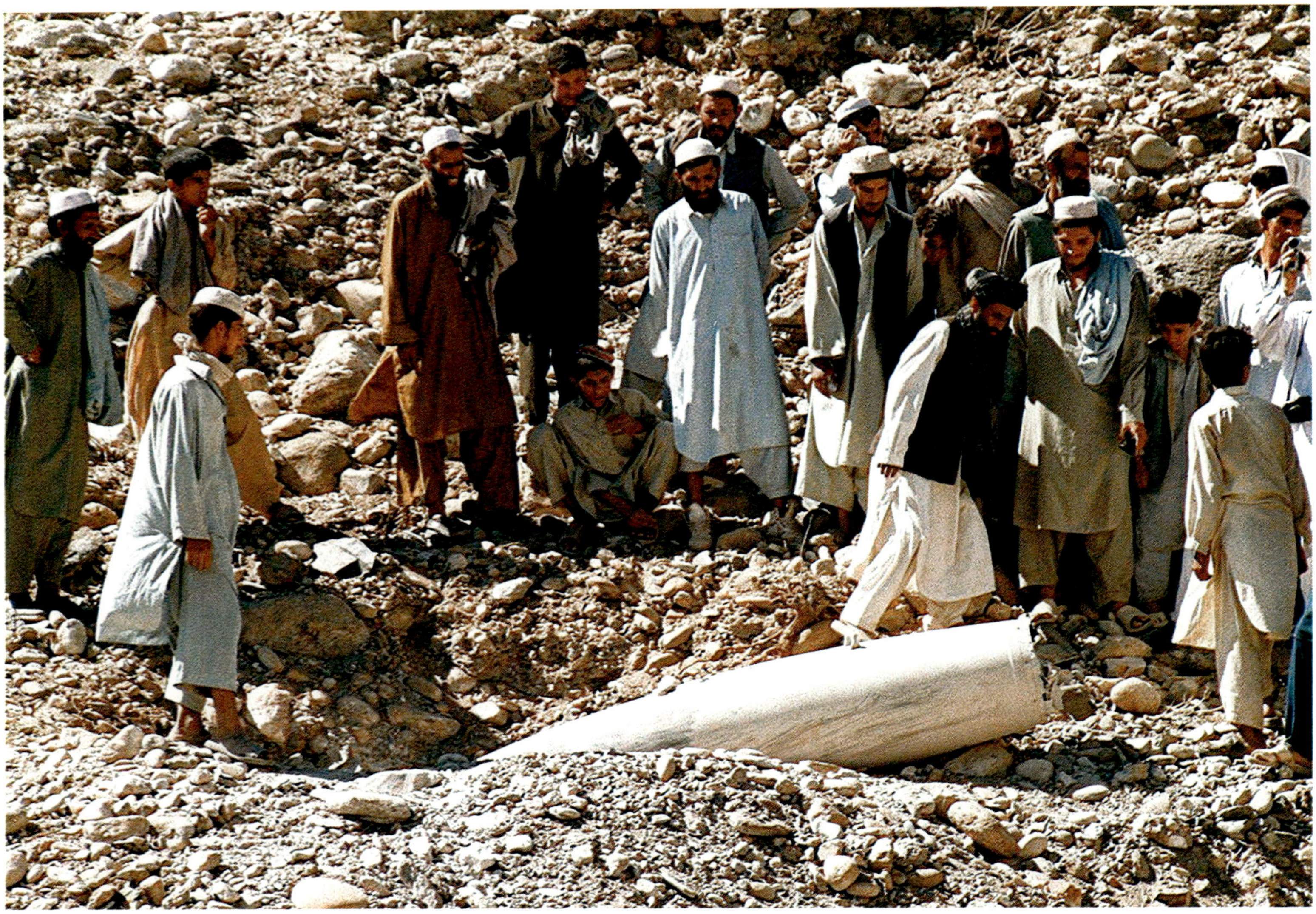

14TH OCTOBER 2001 – KADAM, AFGHANISTAN – AFGHANS GATHER AROUND AN UNEXPLODED MISSILE NEAR THE AFGHAN CITY JALALABAD.

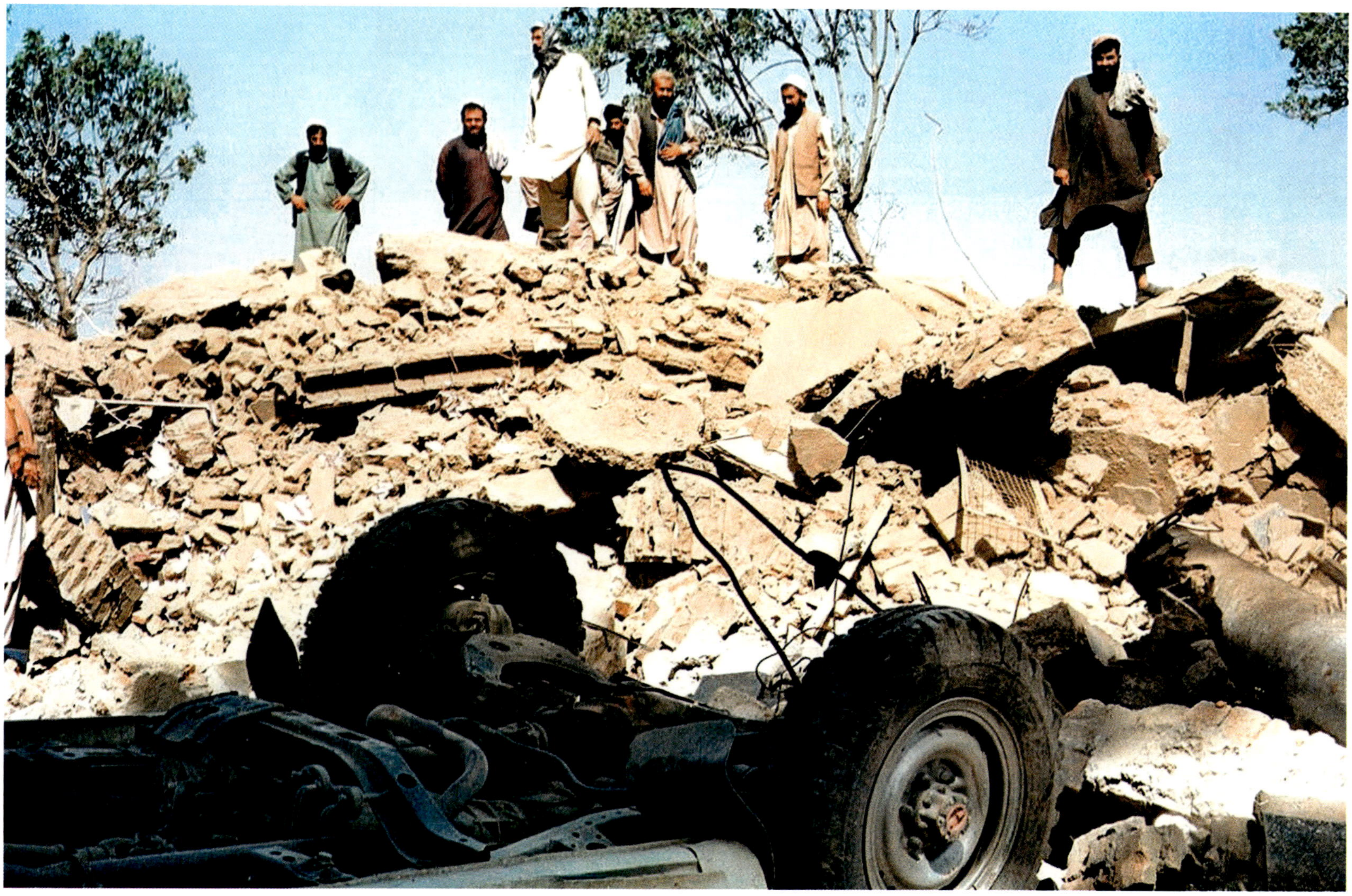

9TH OCTOBER 2001 – KABUL, AFGHANISTAN – AFGHANS INSPECT THE REMAINS OF THE AFGHAN TECHNICAL CONSULTANTS OFFICE, WHICH WAS DESTROYED BY A US BOMB, KILLING FOUR MEMBERS OF STAFF. (SAID MOHAMMAD AZAM)

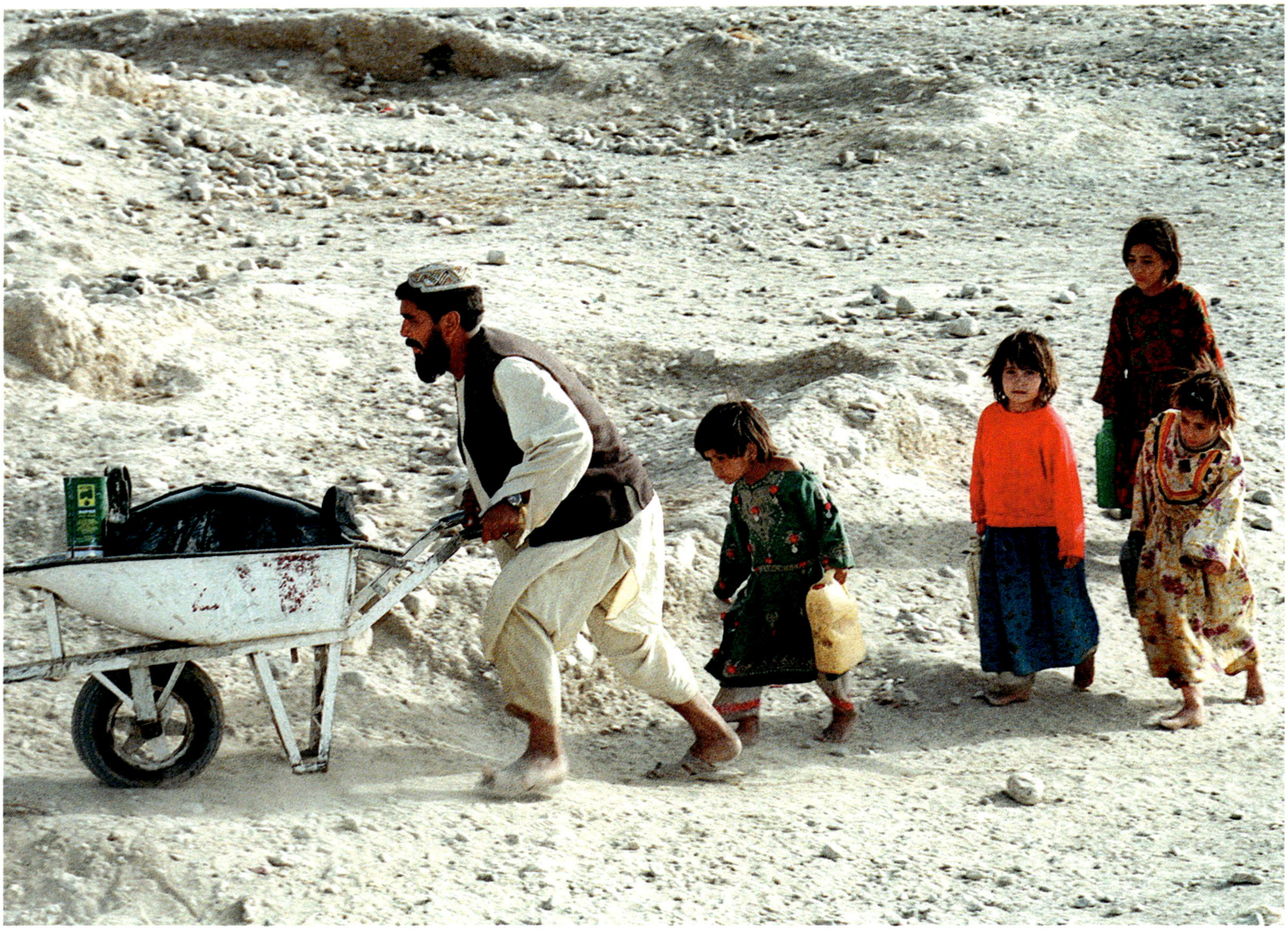

17TH SEPTEMBER 2001
– CHAMAN, PAKISTAN –
AN AFGHAN FAMILY ON THEIR WAY TO A REFUGEE CAMP ON THE PAKISTAN-AFGHANISTAN BORDER. (BANARAS KHAN)

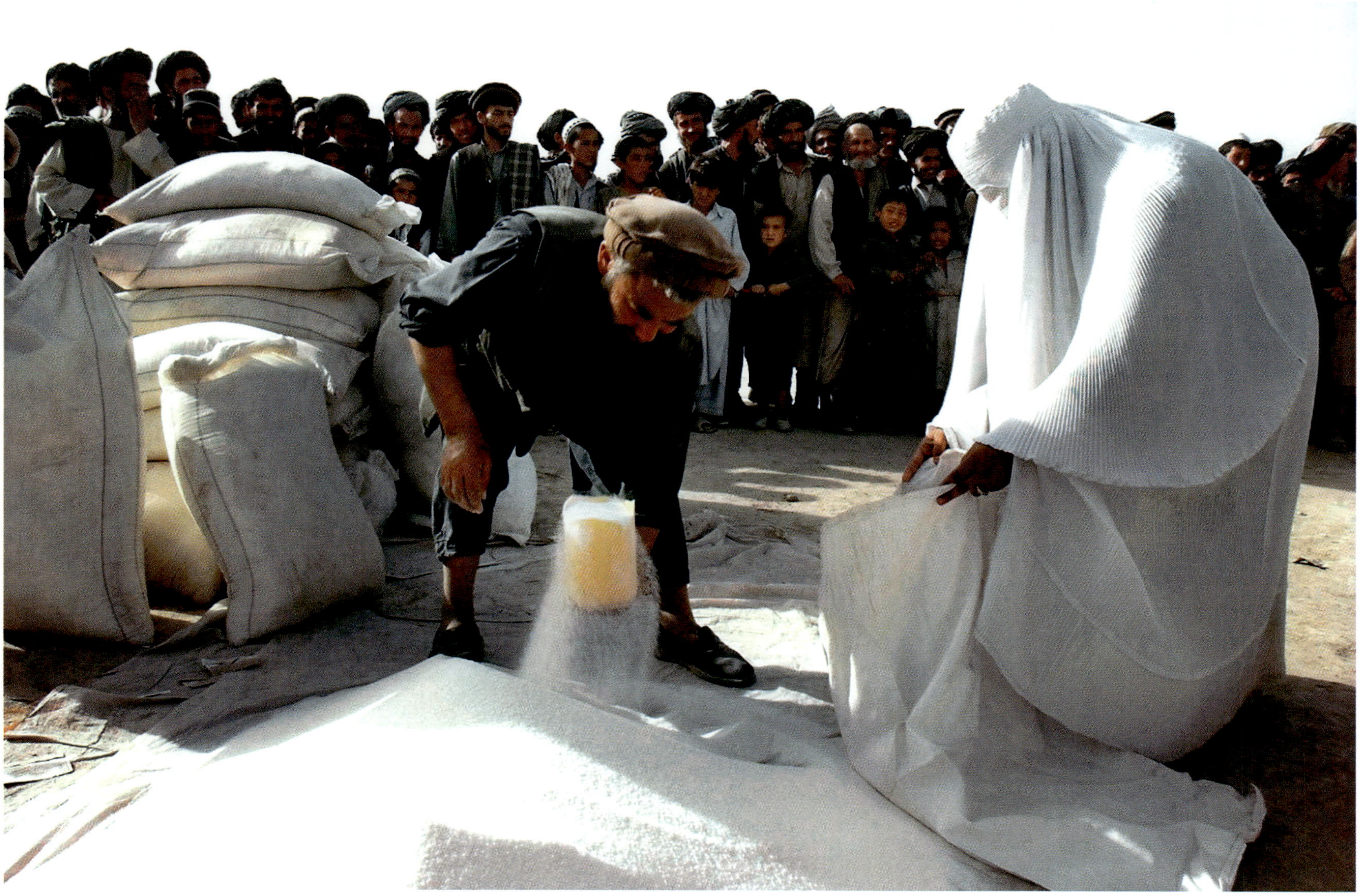

8TH OCTOBER 2001 – KHWAJA BAHAUDDIN, AFGHANISTAN – AN AFGHANI WOMAN RECEIVING EMERGENCY SUPPLIES AT A HANDOUT POST OPERATED BY A FRENCH AID ORGANISATION. (JACK GUEZ)

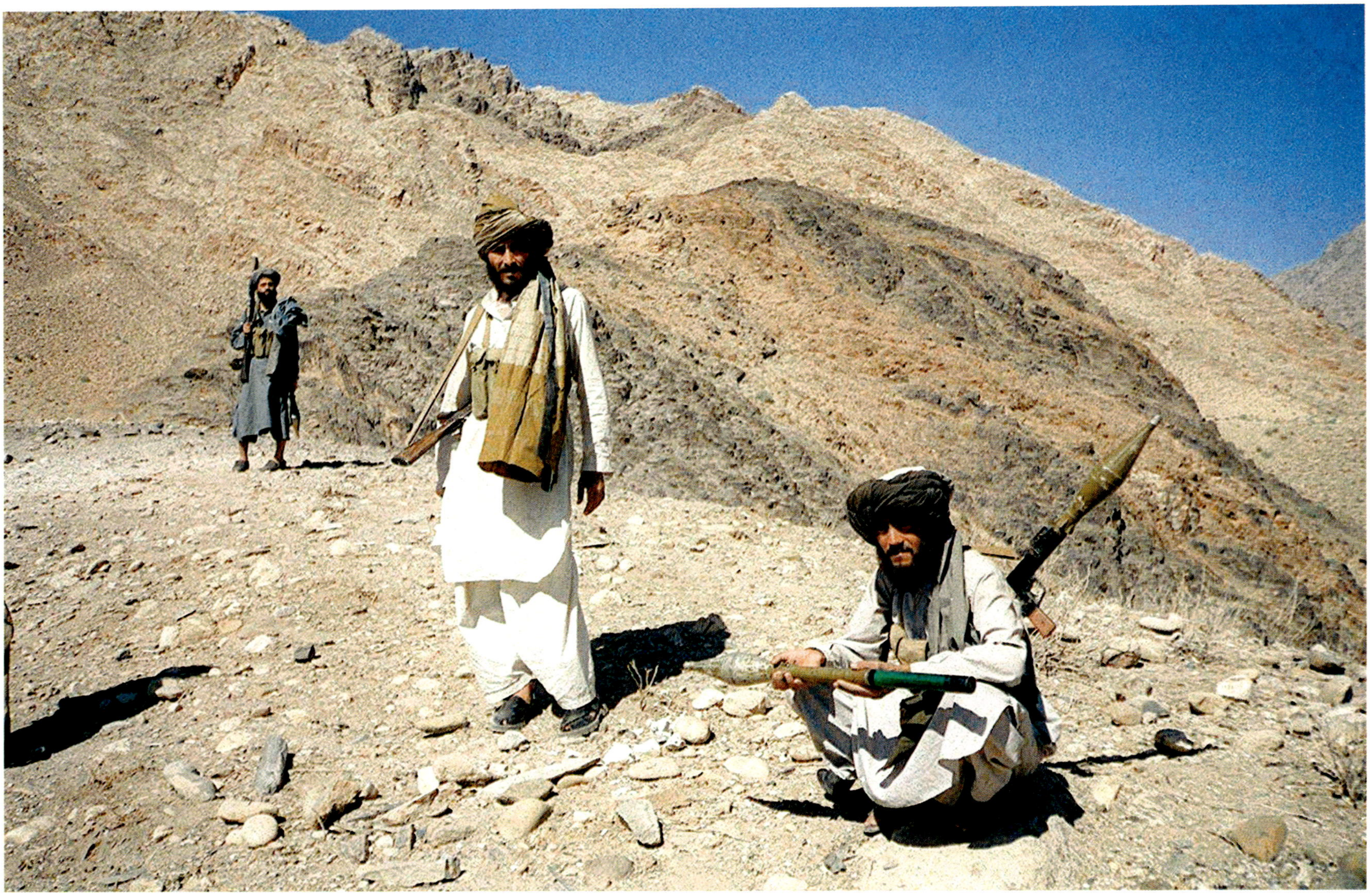

14TH OCTOBER 2001
– KADAM, AFGHANISTAN –
TALIBAN FIGHTERS POSE ON
A HILLTOP NEAR JALALABAD.
(TARIQ MAHMOOD)

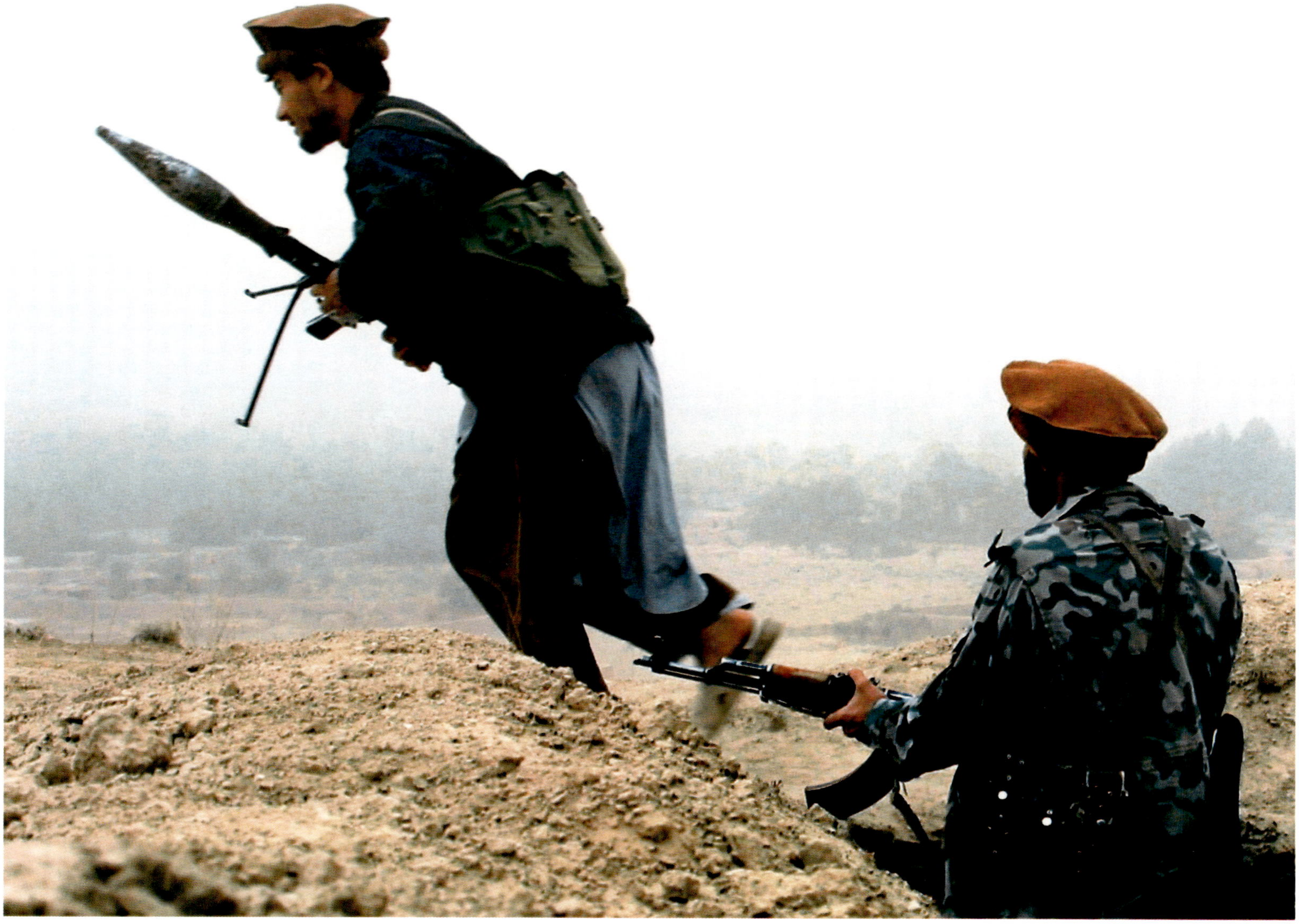

10TH OCTOBER 2001 – QURUQ, AFGHANISTAN – A NORTHERN ALLIANCE FIGHTER FIRING ON TALIBAN POSITIONS, 700M AWAY. (ALEXANDER NEMENOV)

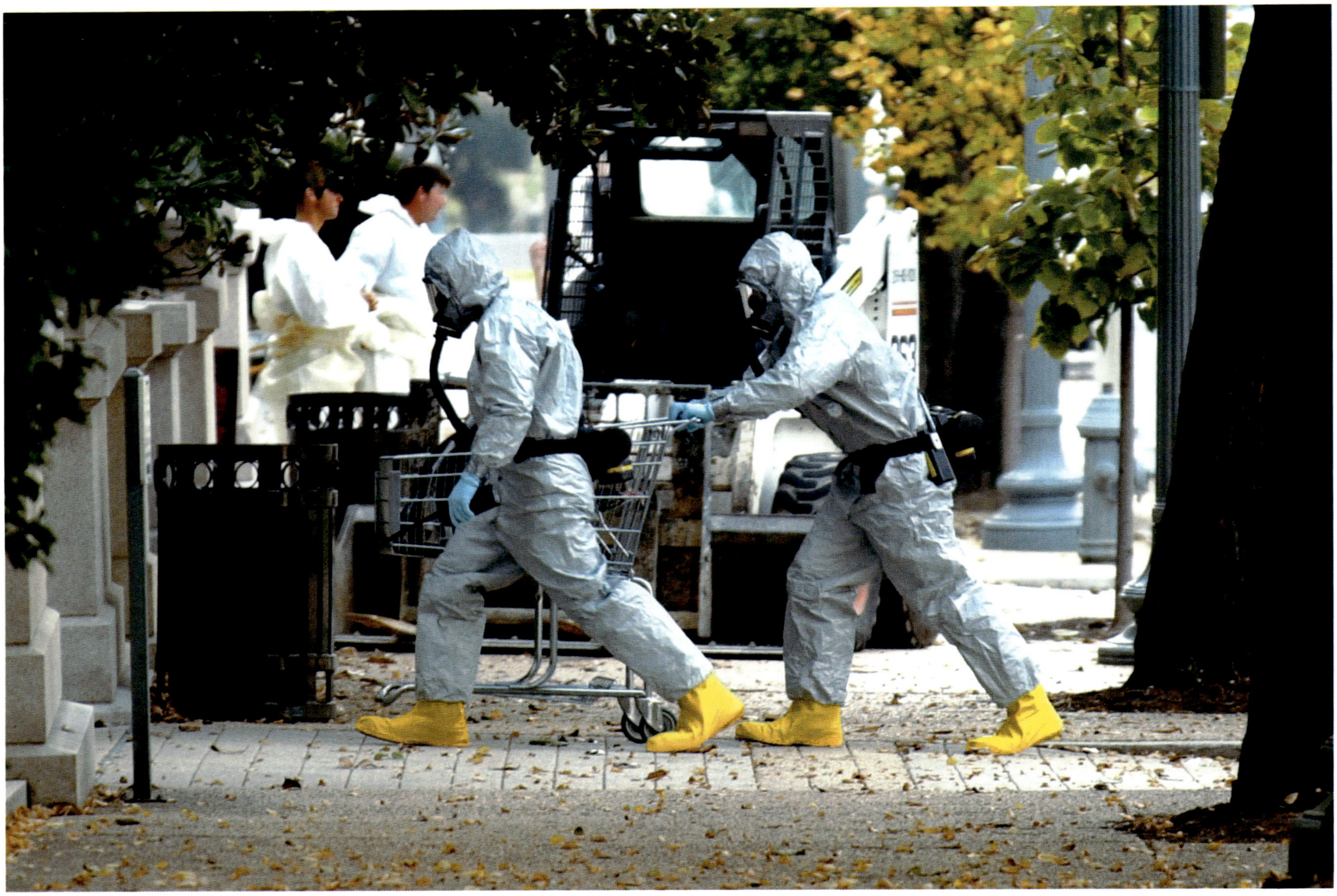

23RD OCTOBER 2001 – WASHINGTON, USA – WORKMEN IN BIOHAZARD SUITS PUSH A CART OF EQUIPMENT INTO THE LONGWORTH HOUSE OFFICE BUILDING ON CAPITOL HILL AMID FEARS OF CONTAMINATION BY AN ANTHRAX ATTACK. (SHAWN THEW)

22ND OCTOBER 2001 – RABAT, AFGHANISTAN – A FIGHTER FROM THE OPPOSITION NORTHERN ALLIANCE WATCHES US WARPLANES BOMB TALIBAN FRONTLINE POSITIONS 50 KILOMETERS NORTH OF KABUL. (JACK GUEZ)

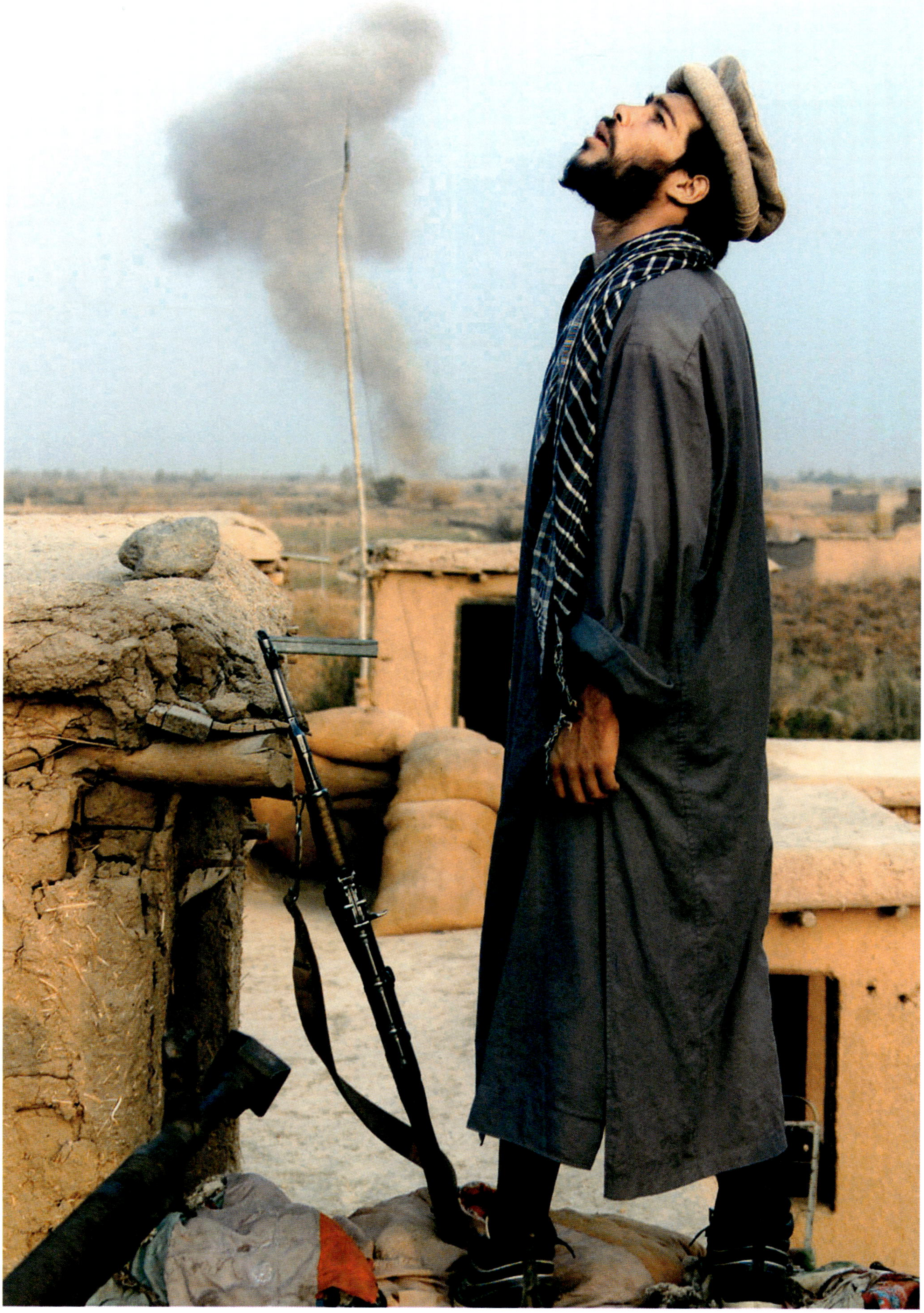

ACKNOWLEDGMENTS

We would like to thank all members of the AFP staff, editorial, and technical departments, who contributed to the production of this book.
Pierre Fernandez, editor-in-chief of the photographic service, was responsible for the overall concept and supervised its production, with the help of Laurence de Surmain and Martina Stanek, who selected the photos to be included.
The service's archives provided invaluable support and the photo laboratory oversaw the quality of the pictures chosen for inclusion.
Elisabeth Friederich was in charge of editing the text and captions, in conjunction with Peter Shard.

Library of Congress Control Number: 2001133127
ISBN 0-8109-3223-7

Published in 2002 by Harry N. Abrams, Incorporated, New York

Printed and bound in France

10 9 8 7 6 5 4 3 2 1

Harry N. Abrams, Inc.
100 Fifth Avenue
New York, N.Y. 10011
www.abramsbooks.com

Abrams is a subsidiary of LA MARTINIÈRE GROUPE